MW01094246

CRISTINA BAKER

A MINUTE OF HOPE

*100 Prayers for Staying
Steadfast Through
Challenges and Change*

THOMAS NELSON®
Since 1798
thomasnelson.com

Published in Nashville, Tennessee, by Thomas Nelson. Thomas Nelson is a registered trademark of HarperCollins Christian Publishing, Inc.

Thomas Nelson titles may be purchased in bulk for educational, business, fundraising, or sales promotional use. For information, please email SpecialMarkets@ThomasNelson.com.

The author photo on the back cover is by Carrin Lewis Photography.

Unless otherwise noted, Scripture quotations are taken from the New King James Version®. Copyright © 1982 by Thomas Nelson. Used by permission. All rights reserved.

Scripture quotations marked AMP are taken from the Amplified Bible (AMP). Copyright © 2015 by The Lockman Foundation. Used by permission. www.lockman.org.

Scripture quotations marked CSB are taken from the Christian Standard Bible®. Copyright © 2017 by Holman Bible Publishers. Used by permission. Christian Standard Bible® and CSB® are federally registered trademarks of Holman Bible Publishers.

Scripture quotations marked ESV are taken from the ESV® Bible (The Holy Bible, English Standard Version®). Copyright © 2001 by Crossway, a publishing ministry of Good News Publishers. All rights reserved.

Scripture quotations marked GNT are taken from the Good News Translation® in Today's English Version—Second Edition. Copyright © 1992 by American Bible Society. Used by permission.

Scripture quotations marked MEV are taken from the Modern English Version. Copyright © 2014 by Military Bible Association. Used by permission. All rights reserved.

Scripture quotations marked MSB are taken from the Majority Standard Bible, public domain.

Scripture quotations marked NASB are taken from the (NASB®) New American Standard Bible®. Copyright © 1960, 1971, 1977, 1995, 2020 by The Lockman Foundation. Used by permission. All rights reserved. www.lockman.org.

Scripture quotations marked NIV are taken from the Holy Bible, New International Version®, NIV®. Copyright © 1973, 1978, 1984, 2011 by Biblica, Inc®. Used by permission of Zondervan. All rights reserved worldwide. www.zondervan.com. The "NIV" and "New International Version" are trademarks registered in the United States Patent and Trademark Office by Biblica, Inc.®

Scripture quotations marked NLT are taken from the Holy Bible, New Living Translation. Copyright © 1996, 2004, 2015 by Tyndale House Foundation. Used by permission of Tyndale House Publishers, Carol Stream, Illinois 60188. All rights reserved.

Any internet addresses, phone numbers, or company or product information printed in this book are offered as a resource and are not intended in any way to be or to imply an endorsement by Thomas Nelson, nor does Thomas Nelson vouch for the existence, content, or services of these sites, phone numbers, companies, or products beyond the life of this book.

ISBN 978-1-4002-5339-5 (HC)
ISBN 978-1-4002-5337-1 (eBook)

Printed in Canada

25 24 23 22 21 FR 6 5 4 3 2 1

To Ryan and Evan, you are the gifts that the Father had waiting for me all my life. Eternity will not be enough to thank Him for the grace He has shown me through my husband and son that He has given me in this life. These prayers are the fruit of the journey of our family, the many mountains, the deepest valleys, the weeping and rejoicing. The Lord has been faithful to us. I love you both so deeply.

God gave us this prayer when Evan was very young. Every time our family leaves each other's presence and before we go to bed, we pray this over one another:

Praise the Lord! Blessed is the man who fears the Lord, who delights greatly in His commandments. His descendants will be mighty in the land; the generation of the upright will be blessed.

PSALM 112:2 MSB

Jesus, I beheld the beauty of Your face through writing this book and these prayers that poured from my heart to Yours for the world that You love. These prayers are to You, for You, and are penned from the love in my heart for You. Holy Spirit, thank You for teaching me the beauty of the interruptible life led by You. This book became a pilgrimage that holds testimonies of healing, hope, salvation, and freedom that I will never forget. What a joy to walk alongside You, my very best friend. I love You, Lord.

CONTENTS

I dedicate this book to my dad, Bill Cabrera. God has used your life to teach me to pray and not lose heart. The Lord is faithful to finish what He started.

When the righteous cry for help, the LORD hears and delivers them out of all their troubles. The LORD is near to the brokenhearted and saves the crushed in spirit. Many are the afflictions of the righteous, but the LORD delivers him out of them all.

PSALM 34:17–19 ESV

INTRODUCTION

I will never forget the day when I realized God was *actually* listening to my prayers.

God wanted to teach me to trust Him even when I couldn't feel or see what He was doing.

One afternoon my husband, Ryan; our young son, Evan; and a family friend made a trip to a local McDonald's. We wanted to pray together for a friend who had walked away from the Lord, and it gave a chance for the children to play in the playscape. I was in a season of learning how to hear the voice of God in prayer, and He was teaching me how to hear His heart when I prayed for others.

Our friend told me that day, "Cristina, you are going to make mistakes. I am going to make mistakes. We will all make mistakes together, but that is the power of His grace. As you pray, when you hear the Word of God or see the Lord show you something while you pray, open up your mouth, and say what He is saying and showing to you." In an instant, I was set free from the fear of saying the wrong words or being driven by perfect performance and saying the right things. God sees and hears our hearts even when the right words don't come out, and what is so beautiful about the Lord is that He loves our faith.

As the three adults sat at a table in a PlayPlace in McDonald's while the children played, we began to pour our hearts out. We prayed fervently for our lost friend, and all of a sudden, I saw a picture of a shofar, which we would know today as a trumpet. I was a first-year Bible college student at the time, and I had very limited knowledge about what the shofar was used for in the Scriptures, but I knew enough to understand what the Lord was showing me in this moment while we prayed. So I blurted out, "Lord! Sound the alarm in our friend's life that she may return to You, her first love!"

Our friend, Ryan, and I continued praying around the table, and, with my eyes closed, I saw that shofar again in my spirit. I said, "Lord, blow the trumpet in her life once again! Sound the alarms! Bring her home!" Suddenly, we could hear Evan and all the children at the playground in McDonald's screaming loudly! We opened our eyes and heard the fire alarms going. The staff was feverishly attempting to turn them off, to no avail.

Ryan looked at our friend and me and said, "Didn't you hear the fire alarms go off the first time? Cristina, when you said, 'Lord, sound the alarms' the first time, they went off and the staff quickly turned them off. Then, when you said it the second time, they went off again!" I had been so caught up in praying for our friend that I didn't hear the alarms the first time, but the second time, I did, and it startled me! In the midst of all the chaos that was happening in that McDonald's in that very moment, the Lord spoke to me so clearly in my spirit, *Cristina, I am listening to your prayers. They matter to Me. I love to hear your voice.*

My hope is that the prayers in this book would

take you deeper into the heart of your loving Father who wants to hear your voice. When I gave my life to Jesus, someone gave me a book of prayers that I still have to this day. I used to march around my home declaring these prayers over my life and family. And let me tell you, the presence of God would flood my little apartment as I declared His Word in faith. His tangible presence would fill my heart with hope and peace during all the calamity and chaos I was facing. He is faithful to come to you when you cry out to Him with your whole heart.

I pray that the power of the Holy Spirit would do the same for you as you read these prayers in your home, at your job, in your car, over your children, over your ministry, over your relationships, or wherever you find yourself. Maybe you'll get loud like I did, or maybe you won't; the good news is that it doesn't matter. Jesus just wants to hear you. I pray that His tangible presence would consume your heart and soul as you pray these prayers of hope and faith, knowing that He is listening to you and that He longs to hear your voice.

PRAYERS OF HOPE
FOR YOUR SOUL

The names of God each unveil a facet of His heart as He reveals Himself to men and women throughout the Scriptures. Through these stories, He gives us a revelation of who He is. In Genesis 16, we are introduced to one of the most intimate names of God that I have held near to my heart over the years through the deepest valleys. A woman named Hagar, who was the servant of Abraham and Sarah, was cast into the wilderness after Sarah became angry with her because Hagar had been forced to conceive a child with Sarah's husband, Abraham. Can you imagine what Hagar was feeling? I imagine feelings of shame, abandonment, betrayal, condemnation, and loss plagued her mind and soul. Yet in her hour of greatest despair, she was met with the angel of the Lord (many theologians believe this was a preincarnate appearance of Jesus), and Genesis 16:13 tells us, "She gave this name to the LORD who spoke to her: 'You are the God who sees me,' for she said, 'I have now seen the One who sees me'" (NIV). What is so beautiful about this passage is that the Hebrew word for *seen* describes that they looked at each other. It is quite clear that He saw her first based on her response, and she gave Him one of the most beautiful names that touched the depths of her heart. Since this woman was an Egyptian, a foreigner, she did not have a covenant with God. Yet He chose a woman He had no relationship with to reveal His heart to!

God sees you today. Whether you are in the deepest valley or on the highest mountain, Jesus longs to hear you. He longs for nearness with you, and He deeply cares about the cries of your heart. Just as Hagar was seen by God, as you pray these prayers, picture Jesus looking right back at you, listening to you, and let faith rise within you.

When You Begin Your Day

Good morning, Jesus. I love You. I give You this day and all that You have in store for me. Thank You for carrying me through the night and waking me up this morning. Lord, I need You more than anything. Help me with all I have planned for this day as well as the unplanned moments I don't know about yet. I pray that I will handle every situation with grace and patience. I recognize that tomorrow is not promised, and today is a gift from You. Jesus, You said, "Give us this day our daily bread."[1] I know that You will provide for me, too, one day at a time.

Help me live an interruptible life, where You know You can count on me to hear You and respond quickly. I want to hear Your voice. I pray that You would remove distractions that keep me from Your purposes being fulfilled today. I ask for Your grace to cover every decision I make. Help me always ask for Your wisdom first. This is the day You have made, and I will be glad and rejoice in it.[2] Jesus, I love You and the life You have given to me. In Jesus' mighty name, amen.

When You Start a New Week

Father, thank You for the week ahead and the gift of life. I give this week and every day to You. I can have joy in every season because I know You are with me. As I start this week, help me remember Your love and promises that are the source of my joy! Father, place people in my path today who need a touch from You—those I can serve, minister to, and be a blessing to in the same way You have blessed me.

Lord, You know what I need before I even open my mouth. I pray that You will provide where I need provision spiritually, emotionally, and financially. Father, I ask You to go before me this week to open doors that need to be opened and close the doors that need to be closed. I don't want to waste the time You have given to me with vain ambitions; I want to be right in the center of Your will in all I do. God, I put You first, and I know You will take care of me. I pray that the opportunities You bring this week would not pass me by. Instead, help me discern when You are speaking and where You are leading me. In the name of Jesus I pray, amen.

When You End Your Day

Lord, Your Word is like honey, and Your love melts my heart when it's become hard and bitter. It's Your kindness that leads me to repentance.[3] Tonight, I ask You for forgiveness for the sins I have committed against You and others. I ask You to free me from any bitterness, strife, and resentment. Jesus, You have made a way for me to come boldly before Your throne,[4] and I pray that You would cleanse and forgive me. Tonight, I pray that You would restore, heal, and strengthen my mind, body, and soul.

Lord, even as I sleep, I want to hear Your voice. Lead me by Your Spirit so I will dream and think on what is pure. Jesus, give my mind rest, and calm any racing thoughts from this day; I release them all to You. I know that when I sleep, You are fighting my battles. Lord, help me rest in You tonight, cover my home with a canopy of Your presence with angels surrounding the four corners of my home. In Jesus' name, amen.

When You Are Tired of Waiting

Jesus, teach me to wait on You, and let Your mercy renew me today. I want You to find me on my knees, surrendered to You, faithful to You, grateful for all You have done, and I want to listen for Your voice at every moment of every day. I don't want to live a day without Your presence. I lay down the regret, shame, and sins that took place yesterday and in the past. I am taking hold of Your grace that empowers me to live in victory.

Lord, I know that when I wait on You, my strength and joy are renewed. As faithful as the rising of the sun, every morning You provide new mercies to me, no matter the sins of yesterday. You love me as You find me, but Your mercy doesn't leave me where You found me. You have looked at me with eyes of love and not of judgment; You have held me close when I have fallen and felt far away. Your love is all I will ever need.

Lord, thank You for the seat You have prepared for me at Your table, where we will be together forever. I honor You, Jesus. Amen.

When You Face Hard Times

Beautiful Jesus, You have proven to me time and time again that You will never let me go. When I thought I was hopeless, You overwhelmed me with Your love. I make a declaration of faith today that You can do exceedingly abundantly above all I can ever think or ask for.[5] Lord, thank You for surrounding me with legions of angels that go to battle for me in the unseen realm.

Today I remember that it is who You are—my defender, my shield, and my protector. I will not fear the arrow that flies by day nor the terror of the night because You are with me.[6] Lord, I ask for fresh faith to be released into my spirit today, the kind of faith David had that caused him to run quickly into battle with Goliath, unafraid, bold, and confident because he knew that the God of heaven was with him. I pray for victory over all adversity facing me, because You have already won the battle. Today, I thank You for the revelation that I am fully known and fully loved by You no matter what may come.[7] Jesus, my entire world is in Your hands, and I rest in the truth that You are faithful. In the mighty name of Jesus I pray, amen.

When You Are Attacked by the Enemy

Lord Jesus, I lift my eyes to You. One look into Your eyes transforms me. You are the King of all hope, and I pray that You would take center stage in my heart. Your Word declares that the Enemy comes to steal, kill, and destroy. But Jesus, You came to give me life in abundance.[8] You give me strength when I am weak, and when all odds are set against me, You raise the sword of Your Word against the Enemy.

Lord, You are strong and mighty, glorious and true. Who is like You? You are the God who sees me in the eye of the storm, You stand with me in fire, You make the mountains bow low, and then you cause the valleys of this life to be raised up. I trust You, Lord!

Jesus, deliver me from the spirit of fear that speaks lies and grip my heart with the truth of Your Word. You declare that He who the Son has set free is "free indeed."[9] In Jesus' name I pray, amen.[10]

When You Want Restoration

Father, I thank You that it is in Your heart to restore what the devil has stolen from Your children. Your Word declares in Romans 8:28 that all things work together for the good of those who love You and are called according to Your purpose. Jesus, I believe You are who You say You are. I believe in Your resurrection power that raises what is dead back to life. Thank You that Your heart is always turned toward restoration. Lord, I thank You for redeeming and restoring everything that has been lost in my life. You are the God of all redemption. Through every season of brokenness that You and I have walked through together, I thank You for restoring my heart, my family, my finances, and all that was taken in that season.

Give me eyes to see the way You do, and purify every area of my heart so I look just like You, Jesus. Today, I declare that it is a new day and a new season of hope. I am so thankful for every blessing You have poured out on me. Jesus, You are my faithful strength, my Wonderful Counselor, and my Savior. In Jesus' mighty name, amen.

When You Are Anxious

Father, in the mighty name of Jesus, I run into Your arms. You are the sovereign Lord, and Your Word is a lamp to my feet and a light to my path.[11] Jesus, I thank You that the mountains melt like wax before You.[12] You tell the sun to stand still, and it does not move.[13] You speak peace to the waves, Lord, and they obey You.[14] Father, I praise You because despite what's impossible for me, I know all things are possible with You.[15] I pray that my eyes would be fixed on You, and my heart would be knit together with Yours. Thank You for the wisdom that You give me to guide me through the valleys and chaos that this world can bring, but today, I choose to rest in Your peace.

Jesus, thank You for fighting my battles, I pray for the light of Your face to shine on me and those I love. Lord, thank You for leading and guiding me today in Your truth. You are the only one who can open doors that no man can shut and close doors that no man can open.[16] Surely goodness and mercy will follow me all the days of my life, and it is all because of You.[17] In Jesus' mighty name, amen.

When You Are Bitter

Father, in the name of Jesus, I bring every hurt and unforgiveness I have held toward others and completely release them to You. Protect me from the subtle offenses that the Enemy brings through false assumptions, accusations, and misunderstandings. I know that bitterness is like a root that sets into my heart that will never produce godly fruit.[18] It produces anger, strife, slander, and resentment. Father, by the power of Your Spirit I pray that You would break every chain that has held me captive. I pray that You will heal my emotions and that my heart would produce the fruit. I desire to walk in the Spirit and forgive others as You have forgiven me.

Lord, thank You for sending Your Holy Spirit, my Comforter and wise Counselor, to lead and to guide me. I trust in You, Lord. I receive Your healing by faith according to Your Word, will, and purpose for my life. Lord, thank You for delivering my heart into Your freedom. In Jesus' mighty name, amen.

When You Are Walking in Humility

Father, Your ways are above my ways and Your thoughts are above my thoughts.[19] I want to be humble like You are humble and reflect the meekness of Your heart. I give this day to You and declare that my eyes belong to You. I pray that I would see others through Your eyes, with eyes of love. Lord, keep me from stumbling. I pray that I would not consider myself greater than others. I am who I am only because of You; every gift that I have, all that I own, and the very breath in my lungs—it all belongs to You.

Help me walk in purity in my thoughts, in my heart, and in the very way that I walk in this world to reflect Your heart, bring glory to You, and cause others to desire to know You. Lord, guard my heart above all things, because out of it flow the issues of life.[20] I pray that the meditations of my heart would be on all that is pleasing to You. I want to meditate on whatever is true, whatever is noble, whatever is right, whatever is pure, whatever is lovely, whatever is admirable; if anything is excellent or praiseworthy, I want to think on these things.[21] In Jesus' name, amen.

The Lord is my shepherd; I shall
not want. He makes me to lie down
in green pastures; He leads me
beside the still waters. He restores
my soul; He leads me in the paths of
righteousness for His name's sake.
Yea, though I walk through the valley
of the shadow of death, I will fear no
evil; for You are with me; Your rod
and Your staff, they comfort me.

You prepare a table before me in the
presence of my enemies; You anoint
my head with oil; My cup runs over.
Surely goodness and mercy shall follow
me all the days of my life; and I will
dwell in the house of the Lord forever.

PSALM 23:1–6

There is a blessing from the Lord that comes when we decide to not quit in the face of adversity, trials, and change. God wants to bring you into the peace and leadership of the Holy Spirit that is cultivated through a life of communion and friendship with the Lord. Trials are a part of this life, and the beauty of walking with Jesus is that you no longer walk through the valleys of life alone, but you have a Good Shepherd who is walking alongside you.

There are seasons when God calls each of us to trust Him when we cannot see beyond the next step in front of us, and these moments reveal our hearts' posture and our faith in Him more than the seasons when we stand on the mountain. It is what happens *in us* in the delay that God is after. But what do you do when it seems like life goes from valley to valley void of a mountaintop experience? The Lord lays hold of our hearts when we find our rest *in Him* rather than in the form of circumstantial peace. Jesus is your peace and desires to be your safe place no matter what is happening in the world around you.

On the other side of the valley of the shadow of death is the depth of God's love for you that reveals the safety you have in His heart where fear does not exist. And there is a Man who has prayed for you: Jesus, your high priest, has interceded for you at the right hand of the Father, and He has walked with you through every valley and scaled every mountain to reveal Himself with a depth He longs for you to know. Today is no different, and what He has done before, He will do again.

Have you ever noticed that God always outdoes Himself in His display of extraordinary love to you over the course of your life? *God prepares a table for you in the presence of your enemies.* Do you know what is special about this passage? David wrote these words in light of the Passover meal before the Lord gave Israel victory over Jericho, when the walls came down. God prepared a meal outside of Jericho right in front of Israel's enemies! Think about that for a moment. God gave His people an opportunity to experience His breakthrough before the walls of opposition ever came down. What a mighty God He is.

Today, the Lord wants to reveal Himself to you as your defender, your safety, your greatest friend, and your Savior. He will lead you beside still waters with the peace that only He can give. Thank Him for the breakthrough before it comes, thank Him for the answered prayers before You see them, thank the Lord for the promises of His Word being fulfilled even before you see them with your eyes! He is faithful to finish what He started in you.

When You Need to Find Peace

Father, there is a peace that this world can never offer, and it is only found in You. I pray for the peace of God that surpasses all understanding to guard my heart and my mind in Christ Jesus.[22] I choose to be still and trust in who You are during the battle. I trust that there are more for me than there are against me.[23] Your Word promises that You will command Your angels to guard and protect me; I believe that no evil will befall me, nor will any plague come near my dwelling.[24] Lord, I pray this over everyone I love, that they would trust You, be still, and know that You are God.[25]

Jesus, I will praise You while I wait for You to move in my life. I choose to worship You through pain and trials because You are worthy. Your Holy Spirit comforts me. You said that You would catch every single one of my tears in a bottle![26] Oh what a love I have found in You, Jesus! My peace will rest in the truth that no matter what comes my way, You are with me, You are for me. You are my fortress, You are my defender, and You are my strength. In Jesus' name I pray with all my heart, amen.

When You Need Strength in Seasons of Change

Father, I am seeking You. Thank You that You have gone before me to make every crooked path straight today.[27] I believe that You have already made a way. Jesus, I know in my heart that when I seek You, I will always find You. Lord, in this season of change and transition, keep my heart connected to Yours. I pray that I will not be moved by what is seen by my eyes; I want to be full of faith and hope for what You have prepared for my future. You are with me now, and You will see me through every season of change. I pray that You would guide and lead me with Your wisdom in every decision I make. My desire is that You would be at the center of it all. Lord, calm my heart when anxiety tries to take over, and cover me with Your peace.

I pray that I would be like Joshua when You told him to be strong and of good courage, and not to be afraid, and it is because You are with me![28] Nothing is impossible with You, Lord, and I thank You for all You are about to do in me and through me. In Jesus' name, amen.

When You Feel Lost

Lord, You are powerful and mighty. There isn't a mountain You can't move, and I know that all things are possible through You. You are the source of my strength, my joy, and every good thing in my life. Today I'm asking that You make a way where there seems to be none. Lord, You are not surprised or caught off guard by the situations I am facing, but I thank You that You have already gone before me, behind me, and all around me. I will not lean on my own understanding, but what I want is to acknowledge You in all my ways, because I know that it is here where You make the crooked paths straight.

Father, I thank You for Your goodness, for Your grace, for Your forgiveness, and for Your kindness, and I thank You that I can do all things through Christ who gives me strength.[29] Lord, thank You for going before me and making a way when the walls seem to be closing in. I trust and know that You already have a plan prepared for me, even if I cannot see it yet, and Your Word will light the way. Lord, I pray that You would give me eyes to see what You see, and ears to hear Your voice. In Jesus' name I pray, amen.

When You Are Desperate for a Breakthrough

Father, in the mighty name of Jesus, thank You that You are the one true God. Only You can deliver me from the circumstances I am facing, and today I am calling on Your name for divine breakthrough. You opened the Red Sea for Your children when they came out of Egypt, and You delivered them from the bondage of slavery. Lord, You made the sun stand still for Joshua because he was a man who was in covenant with You. I know there is nothing You cannot do. I will not fear because You are walking with me through this trial. I pray that You would give my heart peace while I wait on You to do what only You can do. So I lift my eyes to You, Lord, and You alone. King David said, "I lift up my eyes to the mountains—where does my help come from? My help comes from the Lord, the Maker of heaven and earth."[30]

I call on the mighty name of the Lord, You hold the keys; all authority is in Your hands, Jesus. I thank You in advance for answered prayers according to Your will. In Jesus' mighty name, amen.

When You Need to Be Forgiven

Jesus, I want to pursue You and receive the grace You have so freely given to me. I praise You for every promise You have spoken over my destiny and what You desire to do in and through me. You knew me before I was even knit in my mother's womb.[31] Lord, I pray that my lamp will be full of oil and full of Your Spirit. Where I have felt weary and brokenhearted, I know that You love to give beauty for ashes, joy for mourning, and a garment of praise for the spirit of heaviness.[32]

Holy Spirit, reveal the Son to me; breathe on my heart that my soul would sing again. Your grace and joy bring me strength! Lord, would You open wide the windows of heaven on my life and family and pour out Your grace? I know You will make a way where there seems to be no way. I ask You to forgive me, and I choose to rest in the grace I can only find in You, Jesus. Amen.

When You Are Worried

Father, in the name of Jesus, thank You that goodness and mercy will follow me all the days of my life.[33] Lord, You are my healer, my hope, and my strength. When I need guidance, You are my greatest Counselor. When I need freedom, You are my deliverer and my shield in the day of adversity.[34] Lord, You are sovereign, and You see the end from the beginning. I know I can trust You in the path You have set before me. You are a good Father, and You watch over my life; there is nothing to fear.

Open my eyes to see that more are for me than there are against me.[35] Calm my anxious heart. I pray that You would remove the worry and fear of the future. I ask that You replace them with faith in You! Thank You for comforting and restoring my heart today. Thank You that while I pray, You are already moving in and through me. Thank You for the angels surrounding me and my family. You rescued me from deep affliction before, and I thank You for lifting the heavy burdens from me now. In Jesus' mighty name, amen.

When You Eagerly Await the Restoration and Redemption of God

Father, in the name of Jesus, I thank You for the opportunity to trust You with all my heart, mind, soul, and strength. Thank You for redeeming and restoring my life. I know that Your heart's desire is to see me fully restored from all past hurt and brokenness. For every season where I have experienced loss and a broken heart, it is Your gentle hand that has come to put the pieces of my heart back together. Thank You that there is always purpose through pain, and You are faithful to make all things work together for good.[36] I trust You with my whole heart, my family, and my entire life.

God, You are near to me. The joy of knowing You is all that I will ever need. Thank You for all You have done, all that You are doing, and all You will do in the future. Father, You have blessed me with the gift of life and You love to restore what the Enemy tried to destroy me with. Lord, I bring all the losses of the past to You and consider it all joy because my greatest reward and prize in this life is to know You.[37] In Jesus' name, amen.

When You Shout the Mighty Name of Jesus

Father, there are some who trust in chariots and some in horses, but I will trust in the mighty name of the Lord.[38] I pray that my heart would be rid of any anxiety, fear, and worry, and that my eyes would be fixed on the one who is faithful and true. Lord, when has impossible ever stopped You? Father, I trust You, I love You, and I lift my heart to You today. I pray that You would overwhelm me with Your love. I want to trust You without bounds and without holding back! Lord, I pray for supernatural faith in my heart to take on everything You've set before me. My entire world, and everything in it, I lift up to You. You are the Lord who moves mountains, and I pray that my trust in You would grow deeper. Help Your Word ignite faith in my spirit to trust You in the face of the most impossible situations. There is nothing You cannot do, Lord! I believe Your promises and that Your Word will not return void, but it will do what You have declared for it to do.[39] Truly, there is no one like You, Jesus. In Your mighty name I pray, amen.

When You Wonder If You Are on the Right Path

Father, in the mighty name of Jesus, thank You for all that You have done. I pray for my heart and my soul to rest in Your presence and Your peace. You are the author and finisher of my faith,[40] and You have written a story that will bring You glory. No matter what circumstances may look like, I believe that Your plans for me are good, and You will bring beauty from ashes.[41]

Father, I ask for times of refreshing as I wait on You to fulfill Your Word and Your desires for my life. I open my heart and lay down every expectation of what I think life will look like, and I surrender this story to You. I pray that my heart would be softened and attentive to Your voice when You speak. I am letting go of all my expectations and I trust that You have good plans to draw me close—Jesus, I trust You with my whole heart. You have turned my mourning into dancing.[42] Thank You for restoring hope in my heart and turning all evil against me into good.[43] In Jesus' mighty name, amen.

When You Need to Be Filled with the Power of God

Father, I ask You to fill me with Your powerful love and presence. I thank You for breaking the power of the Enemy over my life in the mighty name of Jesus. Where the battle rages, it is You who raises a standard against him, and You strengthen me.[44] Father, I pray that I would have faith like the generation of Joshua who entered the promised land. They rose up with courage and chose to trust You with all their hearts, minds, souls, and strength. You see my victory through the fiercest trials, and You have already given me the greatest reward—Your glorious presence. I will not doubt You. You are the God of Abraham, Isaac, and Jacob, and I know that You will do what You said You will do. I stand boldly with You, Lord, unafraid of what may come, because there is safety and refuge in Your presence. I let go of all bitterness, offense, unforgiveness, and works of the flesh that prevent me from walking in the Spirit according to Your Word. Lord, I want to be filled with the strength and power that only Your Word can give me. You are the one true God who keeps His promises, and I am so grateful to know You. In Jesus' name, amen.

PRAYERS OF HOPE FOR YOUR HEART

Years ago, the Lord spoke deeply into my spirit: If I would give Him preeminence over every part of my life, no matter what came, He would protect my heart. God didn't promise that everything would be a bed of roses, but He promised to be with us and that He would never leave or forsake us. Everything in life hinges on our relationship with Jesus, and the words that we pray matter to Him.

Can you imagine that? The God of the entire universe cares about what you say to Him, and He listens attentively to you. This thought alone always sends me into a tailspin of awe and wonder at the goodness and greatness of our God. He is the God who desires to be with us. He wants to dwell with us, to talk to us, and for us to come near to Him. It was His desire from the very beginning. Adam and Eve fellowshipped with God and walked with Him in the cool of the day (Genesis 3:8). Jesus Christ came to restore that garden experience with our Father, and He loves to hear your voice.

When You Have a Broken Heart

Jesus, how I love Your name. Through the night, You are faithful and near to me. I don't have to feel it or see it; by faith I believe because Your Word promises that You are near the brokenhearted.[45] Father, I pray that You would mend my heart where it's been broken by disappointment and pain. You extended Your hand to Peter when he began to sink and pulled him out of the raging waters, and he walked with You. Today, I choose to fix my eyes on You like he did. Through change, hardship, challenge, and pain, Jesus, I declare that You are my rock and my strong tower.

Father, if there is any trauma from my past, I ask that You heal me wholly and completely. Right now, I repent of every wrong motive and sin, even the ones I may not see or be aware of; I ask that You forgive me. Lord, break every chain in my life and destroy the works of darkness that seek to steal, kill, and destroy the life You breathed into me. Today, I am stepping into the abundant life You promised me. In the mighty and powerful name that is above all names, Jesus my beloved, amen.

When You Feel Alone

Father, I thank You for the companionship I find in You when I am alone. Your Word declares that You put the lonely in families.[46] A full life comes through the connection that we have with our brothers and sisters in Christ. I pray that You would send godly friends into my life that love You and are friends to the destiny and purpose that You have for my life. Lord, I ask that You bring me into fellowship with other believers that love You with all their hearts, minds, souls, and strength. Lord, thank You for the friendships and family in Your kingdom that You will bring to walk with me, and I pray that You would be at the center of every friendship and relationship that comes into my life. My hope is in You, my strength is in You, and all that I will ever need is found in You, Jesus. You are still my first love, and by faith I receive all I have prayed for today. In Jesus' name, amen.

When You Have a Heavy Heart

Jesus, my heart is Yours, and I thank You that I am Your delight, and You are mine. I willingly open my heart to be pruned, purified, and refined by Your Holy Spirit. You are the vine; I am the branch,[47] and today I surrender every area of my life that hinders Your love from reaching the depths of what You desire for me. Teach me to say yes to You quickly, without reservation. I pray that You would remove the distractions that weigh on my heart. I give them to You. Lord, I pray that You will keep the flame of Your love lit in my heart even when everything around me is changing and life seems to be shaking. I declare today that I find my rest in You even when chaos is all around me. Impress on my heart the only thing that never changes in this world, and that is Your deep love for me, Father. You are the uncreated, unchanging, eternal God, and Your Word declares that You are the same yesterday, today, and forever.[48] If there is any apathy in my heart, no matter how subtle it may be, I pray that You would break the power of it over me and that You would release resurrection power over my life. In Jesus' name, amen.

When You Have Been Betrayed

Jesus, You are the Good Shepherd, and I am the sheep of Your pasture. Lord, teach my heart to trust You even when nothing makes sense in my life. Where trust has been broken in my relationships, I pray that You would restore those broken areas and make them whole. I find peace and rest in the truth of Your Word that declares that You are faithful and not a liar.[49] You are loyal to me, and You will never betray me.

Father, I pray that You would help me release all the people in my life—past, present, and future—who have betrayed or abandoned me. Your response to those who betrayed You was forgiveness, and I want to forgive the same way You did. Today I release all the debts, betrayals, and sins that others have committed against me. Father, forgive me for holding others captive because of hurt I've held in my heart. Just as You have forgiven me for all my sins, help me forgive fully. I release it all to You, Jesus. Set my heart on fire for You and others as I forgive and give mercy to others the way You have given to me. I exalt You, high Lord, because You are worthy. In Jesus' name I pray, amen.

When You Need Protection over Those You Love

Jesus, I lift Your name today, and I thank You that Your mercy and kindness will never fail. You have called me to walk on the waters by faith, and my prayer is that my eyes would stay fixed on You. I pray for a deeper revelation of Your Word in my life and that I would keep You at the center of everything I am and I do. Jesus, my desire is to see You!

I pray for the same faith David had to run into the battle with Goliath, knowing the God of heaven, the commander of heaven's armies, was with him! I speak to every giant in my life today by the power of Your Word to be overtaken by Your victory! I pray for miracles to reverse illnesses and infirmities, bring home prodigal children and family members who have walked away from You, and heal their hearts and souls. Today, I pray for the people I love, the family You have given me, and trust that You will move in Your perfect timing. Lord, thank You for strengthening me. I look to You in all things, and I thank You in advance for all You will do. In Jesus' mighty name, amen.

When You Need Help Guarding Your Heart

Lord, You reign high above the heavens and high above the earth. Today, I choose to trust You, and I know that my entire life is in Your hands. Your Word declares that despite what is impossible for humans, all things are possible with You.[50] You are the God of miracles, and there is no one like You. Lord, I pray that You will guard my heart and my mind in Christ. Jesus, You protect me when I am standing in the furnace of affliction.[51] Lord, just to know that You are with me is all that I will ever need. Jesus, You are the balm that covers my heart from the arrows of affliction that come my way.

Today, I pray that You would protect me from the devil's schemes to open doors to anger, unforgiveness, and bitterness and cause me to stumble and disconnect my heart from Yours. Lord, keep me from stumbling and falling into murmuring and complaining when life does not go as planned. Would You fill me with Your presence? I want to pursue You, and I want to know You. Jesus, You are faithful. In Your name I pray, amen.

When You Need Hope

Father, Your Word is life to me. It breathes energy into my body, soul, and spirit. Today, I pray that You would anoint me with the power of Your presence. I long for the embers of Your love to burn brightly for all the world to see. Lord, You give me beauty for ashes, joy for the seasons of mourning.[52] Jesus, I ask that You break the power of despair over past seasons I have walked through and that Your hope would arise in my heart. I want to see all things through Your eyes and live in light of eternity. Where my hope has been delayed, thank You that Your desires were being fulfilled first. I pray that You would bring to pass that tree of life that is filled with Your promises,[53] in Your perfect timing. Help me trust You more.

Jesus, thank You for filling my heart with hope even as I pray these words from my heart. You are faithful to finish what You started. Give me eyes to see You. Give me ears to hear You and to be attentive to Your Word. I was made for You, Jesus. Thank You for knitting my heart together with Yours. It's in Your name I pray, Jesus, amen.

When You Are Suffering

Father, one of the greatest gifts I could ever receive is coming to the end of myself. It is here that I find You. God, I ask You to deliver me from striving and living from my own strength and power. I pray that the cry of my heart would be to know You—the power of Your resurrection and the fellowship of Your sufferings. Awaken my spirit. Help me get my eyes off temporary suffering and look at this life with an eternal perspective. This is the moment in the grand scheme of eternity where I get to worship You through trials. I get to choose to have joy because I have You. One day, You will wipe away every tear from my eyes,[54] but until that day, I choose joy despite the fiery furnace I am standing in right now. I get to choose the faith of the three Hebrew boys in the fire who You stood with in the book of Daniel. You were the fourth Man in the fire with them,[55] and You are the Man standing in the fire with me now. I love You, Lord. Come what may, I am alive in You forever. To live is Christ and to die is gain.[56] In Jesus' name I pray, amen.

When You Are Grieving

Father, thank You for the precious blood of Your Son Jesus, which has justified, cleansed, and redeemed me. I have been bought with a price,[57] and I just want to thank You, Lord. By Your grace I have been made whole, and it is Your love that brings me to repentance. Today, I bring my heart to You and ask that You would restore every part of it that has been fragmented and make it whole. Jesus, You shed Your blood so I could be restored to my heavenly Father. You died for me, You made a way for me, You did what no man could do, and I know that You are healing and restoring my heart into total freedom. I pray that my spirit, soul, and body will be whole in You.

Jesus, You made a way for You and me to be face-to-face, and when I behold You, there is healing in Your eyes. There is restoration for my heart and healing to my soul. Keep me in this place of complete surrender; I want none beside You, and none before You. My joy is in You, and Your love heals me. Lord, I will be still and know that You are God.[58] In Jesus' name, amen.

When You Long for a Friend
to Accept Jesus as Lord

Father, I pray for my friend and stand in the gap today for them. I want to intercede on their behalf, and I bring them before Your throne of grace. Help those I love who are walking in unforgiveness and deliver their hearts from the hurt they have experienced. I pray for everyone I know to find You, and that You would grip their hearts with Your love that is deep and unending. Help them see You as You really are, and if they have been hurt by people they trusted, I pray for complete healing in them so they would return to You.

Lord, You are a good Father, and I believe that You will finish the good work that You started in my friend.[59] Father, I pray that You would reveal Your heart and Your love for them. Even though I may not see it yet, I believe that You have a plan of salvation for them. I take hold of the hope that is found in the power of prayer as I lift them up, that they would know You and spend eternity with You. In the mighty name of Jesus I pray, amen.

And it happened, as she continued praying before the LORD, that Eli watched her mouth. Now Hannah spoke in her heart; only her lips moved, but her voice was not heard. Therefore Eli thought she was drunk. So Eli said to her, "How long will you be drunk? Put your wine away from you!"

But Hannah answered and said, "No, my lord, I am a woman of sorrowful spirit. I have drunk neither wine nor intoxicating drink, but have poured out my soul before the LORD. Do not consider your maidservant a wicked woman, for out of the abundance of my complaint and grief I have spoken until now."

Then Eli answered and said, "Go in peace, and may the God of Israel grant your petition which you have asked of Him."

And she said, "Let your maidservant find favor in your sight." So the woman went her way and ate, and her face was no longer sad.

1 SAMUEL 1:12–18

There are prayers that go beyond words and straight to the heart of God. Sometimes it looks like Hannah's prayer for the Lord to bless her with a child; her lips were moving as she prayed and wept, but words didn't come out.

Sometimes it looks like a whisper, because words are few, but God sees and knows your heart, and He knows what you need before you even open your mouth.

Sometimes prayers are bold and tenacious, where you find yourself pacing the room, declaring the power of the Word of God over your situation.

At the end of the day, where there is faith in God and passion in your heart, it isn't about eloquent words, how your prayer sounds, or what it looks like; the prayers that shake the heavens are the ones that come from your heart, straight into the heart of God.

When You Want to Cultivate a Life of Friendship with God

Father, I thank You that having fellowship and friendship with You is not supposed to be a difficult process. I am so thankful that You know my innermost being and that I can be myself with You.[60] Jesus, thank You for the gift that You've given to me to look into Your eyes and the treasure of knowing Your heart. There is nothing hidden from You in my heart, and I am grateful that You have opened the door for me to come to You at any time and share what I'm going through.

Lord, from the beginning of time, Your deepest heart's desire was to have fellowship and friendship with me, and You gave Your life to make my heart a place where You can dwell. Help me remember that prayer is about having a relationship with You and is a conversation that will never end. Heal any experiences from my past that keep me from fully opening up to You, offering my heart, and being open with You. In Jesus' name, amen.

When You Are Grateful

Father, You have been so good to me. I remember how far You have brought me, and I am overwhelmed by Your mercy. You have never let me go, even when I've tried to run away from Your presence. Your love has kept me; Your love has pursued me. You have relentlessly fought for me, and there is truly no other love that has tenderized my heart the way Yours has.

I want to thank You for blessing me with the daily bread You provide, the people You have placed in my life to lead me to You, and most of all, the love You have for me. Your Son laid down His life to open the door for us to be together forever. I love You, Lord, and there is no one like You in all the earth. I want to thank You for all the prayers You have answered so faithfully, but I also want to thank You for the prayers You answered with a "no" or "not yet" because You were protecting me. What a mighty God You are. I could go on forever because of the gratitude in my heart for all You have done. I give You my life and everything in it. In Jesus' mighty name, amen.

When You Long to Receive the Love of God

Lord, forgive me for searching for love in all the wrong places. You are the God of love, the one who satisfies my heart and soul like no other. This entire world could not offer me the peace and refuge that You give to my heart. Father, where I have resisted You, help me receive and encounter Your heart, because I know You long to show me how much You love me.

If there is fear of letting You in, whatever that root may be from my past, I pray that You would remove it and replace it with the balm of Your love that gives me peace. I pray for my heart to be open wherever I didn't want You or anyone to see disappointment, pain, and delayed hope. Father, You have waited so patiently for me to come to You, so here I am. God, I need Your voice, and I pray that You would bind up my heart where it's been broken. Save me when my spirit has been crushed. Holy Spirit, help me soften my heart. I release it all to You, Lord, I let You into those secret places that no one knows of; I am opening the door right now to You once and for all. Amen.

When You Need Direction
for a Troubled Marriage

Father, in the name of Jesus, I come boldly before Your throne of grace and ask that You would heal and restore my marriage. Lord, I ask that You rebuke and dismantle the plans of the Enemy to destroy and divide my family and that Your will would reign supreme over every area of our lives. Lord, what You have joined together, let no one separate.[61] I pray that Your Spirit will heal and bring life to every area. Give us both the grace to forgive one another. Today, I pray that You would heal the pain of the past caused by words that were spoken in anger, haste, bitterness, and unforgiveness.

Lord, thank You for my spouse, and I pray that You would break the power of division over our marriage. Thank You for healing our hearts where we have been broken and restoring unity in us again. In the mighty name of Jesus I pray, amen.

When You Need Endurance

Father, I believe You will give me the strength to run my race. I declare over my life that Your grace is sufficient for me.[62] Even when nothing makes sense, I trust that You are leading me into Your perfect will and purpose for my life. Jesus, You are the Bread of Life that nourishes my body, heart, and soul. All I need is Your presence, and I know that You will see me through to the other side of this season. I can do all things through Christ who gives me strength.[63] You are the source of my joy, the source of my life, and You hold me together when it seems like I should be falling apart. In these moments when I may feel the weakest, You reveal Your strength. Your strength is perfected in my weakness.[64] I know that You will be the one who sees me through this season no matter how difficult or impossible it may seem. I rest in the truth that Your grace is what gives me the strength to do all You have called me to do. Keep my heart inside Yours—protected, pure, and without compromise. In Your mighty name I pray, Jesus, amen.

When You Need Protection from the Enemy

Father, You are the almighty God, and the safety You provide me is my refuge and strength. Your Word declares in Isaiah 54:17, "'No weapon formed against you shall prosper, and every tongue which rises against you in judgment you shall condemn. This is the heritage of the servants of the Lord, and their righteousness is from Me,' says the Lord."[65] Father, I lift the shield of faith to extinguish every fiery arrow of the Enemy that comes against my life, my family and other relationships, and all You have entrusted for me to be a steward of.[66]

I pray that You would give me grace to continually walk in forgiveness, and that I would not be unaware of the Enemy's schemes. Help me forgive people who have spoken words against me and protect me from becoming offended. I let go of resentment and anger and forgive them as I have been forgiven by You. Thank You for a canopy of protection over my entire family that only You can give. In Jesus' mighty name, amen.

When You Need God's Presence to Increase

Father, thank You for the spirit of wisdom and revelation to open my eyes and heart. I pray that You would shed light on Your Word so I may see Jesus. I long to see You so I can respond to Your thoughts and Your ways. I long to commune and be in fellowship with You. Lord, I thank You for the privilege to move Your heart. Thank You, Jesus, for Your humility. You are all in all, and yet You still reveal Yourself.

Father, I pray that You would tenderize my heart and let the words of Hosea 10:12 come alive in my spirit today: "Sow for yourselves righteousness; reap in mercy; break up your fallow ground, for it is time to seek the LORD, till He comes and rains righteousness on you."[67] Lord, I ask that You break up any fallow ground or hardness of heart so I may seek and love You with all my heart, with all my soul, with all my mind, and with all my strength. Overtake me with Your presence so I can be a witness to others who don't know You. I want my life to be used by You! In Jesus' mighty name, amen.

When You Want to Give Your Life to Jesus

Lord, I confess my sins to You. My desire is to love You. I want to be set free from every chain that has held me in bondage and captivity. Jesus, You hold the keys to death and the grave.[68] I want my heart to be Your home where You can dwell. I want to have fellowship with You every moment of every day. I open my heart to You, Jesus, and I pray that You would remove any pain or fear of rejection and intimate fellowship with You because of the trauma from my past. I repent of not allowing You in, and today I give You all that I am and place my heart into Your gentle hands.

Lord, come into my heart. You are my Lord and Savior. I believe that You gave Your life, and I declare with my mouth, Jesus, that You are Lord, and that You were raised from the dead.[69] Thank You for laying down Your life for me so You could open the door to everlasting friendship and relationship with You. All the power, the glory, and the honor belong to You, Jesus. In Your powerful name I pray, amen.

When You Need to Overcome Resentment

Father, this day is a gift from You, and today I declare Your Word over every moment You have given to me. This is the day that You have made, I will be glad and rejoice in it.[70] I set my heart on You and choose to bring an offering of praise and gratitude to You. I set my eyes on Jesus, and not what is on the earth. Jesus, when I look at You, the issues of this world begin to fade into the background like images in the rearview mirror of a car. Lord, would You remove every distraction that keeps me from fully entering the joy of Your presence? Help me resist the temptation the Enemy brings every day to look at what I don't have instead of looking at all You have blessed me with.

Father, I ask that You would cover and protect my heart from resentment and bitterness toward myself and others. Help me discern when the Enemy is attempting to sow seeds of discord in my heart and to turn away from it quickly. You have been so good to me, and eternity itself will not be enough to thank You for the miracles You have done in my life and in the lives of the people I love. Thank You, Jesus. You are worthy.

When You Need God's Peace

Father, Your peace binds my heart to Yours. Your peace is my weapon against the Enemy, and Your desire is for my heart to rest in Yours. Deliver me from the cares of this world that attempt to steal what You promised You would leave with me when You went to heaven after Your crucifixion. Jesus, You said, "Peace I leave with you, My peace I give to you; not as the world gives do I give to you. Let not your heart be troubled, neither let it be afraid."[71] Lord, help me abide in Your peace and stay calm in this day and resist the temptation to become fearful or upset when chaos is all around me. I know the Enemy's desire is to steal the peace You have given me, to steal my joy because Your Word declares that Your joy will be my strength.[72] I need Your strength to move from season to season and not become weary!

I am reminded of the words You spoke to Moses in Numbers 6:24–27, when he blessed Israel, saying, "The Lord bless you and keep you; the Lord make His face shine upon you, and be gracious to you; the Lord lift up His countenance upon you, and give you peace." Father, thank You for the peace that covers and protects me and the ones that I love. In Jesus' name, amen.

PRAYERS OF HOPE FOR YOUR PHYSICAL BODY

You know those moments in life that mark you forever? Sometimes they are good moments, like my experience praying at McDonald's, but life is riddled with so many difficult moments as well. Jesus told us that in this world we would have tribulation, but to take heart, because He has overcome the world (John 16:33). What a promise He has given us! Through the years, I have learned that God's glory and goodness assuredly go hand in hand with the perils, trials, and tribulations that life brings. But here is the good news: As we abide in Him, we are victorious because He holds the victor's crown! What a hope we have in Jesus! But here is the key: Our hearts need to remain connected to Him, and this happens in communion with Him; it happens when we walk with God, when we talk to God and pray.

When You Need a Miracle

Lord, today I remember how You have delivered me. Whether I knew it or not, You were always there. Your eyes were always set on me; even before I was knit in my mother's womb, You knew me.[73] You said that You would never leave or forsake me.[74] You are carrying me now, and I know that Your faithfulness will carry me through to the other side of this season. Lord, You have never failed me!

Jesus, Your miracles are memorials that I can look back on and be reminded that if You did it once, You will do it again! You are loyal; You are forgiving; You never break Your promises. My confidence is in who You are. You delivered Daniel from the mouths of the lions, You opened up the Red Sea for Your children to pass through, You gave up Your life and conquered death and the grave!

Lord, I lay every impossible situation at Your feet; help me never forget where You brought me from. I give all that I am to You. You are the King of kings and Lord of lords. You are the miracle-working God who never fails. In Jesus' mighty name, amen.

When You Feel Weak

Father, Your Word declares that what You desire is a broken and contrite heart.[75] Thank You for not turning Your face away from me when I am weak. It is in these moments when Your strength comes and fills me. Your Word declares, "Let the weak say, 'I am strong.'"[76] So today I pray that my heart will be made of flesh and not of stone.[77]

Lord, where would I be without Your grace? It carries me through the trials of this life. Your grace ripped me from the grasp of sin and death, and You have wrapped me in Your arms and declared that I am Yours. Even as I pray right now, I ask Your Holy Spirit to consume every part of my soul that is weak and replace it with heavenly strength that only comes from You! Your Spirit brings Your resurrection power over me when I am at my weakest. Help me be vulnerable toward You and the people that You have put in my life. I want a heart that is open and always listening for Your voice. Help me be sensitive to Your still, small voice today. In Jesus' name, amen.

When You Need God to Strengthen Your Body

Father, thank You that there is nothing that is impossible for You. Lord, I pray that You would release Your strength over me today. I have been weak, and I need a fresh touch from You. I pray for Your Spirit to fill and strengthen every bone, ligament, tendon, and cell in my body. Lord, I ask that You remove any and all pain and discomfort that is keeping my body from being able to fully rest. Today, I long to rest in Your presence. Father, I ask that You strengthen me through the power of the Holy Spirit indwelling my innermost being. You are my strength, and I declare in this moment of weakness that I will be strong in the Lord and in the power of Your might!

Your Word is fortifying me right now. Even as I pray, cause faith to begin to rise within me, and release supernatural strength over the weariness of my body and soul. Your Word is life; it fortifies me and it strengthens me on the darkest days. By faith, I receive the strength only You can give. In the mighty, powerful, strong name of Jesus I pray, amen.

When You Need Rest

Father, I look to You today, and I am so thankful You are the author and the finisher of my faith.[78] I pray for my heart to rest in You. This season has been long and tiring, and there are times I am not sure where I am going to receive strength to keep moving forward. But You are faithful, and I pray You would cause my heart to rest. I am leaving everything at the foot of the cross. I am letting go of all the weights that have brought me down, and I am inviting You into the places that have been difficult for me to let go of.

Father, thank You for a revelation in my heart that everything I need, everything I desire in the present, and everything I will ever want is found in You. Teach me to rest in You through every moment, and that having peace and rest in my heart is not contingent on the circumstances in my life. I have peace because You have already provided it to me through Your presence. I receive it right now, Lord. Thank You for delivering my heart from strife, restlessness, and worry. I thank You for the rest You are giving me now. In Jesus' name, amen.

When You Want Courage

Father, thank You for going before me, behind me, and all around me today. Lord, I pray that You would break the power of fear and unbelief and empower me through Your grace to rise in faith and courage, knowing that You have already made a way for me. Father, You are the Great I Am, You are who You say You are, and I am so thankful for the Holy Spirit's guidance in every step I take. You are my anchor, Jesus, and You hold the victor's crown. What could I possibly fear when I know You are for me and not against me?

Lord, thank You that just like You told Joshua, I, too, will be strong and of good courage; I will not be afraid, because You are with me.[79] Give me boldness that causes me to run into the battles of life with a revelation in my heart like David had of You. He knew that You were for him and trusted You with everything inside him. He knew in his heart that the mighty God of Israel was with him.[80] Today, I take on the courage that You have already given me, and I will run straight into the battle knowing that the Lord of Hosts is with me. In Jesus' mighty name, amen.

When You Need Help Healing from Past Shame

Father, thank You for Your extravagant love that reached down into the depths of hell to save me. Lord, today I pray for a fresh surrender in my heart, and I ask You to forgive me for my sins, known and unknown. You see me as I am, and Your Word says that even though people may see the outward appearance of a person, it is You, Lord, who looks at my heart.[81] I'm so thankful for this truth. You look at me and know the depths of who I am; nothing is hidden from You.

Today, I pray that You would heal my heart entirely from the shame of my past. Restore my mind and heart in such a way that the memories of what has passed would be covered under the precious blood of Jesus. I am a new creation in You; I am crucified with Christ and it is no longer I who live, but Christ in me![82] Father, restore my mind, body, spirit, and soul from the sins of the past, and give me the grace to walk, commune, and fellowship with You all the days of my life. You are my healer; You are the restorer of my heart. I love You, Jesus. Amen.

When You Are Vulnerable

Lord Jesus, You reign, and I thank You for this day. Your Word gives me strength when I feel like I cannot move on anymore. Just when I feel like every wall is closing in on me, here You come with power only You can give. I pray for a refreshing in my spirit that would take away the weariness in me. Your Word declares, "The LORD will perfect that which concerns me."[83] You care about what others may consider "the small stuff." You care when I am hurting and alone. You see me, Lord. You hold my future in Your hands, and I ask You to remove the worries that are on my mind today, giving me Your peace.

Lord, You withhold no good thing from those who walk uprightly.[84] I want to walk in purity without compromise; my connection to Your heart is what matters most to me. Lord, I pray for strength and boldness, because Your Word says, "The wicked flee when no one pursues them, but the righteous are as bold as a lion."[85] I pray for faith like the Roman centurion who called out to You, knowing You could do the impossible.[86] Thank You for the strength You have already released as I pray to You now, Jesus. Amen.

When You Need Freedom from Addiction

God, I pray that You would fill me with Your Spirit and the hope that can only come from You. Lord, I ask that You purify my heart and remove the hindrances that keep me from walking in Your ways. Please deliver me from all the addictions, all the pain, all the shame, all the guilt, and all the darkness that have held me captive in chains. I pray for a complete breakthrough in my life so I can walk in the freedom You have provided for me through the power of Your blood shed at the cross.

Lord, I pray that You would remove the desires that these addictions have held me in bondage to, and give me a desire for Your presence. I pray for every void in my heart to be filled with the joy of knowing You, and I ask that You would close the doors in my life that are open to sin. Father, remove ungodly alignments and influences in my life that have led me onto the path of destruction, and lead me on the narrow path that leads to life with You.[87] Thank You, Father, for watching over me and delivering me from every chain and addiction from my past. In Jesus' powerful name, amen.

When You Seek God's Protection for Your Life and Family

Father, I thank You today for Your great grace. You have opened my eyes to see that You are for me. Lord, thank You that I don't have to fear the arrow by day nor the terror by night.[88] I know that I am hidden in the shadow of Your wings.[89] There is safety in close proximity to Your presence, as You promised in Psalm 91. Father, thank You for placing Your mighty hand of protection over me and sending angels to protect me in my comings and in my goings.

Thank You for bringing me in, for tearing the veil so we could be face-to-face and so I could be near You forever. I am so thankful that Your shadow provides me with shelter and protection. I pray this over my family and the ones that I love. Help me not to grow weary in doing good, but to trust You that in due season, by Your grace, I won't give up, and I will reap the harvest that You have promised in Your Word.[90] I pray this over my family today, and I thank You, Lord, that You are with me. In Jesus' mighty name, amen.

When You Need Help Resisting Temptation

Father, the blood of Your Son Jesus has set me free. I come boldly before the throne of grace for mercy and help in time of need.[91] My spirit is willing, but my flesh has been weak,[92] and I need Your power to set me free. You are triumphant in my life over the addictions that have held me captive. Lord, I pray that You would set me free from the addiction of [name the addiction] and shatter every stronghold that is attempting to destroy me. You declared in Your Word, "If the Son sets you free, you will be free indeed."[93] I know that the plans of the Enemy are to steal, kill, and destroy what You desire for my life.[94] Lord, I pray that You would send warring and ministering angels to surround me. Give me strength to overcome temptation when it comes my way.

Father, I humble myself under Your mighty hand. Help me resist the devil, and I know he will flee.[95] Deliver me from desires to escape my current reality and the memories of the past. Today, I pray that you would release me from the bondage that has kept me from living in the fullness of life that is only found in You. In Jesus' mighty name, amen.

Be still, and know that I am God; I
will be exalted among the nations,
I will be exalted in the earth.

PSALM 46:10

Did you know that the original Hebrew root of "be still" doesn't mean "be quiet"? It means "*let go.*"⁹⁶ Let go and know that He is God. There is freedom in a surrendered heart, and through it God will move in your life in a mighty way and do what only He can do.

I remember a moment in my life where it seemed like the "night season" would never be over. I walked outside and asked the Lord to help us with an impossible situation in which we knew that if God did not intervene, the curtains would close right in front of us. I could hear the scripture: "The steps of a good man are ordered by the LORD, and He delights in his way" (Psalm 37:23). Immediately in my spirit, I knew that the Lord was trying to get a point across to me. God began to remind me of His faithfulness to my family and me over the years. There was a season where I was practically bedridden for almost nine months, and there wasn't a month where He did not miraculously provide for us.

We never knew how God would sustain us, but as each month passed, there was no denying that we knew that God was not going to let us go, and somehow, someway, He was going to take care of us. This season gave us a revelation of how important it is for us to grow in our relationship with the Lord where we go from believing to knowing. See, there is a big difference between believing and knowing. The Bible says that even the demons believe, but where does just believing get anyone? When we know something, we begin to live from that place in our hearts. Walking in godly confidence is tangible and rooted in faith. God wants each of us to go from believing in Him to truly knowing Him. When you know that God has your back, you have nothing to fear, because you know that the Commander of heaven's armies is with you. Being still and waiting on the Lord is hopeful and expectant, even though you do not know what God will do.

The three Hebrew boys in the fire demonstrated to us what this looks like. These boys were thrown into the furnace but knew that God could deliver them from the fire. Yet still, they declared that even if God did not deliver them, they would not bow down to a false God, even if they perished (Daniel 3:1–30)! What an incredible model for us to remember every day. So no matter what stands in front of you today, when your heart is knit together with the Lord's, you can never miss what He has for you, because your steps are ordered by Him. When your heart's desire is to love and follow Him, His Word promises that He will make every crooked path straight for you (Proverbs 3:5–6).

When You Seek Peace in the Lord's Provision

Father, thank You for providing for me in every way. Thank You that I can have confidence in You that You will supply all my needs according to Your riches and glory in Christ Jesus.[97] I choose to believe that what You call me to, You will provide for. You own the cattle on a thousand hills, and the gold and silver of this entire world belongs to You.[98] Lord, You are a covenant-keeping, promise-keeping God, and I know You will not withhold any good thing from those You are in covenant with.[99]

Lord, I want to thank You for Your kindness to me and my family. You have always been faithful to make a way where there seemed to be no way, and I rejoice in Your faithfulness with my heart overflowing with gratitude. Lord, You know my needs and the provision I am praying for today, and I ask that You would help me resist the temptation to worry about what will happen or how You will work things out for me. I rest in the truth that You are watching over me with those kind, loving eyes. My life is a testament to Your wondrous provision. Lord, forgive me for doubting. You will never fail. Jesus, it's in Your mighty name I pray, amen.

When You Are Under Pressure

Father, thank You that You didn't just call us sons and daughters, but You have called us heirs.[100] Holy Spirit, come and inhabit my praises to You. I pray that You would give me Your thoughts and bind my will and mind to the mind of Jesus. God, Your Word declares, "Let everything that has breath praise the Lord."[101] Lord, You have given me the weapon of praise to overcome the works of darkness. I will not wait for the rocks to cry out;[102] I will lift the voice You have given me in worship even when my mind, my flesh, my heart, and my body may fail me. I pray for every part of me to submit to Your will as Jesus did in the garden when He said, "Father . . . not my will, but yours be done."[103] I will declare of Your works in the night, because I know that the night will not last forever. Lord, I pray that I will learn everything that You want me to learn in this season where I am pressed on every side, but I thank You that I will not be crushed![104] By Your grace, I will receive all You have prepared for me. In the mighty name of Jesus I pray, amen.

When You Need God to Make You Safe

Father, You are the King of glory, and I lift my heart up to You today. Thank You for the invitation to Your table to see the awe and splendor of Your presence. You made a way for me to come into fellowship with You when You gave Your life for me. You tore the veil, You shed Your blood, You gave Your life, just for me. There aren't enough thank-Yous in all eternity for what You have done for me. But what I have to give to You, it's Yours. I give it all to You: I give You my surrendered heart; I give You every part of me that is broken and bruised; I bring You my mind; and I pray that I would have the mind of Christ and that I would be made whole.

Thank You for a seat at Your table where I will never hunger or thirst again. I don't want anything or anyone else in this world but You. Your Word declares that You prepare a table for me in the presence of my enemies.[105] I know that trusting in You is the safest place in this world, and I choose to rest in You. In Jesus' name I pray, amen.

When You Need Comfort

Lord, I lift my eyes to You, God of my salvation. Thank You that I will see the goodness of the Lord in the land of the living.[106] Jesus, when I look at You, I know that I will not lose heart. I believe You will strengthen me in every trial. I pray for fervor and endurance, and that I would not lose heart and be tempted to quit. Lord, give me strength to run this race with You in holiness, purity, and with my soul connected to Yours. One touch from You lifts the weariness of my body. One look into Your eyes gives me the strength to keep moving. You are my provider, You are my healer, You are my Savior, and I lack nothing because I have You. Your mercy is new every morning,[107] and I am taking hold of all You have for me.

You know my heart fully, and as I lift my eyes to You, Jesus, I find my identity and who You have made me to be in You. Father, You have seated me with Your Son in heavenly places.[108] I have nothing to fear because I am hidden in the shelter of the Most High God.[109] Thank You for the gift of being hidden in Your presence today. In Jesus' mighty name, amen.

When You Are Moving into a New Home

Father, today I declare over my home, "As for me and my house, we will serve the Lord."[110] I pray that my new home will be filled with Your glory and presence. Let my home be a place of refuge that is marked with purity and holiness. When others step foot into this home, I hope they experience Your presence and know, "The Lord is in this place." I pray that You would drive the Enemy out of my house and crown our home with Your glory and peace.

Your Word declares You give Your beloved rest.[111] I pray that worship would echo through the atmosphere, not just in music or sound, but by the words I speak. Lord, this home belongs to You. You are the covering of my home, the King of this house. I ask that you cleanse this home of anything that is not of You. Make this home a house of prayer, a beacon of Your light to my neighbors, an oasis where people can find peace, a resting place for Your presence, me, my loved ones, and every person who steps foot through the front door. In Jesus' name, amen.

When You Need Financial Provision

Lord, I ask that You open my eyes to see You as You really are. You are my provider, and You care for me, Jesus. You said, "Look at the birds of the air, for they neither sow nor reap nor gather into barns; yet your heavenly Father feeds them. Are you not of more value than they?"[112] You care for all my needs, and I rebuke every lie of the Enemy that says You will not provide for my needs. You are a wonderful Father. You are and have been so good to me. I declare that I lack no good thing.[113] Only goodness and mercy will follow me all the days of my life.[114]

Father, I pray that You would supernaturally provide for me and my family. I am calling out to You because You are the Lord who has already provided what I need, even if I haven't seen it yet. Without faith, how could I please You? I release my faith and trust that when I "seek first the kingdom of God and his righteousness . . . all these things will be added to [me]."[115] Lord, I know You will take care of me in every way, and You will never withhold any good thing from those that walk uprightly.[116] In Jesus' mighty name, amen.

When You Wish to Feel the Nearness of Jesus

Father, You gave Your all, Your one and only Son, for me. My heart explodes with gratitude. Jesus, the value of Your nearness is all I need. You will always be my first love. If my heart has grown cold, bitter, or drawn away from You in any way, I ask for Your forgiveness. Your nearness is what satisfies me more than anything in this world.

Lord, money, power, and fame will never satisfy me the way You do. You are my greatest treasure, and I pray that all my days would be full of Your presence. I ask for Your Spirit to be tangible to every person I meet today, to those who know You and do not know You. Lord, my life is for Your glory. I want to be all You want me to be. I will not forget where I was or where I am now. Awaken my heart to the nearness and beauty that are only found in You. Help me remember that my position in You is and will always be a child of God. My entire existence is to know You. In Jesus' name, amen.

When You Need to Make a Decision

Father, I boast in Your strength and Your power alone. You are the God who opens doors that no person can shut, and You close doors that no person can open.[117] I pray for Your will to be done in the situation that I am facing today. There are decisions that I rely on You for, and I need to see what You desire most in my life. I lay down what I think is right and best and surrender to Your will and purpose for the season ahead. You know the beginning from the end, and the end from the beginning.[118] I do not want to take a single step forward without You being the one to open doors. I am asking that You also close the doors that are not of You. Remove any veil of deception and allow for me to see through Your eyes and discern Your voice and Your heart in the decisions I make. I pray that I would not be led by desires of the flesh, but that I would only be led by Your Spirit. I give You my will; I lay down any desire to be right and ask that You would make Your will known to me. Father, I pray that no weapon formed against me would prosper.[119] In Jesus' mighty name, amen.

When You Need to Overcome Temptation

Father, Your Word declares that we have been adopted as sons and daughters through Your Son, Jesus Christ.[120] Your blood has covered my sins, and today I pray that I would wholeheartedly receive Your grace by faith to overcome temptation. Your Word declares, "God is faithful; he will not let you be tempted beyond what you can bear. But when you are tempted, he will also provide a way out so that you can endure it."[121] Your grace empowers me to overcome sin, temptation, and the works of the devil. I lift my heart and my hands in complete surrender to You because You are the one and only true God of love who sees me and cares. I lift my hands in victory and thank You that I am triumphant in You. I call on the name of Jesus that is above every name and god of this world, and I pray that You would fill my life with Your grace. Lord, You always provide a way of escape from temptation and sin that attempt to ensnare me. Lord, thank You for covering me with Your precious blood. In the mighty name of Jesus I pray, amen.

When You Are Looking for Peace

Father, thank You for sending us Your Holy Spirit to lead and guide us into all truth. In Colossians 3:15, Paul said, "Let the peace of God rule in your hearts, to which also you were called in one body; and be thankful."[122] Your peace is like a compass that leads me into Your will. I pray that I would have spiritual discernment to know the difference between You and temporary comfort from the world. Jesus, take me deeper into Your heart, because to know You is to know the peace only You can give.

Father, I surrender my desires to You for my life. No matter what it costs, I want what You want. Your will for me is my home, and I thank You for the peace that covers my heart and mind. I pray for forgiveness for the times I made decisions without inquiring of You first. Through these experiences, You have taught me what it means to be led by You. Jesus, You are the Prince of Peace, and I thank You that You lead me beside the still waters of peace.[123] Help me become more like You and listen to You when You speak. In Jesus' name, amen.

PRAYERS OF HOPE FOR PEACE OVER YOUR THOUGHTS

It's interesting to me that in Luke 11, the disciples came to Jesus asking Him to teach them how to pray. They didn't ask Him how to teach, preach, cast out demons, or prophesy. All that is wonderful, and the gifts God gives have a specific purpose for His glory. But what the disciples wanted was to learn how to pray the way He did. In other words, the disciples saw something in Jesus that they desired deeply, and it was His friendship with God.

I believe the disciples understood that all the other aspects of life and ministry flowed from the place of friendship and intimacy with the Father. Somehow, they figured out that there was something about Jesus' prayer life that unlocked the supernatural life He lived on full display before the world. Now, I am not undermining the gifts of the Spirit in any way; I love the gifts that the Lord has given to the body of Christ and desire them earnestly! But I am saying that all things flow from communion with the Lord in prayer when we fellowship with Him. And when you speak, He is listening to you!

When you spend time in prayer and fellowship with Jesus, He begins to transform your thoughts and your mind. The Scriptures tell us that His ways are higher than our ways and His thoughts are higher than our thoughts.[124]

When You Need Peace for Your Mind

Father, Your Word promises in Isaiah 26:3, "You will keep in perfect peace all who trust in you, all whose thoughts are fixed on you!"[125] Today, I am fixing my gaze and thoughts on You. My desire is that the meditations of my heart and mind would be on Your Word that sets me free. I give every anxious thought to You. Jesus, You are God, and my life is entirely in Your hands. I surrender every situation I can't control.

Lord, thank You for the peace of Your presence that removes fear of the unknown, dread of the future, and fear of what may come. I will wait on You in expectant hope and rest in the promise that when I wait on You, my strength is renewed![126] I will not be anxious or afraid because, Jesus, You are the Lord of all the earth, and You are walking with me!

Lord, You strengthen me in my weakness and give life to my soul when I feel like I can't go on another day. I know that every good and perfect thing comes from You, the Father of lights.[127] You have not given me a spirit of fear, but of power, love, and a sound mind.[128] I trust You, Lord. In Jesus' name, amen.

When You Need Freedom from Guilt and Shame

Jesus, You are beautiful, and my heart is overwhelmed when I see Your face. You see me like no one does. I choose to believe what You see and not what my past or even what my present situation may be. I pray that You would reveal my identity that is found in You. Your thoughts toward me are good, not to do me harm, but to give me hope and a future.[129] I want to know the dreams in Your heart that You had before I was knit in my mother's womb.[130]

Father, I pray that You would remove from my mind words spoken against me or words I have spoken and believed about myself that don't align with Your Word. Lord, deliver me from shame, guilt, and condemnation that the Enemy has sought to torment my mind with, and cover me with Your love. Your Word says that love covers a multitude of sins.[131] I ask that You set me free from every shackle of guilt and shame that has kept me bound by the past. By Your grace, I will not fear, fret, or worry. Come, Lord Jesus, I wait for You. In Jesus' name, amen.

When You Face Impossible Situations

Jesus, You are my promise-keeping friend and Savior. Today, I pray that the light of Your face will shine on me. Lord, You declared in Your Word that despite what's impossible for man, all things are possible with You.[132] I am facing impossible situations today in which my heart is crying out for a divine intervention from You. You made the sun stand still for Joshua because of Your relationship with him.[133] I turn to You because I know that You are able to do exceedingly abundantly above all that I can think or ask for.[134]

Help me recognize that the adversities of this life are an invitation to draw close to You. I will not retreat in fear, but today I choose to lean into Your heart and believe that You will never leave me. Today, I remember all the impossible situations You brought me through before, and I believe You will do it again!

Lord, take my faith to new heights and disrupt the plans of the Enemy! In this moment of what seems impossible, I believe that You will open the doors that need to be opened and close the doors that need to be closed.[135] In Jesus' name, amen.

When You Need Help Letting Go

God, thank You for giving me the grace that I need while I am in the process of letting go of anything and everything that has held me captive to the past. You know my struggles and the battles I have faced. Today, I need Your strength to overcome once and for all. I ask You to show me the next step I am to take as my life is shifting and changing so quickly. I do not want to hold on to the old baggage of yesterday. I want to take hold of the new season that You have ahead of me without looking back.

Lord, give me the grace I need to start moving forward today, and keep me encouraged and focused so I can run my race with endurance.[136] I pray for the strength to be strong spiritually, emotionally, mentally, and physically. Jesus, You watch over and take care of me. I don't want to go backward and feel like I have failed again, so I pray for grace and strength to let go of the past and move into this new moment, without grief or sorrow. Thank You for the joy only You can give. In Jesus' mighty name, amen.

When You Want to Make the Most of Your Time

Father, Your Word teaches us to not worry about what will happen tomorrow because tomorrow will have worries and anxieties of its own.[137] Your Word tells us that this life is like a vapor,[138] a short glimpse of what is to come. Help me make the most of every moment of every day and know that this day is a gift from You.

Father, the days of my life are counted, and I want to bring You glory and lead others to You with the time I have on earth. Holy Spirit, remind me of the power of living one day at a time with gratitude in my heart. I'm not where I was, I'm not where I'm going, but You and I are on a journey together led by Your peace where I get to know You deeper. Thank You that You are just as much in the journey as You are in the destination where You desire us to go together. Holy Spirit, I pray that You will help me let go of the past and the regrets of what I've done or not done. Today is all that I have, and I trust that You will keep me in thankfulness for all You have blessed me with today. In Jesus' mighty name, amen.

When You Feel Like You Need Control

Father, You are awesome in all Your ways; You know and see all things. Today, I pray for the peace that passes all understanding to surround my heart and my home.[139] In everything that I do, I pray for You to be like a compass in my heart. You are my refuge and strength, a very present help in the day of trouble.[140] You alone, Lord, can make all things work together for good, and I pray for that today in every relationship You have given me.

I pray for bold faith as I trust You with every circumstance in my life. Help me to not be surprised when adversity comes my way, because You said that trials and peril would be a part of this world. But You also said to take heart, because You have already over-come the world.[141] Father, nothing in this life compares to the hope that only You can give, the hope found in Jesus, and for that I am so grateful! No matter how difficult or how painful it is, I know there is freedom when I surrender it all to You, Lord. In Jesus' mighty name, amen.

When You Seek Direction in Your Life

Father, I am so thankful for the wisdom You freely give when I ask You. I want to walk step by step with You. I know that You are guiding my every move, and I can rest in the truth that when my heart is set on You, God, You will always make the right doors open and close the doors You don't want me to walk through. You will not allow me to stumble when I abide in Your shelter. In the shadow of Your presence, there is safety and protection.[142]

Lord, lead me in paths of righteousness for Your name's sake.[143] Thank You that I am not led by the flesh, reason, or wisdom of the world, but I am led only by Your Spirit. Draw me into Your understanding, and keep my heart tender so I will always seek Your face for every decision I make in the days ahead. Jesus, You are leading me; You are the Good Shepherd, and I know You will never lead me astray. Thank You for the next step You will have me take in faith, because that is what pleases You—that I trust You with my whole heart. In Jesus' mighty name, amen.

When You Need Discernment

Father, thank You for giving me Your Holy Spirit to live within my heart. It's incomprehensible that Your greatest desire from the very beginning was to dwell with Your people. Holy Spirit, I treasure the gift of discernment and the ability to tell truth from the lies of the Enemy. I pray that You would increase discernment in my life in this season to know Your Spirit from every other spirit. I ask for eyes to see and ears to hear You. Your Word brings revelation, and through it, You impart truth into my spirit, allowing me to see the difference between the truth of Your Word and deception. I pray that when I open Your Word, the attacks against my mind to blind me from the truth would not succeed, but that Your Holy Spirit would bring the light of revelation. I pray for the spirit of wisdom and understanding that reveal who You are.

Jesus, to know You and hear Your voice is the greatest treasure of this life. My heart longs to know You, and to know You is to know the truth and the power of Your resurrection. In the mighty name of Jesus I pray, amen.

When You Need Patience

Father, thank You for the expectation that is being produced in my heart as I wait on You. Lord, I pray for abiding trust in You no matter what I may see with my natural eyes. Jesus, You have led me, You have taken care of me, You have guided me through the deepest valleys, and I am forever grateful for Your great faithfulness to me. You have taken me by the hand and given me Your grace. Through every fall I have taken, You have picked me up, and I know You are not done with me. Thank You for believing in me the way You do and seeing me for who I will become. No one sees me the way You do, Lord. I love You, Jesus.

Today, I pray that You would cast off all fear, worry, fret, and anxiety from me. Help me abide in You and in the peace that only You can give. Lord, keep my heart connected to Yours during the moments my faith fails and the Enemy attempts to sow seeds of doubt. Help me rise in faith and trust that Your Word is the final word, no matter what is said or what I see. Thank You for the strength that comes when I wait on You. In Jesus' name I pray, amen.

When You Need to Fight Weariness

Lord Jesus, You are my peace in the midst of every storm in life. Lord, You calm the winds and the waves in my life, and I pray for my family, that You would fill their hearts and fill our homes with Your glorious presence in the mighty name of Jesus.

Lord, thank You that Your Word promises me that when I wait upon You, You will renew my strength, and I will mount up on wings like eagles, I will run and not be weary, I will walk and not faint.[144] I pray today that I will be full of Your strength and joy. Lord, give me peace in the waiting.

I thank You, Lord, that You always come through for me; You are perfect in all Your ways.[145] You never fail, and I know You never will. You're the same yesterday, today, and forever.[146] I pray that You would fill me with the power of Your presence. In Jesus' mighty name, amen.

> "Because he loves me," says the LORD, "I will rescue him, I will protect him, for he acknowledges my name. He will call on me, and I will answer him. I will be with him in trouble, I will deliver him and honor him. With long life I will satisfy him and show him my salvation."
>
> PSALM 91:14–16 NIV

Psalm 91 is a weapon given to us in Scripture where the Lord teaches us what happens when we abide in the shadow of His presence. God wants you to see Him as your source of peace, safety, friendship, and hope regardless of the circumstances taking place around you. The eye of the storm is an invitation to connect with the heart of Jesus in the secret place of His presence.

We always become what we behold. When we look at Jesus and when we worship Him through the trials and valleys we face in life, we become more like Him! Think about it: This is the only time in all eternity where you and I will have the opportunity to worship God through pain. One day, Jesus will establish His kingdom in the new earth and there will be no more tears and no more pain. "And God will wipe away every tear from their eyes; there shall be no more death, nor sorrow, nor crying. There shall be no more pain, for the former things have passed away" (Revelation 4:21). We get to choose Jesus through the adversities of this life, and He promises to give us beauty for ashes, joy for mourning, and praise for heaviness through the darkest seasons.

Choosing to draw near to God despite our circumstances reveals our heart. It displays our faith (or lack thereof) in the moments that are meant to destroy us. I think about how it must move God's heart to see us respond to Him in faith no matter what our circumstances look like. And when we choose to abide in the shadow of His presence, our hearts are knit together with His. God provides us with divine protection, safety, deliverance from evil, and His great love that covers us no matter what we face in life.

When You Need to See Jesus

Father, You are the one who loves me through every valley. I thank You for Your Son, Jesus—everything I want and everything I will ever need. You have stormed the gates of my heart and rescued me from the darkness that pursued me. Lord, I want to know what moves Your heart, and I pray that my life would bring You glory. Pour out Your Spirit over me. Lord, I pray that I would be full of faith in You so that I can stand strong in the fiercest battle.

You are my healer, You have delivered my soul, You have redeemed me, You are my everything, Jesus. I want to abide in You and trust in You in the darkest of days, through trial and through change. Father, no matter what may come my way, I have the assurance that You are with me. "One thing I ask from the LORD, this only do I seek: that I may dwell in the house of the LORD all the days of my life, to gaze on the beauty of the LORD and to seek him in his temple."[147] Jesus, show me the beauty of Your heart. I want to behold Your face in this season like never before. Amen.

When You Need Mountains Moved

Father, I remember everything that You have done for me, and I remember the impossible situations that You made possible. Lord, I will never forget how You have blessed me, and I thank You for Your grace over my life and those I love. Today, I pray for a revelation and for there to be a bursting of knowledge of Your Son Jesus in my heart.

Thank You for surrounding me with angels and for being with me always. I yearn for the wisdom and clarity to see Your will. Lord, thank You for everything You have set before me today. I pray that You would move in miracles that bring Your name glory, and that You would be known. I am believing You for healing over every area of my life. Lord, I thank You that You are my healer. I am believing You for a breakthrough. You are the God who goes before me and opens doors that no human can shut. Lord, I pray that You would bless the work of my hands mightily in this season for Your purpose.[148] I eagerly await Your kingdom, and for Your will to be done, on earth as it is in heaven.[149] Cover me with Your presence, Lord. In Jesus' mighty name, amen.

When You Are Overwhelmed with Gratitude

This is my prayer to the love of my life, Jesus. Every breath I take, it comes from You. You are the light in the darkness and the source of the joy in my heart. Lord, You loved me first; You are the first and the last,[150] and I am so thankful I get to respond to Your love. Remembering Your miracles, Your goodness, and how You loved me when I rejected You overwhelms my heart with thankfulness, and it protects my heart from growing hard and cold. I never want to forget what You have done to break the power of the Enemy over my life. I never want to forget the testimony of how You delivered me when I was lost. I never want to forget the truth of Your Word when Paul declared, "God demonstrates his own love for us in this: While we were still sinners, Christ died for us."[151] Jesus, You died for me; Your blood is, was, and will always be enough! How can I thank You adequately? Your love covers a multitude of sins,[152] and even now as I pray, it is covering and protecting my heart from the cares, the attacks, and the troubles of this world. In Jesus' mighty name, amen.

When You Want Help to Guard Your Words

Lord, You said that death and life are in the power of the tongue.[153] I have been made in Your image, and I thank You for Your Word and Holy Spirit. I pray that You will guard my tongue from harsh words. Your Word says that on the day of judgment, I will be accountable for every idle word I have ever spoken.[154] I pray that the words that come from my mouth would speak life and that my lips would be used as a vessel of righteousness for Your glory. Lord, help me be quick to listen and slow to speak.[155]

Jesus, You only spoke the words You heard the Father speak,[156] and my desire today is to walk in Your ways. Make me aware of when the Enemy brings temptation to cause me to become angry and speak words that are detrimental. Lord, Your grace gives me the privilege to repent quickly and turn away from sin. You said in Your Word, "There is now no condemnation for those who are in Christ Jesus."[157] I receive Your forgiveness, and I pray that my mouth would only speak truth and words that bring you glory. In the name of Jesus I pray, amen.

When You Need Freedom from Sin

Father, in Jesus' name I thank You for Your goodness. Thank You for Your abundant blessing over this season. Lord, I pray that You would help me to always seek Your counsel and inquire of Your heart for Your will, to know Your ways. Today, I cry out to You as Moses did, "Show me Your glory!"[158]

Where my heart has been held captive, Lord, I thank You that Your Word says, "If the Son sets you free, you will be free indeed"![159] Today I declare freedom over my heart and freedom from sin. Jesus, I pray that my heart would be quick to repent of sin and receive Your forgiveness without shame and condemnation. Father, I ask You for forgiveness and pray that You would cleanse me of all unrighteousness according to Your Word in 1 John 1:9.

Lord, You will never tempt me with sin, but when the opportunity comes, Your grace and goodness always provide a way of escape.[160] I pray for grace to choose Your will, obey Your Word, and walk in Your ways. In Jesus' mighty name, amen.

When You Want Help Overcoming Discouragement

Father, in the mighty name of Jesus, I pray for more of You and less of me. Thank You for all the people You have sent into my life who have been a blessing. Right now, I am facing a battle that only You can fight on my behalf. I put my entire life into Your mighty hands and declare that I will trust in You, and You alone, Lord! Fill me afresh when I am weary and help me not take matters into my own hands but truly trust in You.

God, You have promised that when I call out to You and pray according to Your will, You hear me.[161] From the top of my head to the soles of my feet, I pray for Your divine protection. Your Spirit gives me a second wind when I am weak, and I want to run this race with You and finish strong! Fill me with Your presence to overflowing so others around me can see You. May the rivers of living water spring forth from my spirit. I pray that Your glory would rest on me. I love You with all my heart, Jesus; You are beautiful in all Your ways. In Your name I pray, amen.

When You Feel Distant from God

Heavenly Father, I want to ask You for forgiveness for disconnecting my heart from Yours. This has caused me to feel far away from You, and I long to hear Your voice again. Lord, I love You, and I receive Your forgiveness in my life. I pray that You would remove the distance I have felt; I want to be near Your heart, and I pray that You would come and fill every empty space with Your glorious presence. There is a space in my heart that only You can fill.

Lord, I receive all that You are, and You can have all that I am. Jesus, You never fail, and instead of running away from what hurts, I run into Your arms. You are my safest place, and You are my best friend, Jesus. You are the one who has never turned Your back on me. Thank You for the gift of repentance that keeps my heart so closely knit with Yours. One day in Your courts is better than thousands elsewhere.[162] Keep me in this place of close fellowship with You, walking with You, talking with You. There is no place I would rather be than here with You. I love You with all my heart, Jesus. Amen.

When You Seek Dependence on the Holy Spirit

Father, I am so grateful for the promises of Your Word that You said I can have by faith. You said that blessed is the man who trusts in the Lord, whose confidence is in You.[163] I believe I will be like a tree planted by the water that spreads out its roots by the stream. I will not fear when heat comes, because the leaves of my tree are always green.[164] When the droughts come, I will not worry because I know I can depend on You, and I will never fail to bear fruit. Holy Spirit, thank You for teaching me what it means to rely on You. There isn't a battle You have ever fought where You have failed, and I can rest in knowing that You will not leave or forsake me.[165] Thank You for the fullness of Your Holy Spirit living within me to empower me to pray and live the life that You have called me to live for You. I have never walked alone. Thank You for the grace You give me each day to look to You for hope, strength, wisdom, direction, and truth. I rest in who You are and the peace You promised to me. Lord, I thank You for leading me into Your will for my life in the days ahead. In Jesus' name, amen.

When You Are Experiencing Spiritual Warfare

Heavenly Father, the book of Ephesians teaches that You have provided me Your mighty armor that is my protection against the attacks of the devil.[166] Today, I claim Your victory over the works of darkness by putting on the full armor of God. I put on the belt of truth so I will stand firm on Your Word, and I will not be deceived by the lies of the Enemy. I put on the breastplate of righteousness so it will guard my heart from evil, and I will remain pure, holy, and protected under the blood of Jesus Christ. I place my feet in the sandals of the gospel of peace so Your peace will shine through me to every person I meet today. I put on the helmet of salvation so my mind is protected from deceit and lies that attempt to alter my thoughts. I take up the shield of faith that protects my entire being from the flaming arrows of the Enemy. I take up the sword of the Spirit so I can discern the tempting lies of the devil. You have prepared me as a warrior in Your kingdom, and I will not be afraid! In Jesus' mighty name, amen.

When You Haven't Put Jesus First

Lord, today I come before You with a repentant heart. Wherever I have allowed anything to turn my gaze away from You—by putting other priorities, work, people, and all the distractions of this world in front of You— Father, forgive me. I don't just want to go through the motions and live a life that is stagnant. Forgive me for spiritual complacency, and Lord, I pray that You would set my heart on fire! Would You rekindle the fire on the altar of my heart to burn brightly again?

Your Word says that we are the salt of the earth.[167] Restore to me the joy of Your salvation where Your name echoed inside me, and I was consumed by the revelation of Your love for the first time. Holy Spirit, come and have Your way in me; purify every area of my life that needs it. Fellowship with You is the oil in my lamp that my heart longs for. Create in me a pure heart, God. Give me a passion to win souls for Your kingdom, and grip me with the spirit of reverence and fear of the Lord. Remove every open door of compromise and let the oil of our friendship burn once again. In the name of Jesus I pray, amen.

PRAYERS OF HOPE
FOR YOUR SPIRIT

The moment of prayer in McDonald's that I wrote about earlier is where one aspect of my life changed forever. For some I can understand that God hearing our prayers is a given, but for this girl who at one time in her life didn't even believe there was a God, I was wrecked. *God is listening to me? God cares about what I have to say to Him? He actually inclines His ear to hear the cry of my heart?* The answer to this is yes, He does.

God gives us words from heaven that we speak into the situations of life. He changes the course of history through our words in prayer to Him! A couple of weeks after the McDonald's prayer time, we received word that the young lady we were praying for that day had made a drastic change in her life and recommitted her life to the Lord.

That moment propelled my life into a journey of faith in prayer. God wanted to lay a solid foundation in my heart. God was listening to me intently and desired to answer the prayers and cries of my heart according to His will. But guess what? He wants to do that for you too! Jesus said, "Most assuredly, I say to you, the Son can do nothing of Himself, but what He sees the Father do; for whatever He does, the Son also does in like manner" (John 5:19). Jesus spent a lot of time in prayer, and the Father would speak to Him and show Him what was in His heart.

When You Want to Rest in God's Assurance

God, I am so thankful for the stream of Your presence that flows through me. Jesus, all my strength and hope are in You. You are my safe place, my refuge, and it is in You that I find rest for my soul. Jesus, You give me the space to breathe, and I will be still and know that You are God.[168] I know You are fighting my battles, and You already have angels on assignment on my behalf.

Jesus, I searched high and low, and found it was You I was searching for all my life. Your love has given me purpose and rest that this world could never offer me. Jesus, You see me, You know me, and You alone are my sure foundation. Thank You for walking with me beside the still waters and putting all my fears to rest. God, in the midst of the storm, You are my Prince of Peace. Genesis 6:8 declares, "Noah found grace in the eyes of the Lord."[169] Lord, thank You for the undeserved grace that You have shown me for my entire life. You hold my whole world in Your hands. In Jesus' mighty name, amen.

When You Struggle with Unbelief

Jesus, You are the victorious risen Lord, and You have delivered me from the snare of the Enemy. Today, I look to You, my King. At times my faith may fail me, but I know that Your grace overpowers the lies that seek to deter me from Your will for my life. Lord, I pray You would fill me with faith that You said would move the mountains of opposition that stand in front of me.[170] At times I feel like the man who fell at Your feet and cried, "Lord, I believe; help my unbelief!"[171] I pray that You would break the power of tormenting thoughts that cause me to retreat in hopelessness and defeat.

Jesus, I declare that You are greater than the lies of the devil. You are above a diagnosis from a doctor, addictions, a child who has walked away from You, a relationship that seems like it cannot be restored, and every impossible situation that I will ever face. Today, You are the one true God, and You lead me beside still waters and give me peace.[172] Help me keep Your Word in my heart that I may not sin against You. In Jesus' name I pray, amen.

When You Need the Lord to Fight for You

Father, there is no one like You—Creator of heaven and earth. Today, I look to You in all things. Father, I ask that You defeat all adversity that has come against me in this hour. God, I trust that You are my defender. You are my strong tower. Your Word declares that You are a mighty warrior, and I thank You that You are fighting my battles. Lord, I want to be like You in times of chaos and peril. You slept in the boat while the winds and the waves crashed all around You and Your disciples.[173] I pray today that Your peace would abide in me no matter what comes my way.

Father, I ask that You go before me, behind me, and all around me. I pray that no weapon formed against me would prosper. I pray that Your angels would surround me and those who I love. Lord, have Your way in me. I want my heart to be yielded and surrendered to You, and You alone. Jesus, I'm giving You all the glory, not just because of what You've done, not just because of what You're doing, not because of what You'll do, but because of who You are. You are worthy of it all because of who You are. In Jesus' name, amen.

When You Struggle with the Darkness of This World

Jesus, You are the word of life, and apart from You, I have nothing. You are the light that shines in the darkness.[174] You speak, and light shines.

I pray that You would redirect every arrow of the Enemy against my life. The darkness of this world will never overcome You, and for that reason I can be confident and not fear. You overcame death and the grave, and I declare Your Word over the life You have given me: If God is for me, who can be against me?[175] Lord, thank You that Your light and presence will shine on every area of my life. I pray that You would remove any scales from my eyes and cause me to see You.

Father, protect me from deception; I want to be led by Your Spirit. The book of Romans teaches us that You are revealed in all of creation,[176] and my prayer is that I would see You in every moment You have gifted me with. Help me live in the present and not be concerned with tomorrow. I have heard You with my ears and I have seen You with my eyes. Today, I behold Your face because You are the Word of life, and I will not be afraid. In Jesus' mighty name, amen.

Likewise the Spirit also helps in our weaknesses. For we do not know what we should pray for as we ought, but the Spirit Himself makes intercession for us with groanings which cannot be uttered. Now He who searches the hearts knows what the mind of the Spirit is, because He makes intercession for the saints according to the will of God. And we know that all things work together for good to those who love God, to those who are the called according to His purpose. For whom He foreknew, He also predestined to be conformed to the image of His Son, that He might be the firstborn among many brethren.

ROMANS 8:26–29

The Enemy of your soul wants you to believe the lie that you don't have any option but to fall into sin. Just remember this: Any area of your life where you feel hopeless is an area where God is revealing a lie to you. Agreements with lies can be very subtle, but the Holy Spirit will reveal these areas so you can have the opportunity to yield and surrender those areas to Him where He can bring healing. Don't be discouraged by the struggle! Even the apostle Paul spoke of the battle between the flesh and the Spirit of God. Struggling is an indicator that God is working with you and leading you where He wants you to go. Lean into the struggle, lean into the moments where conviction of sin brings you to repentance. And through the power of the Holy Spirit, God desires to heal those areas of your heart that He desires to make whole.

The internal battle is proof that God is purifying and cleansing, and the Spirit of God will give you the power to put the desires of flesh to death and give you a way of escape. God desires for you to walk in freedom, not condemnation or shame. Today, I want to encourage you to keep struggling, keep praying, keep fasting, keep getting back up after a fall. Fix your eyes on Jesus, the Author and Finisher of your faith. God didn't bring you this far to leave you, and He will finish what He started in your life as you continue to walk with Him with a surrendered heart.

God is working in your life, so don't let the Enemy feed the lie to you that your struggle is sinful. In fact, it's quite the opposite. The struggles you go through reveal that God is at work in your life, and He loves you too much to leave you where He found you.

When You Seek a Deeper Friendship with Jesus

Jesus, thank You for laying down Your life for me. Lord, You opened the door for us to walk together, talk to each other, and have an everlasting friendship. Lord, I pray that You would heal areas of my heart where I have distanced myself from You. Father, remove any fear because of the past where others may have hurt me or abused my trust. I know You love me. You are gentle and faithful.

Lord, this life is like a vapor, but friendship with You is forever. My heart's desire is to know Your heart and to know Your ways, and You even reward those who diligently seek You.[177] God, I want to shine as a light for You filled with faith. I trust that You are making all things work together for good. Jesus, I searched the entire world and all that it has to offer, but there is no one who compares to You or the love that You give me every day. You never withheld Your heart, or Your love from me, even in my deepest sin. Thank You Jesus, I love You. Amen.

When You Need Faith in God's Plan for Your Life

Lord, You long for me to be near to Your heart. I pray that You would anoint me today with Your presence. I want to be used by You for Your glory. Father, I ask You to forgive me for the moments I have resisted Your will for my life. Forgive me for not trusting You. I ask that You deliver my heart from faithlessness and fear. I trust that Your plans for me are good, with a future full of hope. I will not partner with the lies of the Enemy that seek to question Your good plans for my life and family.

You said that I am fearfully and wonderfully made.[178] Lord, and I am so thankful that You delight in me as Your child. I was created in Your image, and I want to say what You say, I want to see what You see. Your Word declares that I have the mind of Christ[179] and that You give me the desires of my heart.[180] Lord, I give You this day and every decision that I make, and I ask that You go before me, behind me, and all around me. Thank You for the future that You have planned for me. I love You, Lord Jesus. Amen.

When You Long to Hear God's Voice

Lord, I pray You would remove the distractions and hindrances that threaten to take me out of Your perfect will for me. Holy Spirit, I pray You would give me sharp discernment to see the subtleties that the Enemy would use to thwart Your plans for my life. Bring me into close fellowship with You because my heart's desire is to be right in the center of Your will and to be in Your midst. You have a future and hope for my life, and I pray I would live out every dream and desire that was in Your heart when You created me.

Holy Spirit, thank You for leading and guiding me in all truth. Help me receive Your Word into my heart by faith. Your Word declares that Your sheep hear Your voice,[181] and Lord, I pray You would silence the mouth of the Enemy and the lies that he speaks. Jesus, I pray that my ears would be attentive to Your voice at every moment of every day. Your faithfulness carried me through my darkest hours and deepest valleys. God, make Your presence known to me. I need You more than anything in this life. In Your mighty name I pray, Jesus, amen.

When You Need God's Justice

Father, You are the Lord of righteousness, and healing is in Your wings.[182] Today, I forgive and release every person who has caused me pain or treated me unjustly. You are the Lord who knows all things, and nothing in this world goes unseen by You. Father, I pray that I would not take justice into my own hands but that I would choose to trust in Your justice, which is perfect. I have hope because I know that You will vindicate and defend me. Whether it is in this world or in eternity with You, one day all truth will be revealed. For this reason, I can trust You with my whole heart!

You said in Your Word that I can come and reason with You and bring my petitions before Your throne.[183] So here I am, Father; my heart is on the altar. With my lips I declare that You are the commander of heaven's armies, and I trust that You will be my defender. Help me remember how much You have forgiven me. I pray that I would not walk in any bitterness or unforgiveness. You are a righteous King, and I thank You for the peace You are giving me while I expectantly wait on You to work all things together for good. In the mighty name of Jesus I pray, amen.

When You Long for the Unshakable Peace of Jesus

Father, thank You that every good and perfect gift comes from You.[184] I know I am loved deeply by You. Your faithfulness has brought me this far, and it is Your grace that will continue to carry me through. This day is Yours, and I pray that every moment of my life would be an offering of worship to You. My future and every part of my life belongs to You! Jesus, You are with me, and You are walking with me every step of this journey. You are the God who lifts the valleys and levels the mountains that stand in front of me.[185] What a mighty God You are!

Jesus, You are the Prince of Peace, and where Your presence is, there is freedom. I pray for the peace that passes all understanding to flood my heart. Lord, I pray for unshakable faith in my heart. I want to stand strong in You as I trust in You with my whole heart. Father, mold me in Your loving hands. You are the Potter, I am the clay, and the safest place that I will ever be is in Your hands. Let every part of my life bring You glory. In Jesus' mighty name, amen.

When You Are Searching
for Hope in Jesus

Jesus, I magnify and glorify Your name. There is no other name like Yours, and there is power in Your name. Today I pray that You would fill me with the fullness of who You are. One day, every knee will bow, and every tongue will confess that You are Lord.[186] You are the God who raises up kings and You also bring them down.

Jesus, I declare that in Your name alone I will put my trust. You are above addictions, sicknesses, broken relationships, failures, regret, condemnation, and every form of destruction that sin brings into this world. You are my gift and reward, and I fix my eyes on You. When the walls are closing in, I know I can trust You. Fill me with boldness and the power of Your Spirit like You did with the prophet Elijah. With faith and abiding trust in You, his prayer caused fire to fall from heaven and reveal You as the one true God of all the earth.[187] I want to trust You wholeheartedly just like he did. I pray that every part of me would live by Your Word, Jesus. Amen.

When You Need the Strength of Jesus

Father, there is no lack and there is no hunger in You. Thank You for the gift of Your Word so that I can taste and see that You are good,[188] no matter what may come against me. Jesus, You are faithful in all Your ways, and I pray today for the spirit of the fear of the Lord to rest on me, because Your Word promises that the fear of the Lord is the beginning of wisdom, and I want to walk in Your wisdom and Your ways.[189]

Thank You for all You have done, for all You are doing, and for all You are going to do. Lord, I want to seek You, I want to know You, and I want the desire of my heart to be like the apostle Paul's when he said, "I want to know Christ—yes, to know the power of his resurrection."[190] I want to know You as my closest friend, Holy Spirit, and I want to look just like You to the world around me. I want to know what moves Your heart. Just like a child whose sole desire is to make her father smile, I want to bring You joy the way You have brought me the joy of salvation through Your Son. Today, I surrender all to You. You can have my heart. It's all Yours. In Jesus' name, amen.

When You Seek God's Will in Your Life

Father, my deepest heart's desire is to walk in Your will and be led by Your Spirit. I pray that You would direct my steps in every moment of every day. Lord, I pray that You would remove any fear of failure or feeling that I am missing out on what You have for me. I am confident that as I seek You with my whole heart, You will always lead me through the right doors. Help me hear Your voice clearly when You are guiding me. Holy Spirit, I pray that You would fill me with the spirit of wisdom and understanding. I want to lift my heart up to You in this season when I am in the valley of decision.

Lord, thank You for freely giving me wisdom and direction daily for my life. I want to be right in the center of what You desire. You sit in eternity and know what lies ahead; You have a purpose for my life, and I trust You. Thank You for guiding me with Your peace and opening doors that only You desire for my life. Holy Spirit, I only want to go where You go, and I only want to be where You are. Lead me wherever You desire because I will follow You anywhere. I love You, Jesus. Amen.

When You Need the Guidance of the Holy Spirit

Lord, You make all things new, and today I want to thank You for this season of life. I believe You are taking me from faith to faith and glory to glory. Today I ask for Your peace to surround me in every way. I pray against all confusion and chaos that the Enemy may try to bring my way.

You are my strength when I am weak and my very best friend through every trial. Holy Spirit, I pray that You would fill the atmosphere around me with the love, peace, and joy that only Your presence can give. I ask for clarity in decisions I will make in the days ahead and for Your peace to lead my heart. God, there is no one like You. I am so thankful for the gift of Your Holy Spirit. He leads me, He guides me, and He shows me the path You have prepared for my life—all for Your glory. I pray that the revelation that Your perfect love casts out all fear would be the anchor in my heart.[191] In Jesus' mighty name, amen.

When You Seek Complete Trust in the Lord

Jesus, in You there is no lack or hunger. You are the Bread of Life, and You have given me the ability to taste and see that You are good. You are faithful in all Your ways. I pray for the Spirit of the fear of the Lord to rest on me. Lord, I want to seek You; I want to know You. I pray in the mighty name of Jesus that You would fill me with the power of Your Spirit. Above all else, I want to trust You with all my heart. I want to know Your heart and Your ways. Help me lean not on my own understanding but acknowledge You in all my ways.[192] I know You will guide me and make every crooked path straight.[193] Your Word declares that whenever I lack wisdom, I can ask it of You and You will never hold back.[194] I pray that You will lead me today and every day. I pray for supernatural wisdom in every decision I make this week, and I thank You for the promise in Psalm 37:23, which says, "The steps of a good man are ordered by the LORD, and He delights in his way."[195] Father, delight Yourself in all my comings and goings so I can bring glory to You in every way. In Jesus' powerful name I pray, amen.

When You Need to Feel God Is with You

Father, great is Your faithfulness. You have made Your Son Jesus the King of all kings and the Lord of all lords. I worship You and I magnify You through my circumstances today. I trust that You will be faithful to me and those I love, as You have always been. You hung every star in the perfect place. Who is like You, Lord? It is You who sits above the circle of the earth and stretches out the heavens like a curtain and spreads them out like a tent to dwell in.[196] You are a mighty God; my entire world is in Your hands today and forever. I repent of all doubt in You. You have been so good to me!

God, Your eye is on me, and no matter what I face, You know me. You see my heart, and You know the tears I have cried in secret. Lord, I am looking at You. No matter what turmoil, calamity, fear, or anxiety comes my way, You are greater. You shut the mouth of the lions for Daniel.[197] I know You are with me today. Today I will find refuge in Your Word: "Many are the afflictions of the righteous, but the Lord delivers him out of them all."[198] I love You, Lord Jesus. Amen.

When You Seek Trust Amid the Unknown

Father, thank You for Your faithfulness to me. I find hope in Your Word that says, "Who is this King of glory? The LORD strong and mighty, the LORD mighty in battle."[199] Today, I ask for fresh strength, a fresh anointing. And Lord, I pray that You would fill me with bold faith. I don't have to know what is on the other side of this moment in this season because I trust You. Father, Your Word is my solid foundation, and I know that whatever may come, You are trustworthy, You are faithful, and the greatest reward of this life is to know You. You are Emmanuel, God with us; You are here with me, and You will be with me always. I have nothing to fear. Thank You, Lord, that You have not given me a spirit of fear, but of power, of love, and of a sound mind.[200]

Jesus, I will trust You with bold faith. Thank You for walking with me and vindicating me with justice that only You can give. Lord, You are wonderful in all Your ways. I am so thankful that You are with me. In Your name, Jesus, I pray, amen.

When You Need Jesus as Your Protector

Jesus, at the mention of Your name, demons tremble and darkness flees. You are my healer and deliverer. Jesus, I have overcome by the blood of the Lamb and the word of my testimony.[201] Hell could not hold You down. There is no authority or power that can overcome the power of Your blood that has healed me. Jesus, thank You for delivering me, healing me, and making me whole in Your presence. You raise what's dead to life spiritually and physically, so today I ask for the resurrection power of Your Spirit over me and every person who needs a touch from You.

Lord, it's You I run to when I feel afraid, and the life of Your Word brings me safety and peace. Thank You for the power of Your presence, for Your power working in and through my life. Your Word declares, "The LORD goes out to fight like a warrior; he is ready and eager for battle."[202] Jesus, I know You are fighting my battles, and I pray that You would break the power of fear and every demonic attack against me for today. Your name is high and lifted up, Jesus. Amen.

When You Need to Trust That God Has Gone Before You

Father, You are good; You are faithful; You are merciful; You are kind; You are awesome and glorious. Thank You for those I love and for the life You have given me. Your Word stands through the ages, and You are the author and the finisher of my faith.[203] I look back on my life and can see Your great faithfulness. I see it today, and I know that You are already in my tomorrow, whatever it may hold. God, You will finish what You started in me. I believe that Your Word is the final word over my life, and against all odds, nothing is over until You say it's over.

Lord, You cover and lead me. There is nothing that has gone unseen by You. I trust that You have already made a way and gone before me. Lord, You are my Shepherd, and You cause me to lie down in green pastures of peace. Father, I pray that You would be with me and that there will be no fear, worry, or anxiety in my heart, knowing that You are the one who goes before me, behind me, and all around me. In Jesus' mighty name, amen.

When You Want to Trust that God Will Restore What's Been Lost

Father, thank You that You are God all by Yourself, and You never fail. You have never let me down, and I know that You never will. I lay down every expectation of what I believe the outcome should be, and I surrender it to You. Your plans are always better than mine! Lord, I pray that You would lift my heart when it feels weary and refresh me with Your hope. Father, I know that You will recover all that has been lost or stolen in the past season. I pray for complete restoration as You provided for Your servant Job. You gave him double for all that was taken from him.[204]

Jesus, I want to thank You for the hope You have given me. You restore my past and renew my heart like no one can. I know that even when I walk through the valley of the shadow of death, I will not fear any evil, because You are with me.[205] Jesus, You encourage and lift my heart like no other. Show me Your face today. I am so grateful to behold You and know that I am deeply loved by You. In Jesus' mighty name, amen.

When You Want to Feel God's Presence

Jesus, You are the one who walks with me through the fire. I'm so thankful that You are with me today. No matter what I see or do not see with my eyes, I know You are working all things together for good.[206] I love You, Lord. No matter what the outcome of my situation is, God, You are faithful, and Your name is above every name. I know I can trust in You with my whole heart.

Lord, it is Your grace that keeps me. You shelter me from the Enemy and keep me in the shadow of Your presence. Jesus, You are who You say You are, and I trust in the promise of Your Word that sustains me through the pain and the trials. The ways You have moved in my life I couldn't even have prayed for because they are so great! You are the one true promise-keeping God! I have seen Your hand in my life, and by Your grace I refuse to give up no matter what comes my way. Lord, open my eyes to see and behold You. In the mighty name of Jesus I pray, amen.

CONCLUSION

To hunger and thirst for the presence of Jesus is a precious gift. When the Holy Spirit draws your heart into His, even the slightest nudge is a display of God's deep longing for you to know His heart and have friendship with Him. Matthew 5:6 says, "Blessed are those who hunger and thirst for righteousness, for they will be filled" (NIV). God desires for our hearts to be moldable so that He can reveal His heart and His plans and display His love to You. God has a purpose for your life, and when we spend time with Him in prayer and in His

Word, we discover the great plans and desires that He had for each of us before we ever even existed! Think about that for a moment: God Himself, who created the universe and all that is in it, wants to sit and fellowship with you and me.

I don't know about you, but wrapping my mind around this truth about God's heart is incomprehensible. It helps me to understand David when he said, "When I consider Your heavens, the work of Your fingers, the moon and the stars, which You have ordained, what is man that You are mindful of him, and the son of man that You visit him?" (Psalm 8:3–4).

But isn't it truly incomprehensible? When the world turns its back on you, the God of glory and all creation wants *you*. He loves you deeply, and from the beginning of time and for all eternity, His desire is to have friendship with you. God invites you into His heart that you may *know* Him. And it doesn't end here. When you speak to Him, He is listening. In fact, the Scriptures tell us that His ear is inclined to the words you say and the prayers that pour out from your heart. "I love the Lord, because He has heard my voice and my supplications. Because He has inclined His ear to me, therefore I will call upon Him as long as I live" (Psalm 116:1–2).

Friend, today Jesus is calling you by name. He is knocking on the door of your heart and calling you to Himself, just as He did with the woman at the well in the Gospel of John. Jesus waited patiently for her to arrive, and she received the greatest gift of this life: Him. Jesus did not judge or condemn her. He simply looked at her and gave her exactly what she needed the most: God's tender love. That day, she received from the well that never runs dry, the living waters of God's love. She finally found what she had been looking for; she finally found her beloved, Jesus. One conversation with Jesus changed her life, and we know this because she left that well after her encounter with Him and set an entire village on fire telling everyone about a Man who changed her!

Jesus loved her not just where she was but also loved her enough to speak truth to her heart to bring her to repentance. *Just one look and one word from Jesus changed everything.*

I have always said, what God does for one, He will do for all. He doesn't play favorites like we humans do;

He will do the same for you that He did for the woman at the well.

So come and meet with Jesus, the Man who will love you as no one else in this world could ever love you. As you pray and commune with Him, He will fill every empty void; He will satisfy every need in your heart, mind, body, soul, and spirit.

Your prayers matter to Him, and He longs to hear your voice today. Pour out your heart to Him. Watch how your prayers move the heart of the living God, and receive from the well that will never run dry.

FRIENDSHIP WITH GOD

LORD, TEACH US TO PRAY

> *Now it came to pass, as He was praying in a certain place, when He ceased, that one of His disciples said to Him, "Lord, teach us to pray, as John also taught his disciples." So He said to them, "When you pray, say: Our Father in heaven, hallowed be Your name. Your kingdom come. Your will be done on earth as it is in heaven. Give us day by day our daily bread. And forgive us our sins, for we also forgive everyone who is indebted to us. And do not lead us into temptation, but deliver us from the evil one."*

LUKE 11:1–4

There was a moment in my life when I had a thought I will never forget: *If there is a God, these people have come face-to-face with Him.* At that moment in time, I didn't believe God existed. I was at the end of my rope and ready to step over the edge and end my life, when a man invited me to a prayer meeting at my job. When I walked into the break room where they were praying, it wasn't what they were praying, how they were praying, or the volume of their voices that caught my attention. It was the fact that it seemed like they were talking to someone they had known all of their lives, as if they were speaking face-to-face. Over the years, I have often reflected on what it was that so captivated me when I heard the prayers of this group of people passionately crying out to God for me. I have come to the conclusion that it was the friendship and closeness they displayed with God, as if they were talking to their very best friend. That is because they were.

Historically, prayer has been viewed as a list, but in Luke's Gospel, Jesus taught the disciples that prayer has nothing to do with a list but everything to do with a person, God Himself. Jesus told them to look up and direct their attention to a Father in heaven who would provide for them, deliver them from the temptation of sin, and forgive their sins! Jesus had friendship with God; the disciples knew this, and they wanted to have what He had.

True friends will look beyond what is external and look for what is within. I will never forget the moment when I was in worship at church and I said, "Lord, You know my heart, and You see right through me." Immediately, the Lord showed me that His desire was for me to see right through Him as well. That moment overwhelmed me because I had never known I had permission to see through Him as well. Now, while some may think this is obvious, at that moment in my life, it was the first time I realized that not only was there an open invitation to know God's heart, but His desire was for me to see right through Him as He sees right through me.

The God of all creation invites you into His heart, and you don't have to jump through hoops to earn His love—you already have it. You don't have to prove anything about who you are either, because He already knows the depths of your being that no one else knows. True friendships are not one sided, and prayer is an ongoing conversation with Jesus that never ends. There aren't formulas or rituals when it comes to prayer. Prayer can begin by speaking straight to Him or by simply listening for God's voice and responding to Him as you walk and talk with Him just as Adam and Eve did in the garden of Eden in the cool of the day.

Jesus gave His life for you and me to have direct access to the Father the way He did. If you could ask God one question, what would you ask Him? My immediate question is why? I believe the answer to this question is that the entirety of Scripture revolves around our heart connection with the Lord.

> Seeing then that we have a great High Priest who has passed through the heavens, Jesus the Son of God, let us hold fast our confession. For we do not have a High Priest who cannot sympathize with our weaknesses, but was in all points tempted as we are, yet without sin. Let us therefore come boldly to the throne of grace, that we may obtain mercy and find grace to help in time of need. (Hebrews 4:14–16)

Do you know what I find so extraordinary about this passage of Scripture? Paul depicted the compassionate nature of Jesus and His heart toward our weaknesses to show that He knows exactly how we feel because He experienced it, too, as a man! But what gets me is that Paul even told us about the attitude we can have when we come before God's throne: boldness. Our confidence is not in ourselves, our good works, or who we are. Our confidence is in the blood of Jesus that has made a way for us to have the friendship and closeness with God that

Jesus had. And this is all God is looking for; He wants friendship with you.

Prayer causes you and me to look at the Son of God, and, as we behold the face of Jesus, we will become more like Him. Did you know your companionship and fellowship actually bless the heart of God? It is why He gave His life for you and me and anyone who would receive Him into their hearts and make Him Lord and Savior of their lives!

I have asked myself this question so many times: *What kind of love is this?* The love of God is incomprehensible to you and me, and Paul said it like this:

For this reason I bow my knees before the Father, from whom every family in heaven and on earth is named, that according to the riches of his glory he may grant you to be strengthened with power through his Spirit in your inner being, so that Christ may dwell in your hearts through faith—that you, being rooted and grounded in love, may have strength to comprehend with all the saints what is the breadth and length and height and depth, and to know the love of Christ that surpasses knowledge, that you may be filled with all the fullness of God.

Now to him who is able to do far more abundantly than all that we ask or think, according to the power at work within us, to him be glory in the church and in Christ Jesus throughout all generations, forever and ever. Amen. (Ephesians 3:14–21 ESV)

God's love is deep and wide; it is a profound mystery that is found in the power of the cross that surpasses all human understanding. Today, He invites you and me into the journey of walking with Him, talking to Him, listening for His voice, and knowing Him deeply.

TRIALS AND ADVERSITY PRODUCE FRUIT IN YOU THAT REMAINS

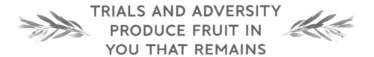

Understanding suffering in the early church is vital in comprehending the heart of God and His desire for us to embrace the trials that we as believers will all face in this world. The book of Acts fully displays the immense persecution that believers experienced as a result of their faith in Jesus Christ. James, Peter, and the writer of Hebrews provide a divine blueprint for us on how we as Christ-followers are to navigate the persecution, suffering, and trials that we are promised as His children. Suffering is not only a New Testament concept but a thread that we see from Genesis to Revelation as a result of the fall in the garden and sin entering into the world. "Many are the afflictions of the righteous, but the LORD delivers him out of them all" (Psalm 34:19). God uses suffering to produce fruit in all circumstances, and unpacking this will help us walk through intense pressure in this world.

The book of Hebrews teaches us that God refines us through His discipline when we suffer as a result of our own sinful decisions. Our heavenly Father loves us, and He uses these moments to display His love to us as we become more like Him. "For they disciplined us for a short time as it seemed best to them, but he disciplines us for our good, so that we may share his holiness" (Hebrews 12:10 ESV). In addition to this, Hebrews 5:8 tells us that the Lord Himself learned obedience through suffering. There is purpose for pain and suffering in this life, and it allows the Holy Spirit to transform us into His likeness. It is incredibly encouraging to think about God's heart for us in that, "for those who love God all things work together for good, for those who are called according to his purpose" (Romans 8:28 ESV). Even when we have opened the door to sin in our lives, God is already at work to cause all things to work together for our good. The book of Hebrews reminds us of what a wonderful Father we have. His heart is always turned toward us, to redeem us, and restore us.

SCRIPTURES OF HOPE

The Lord is my strength and song, and He has become my salvation; He is my God, and I will praise Him; My father's God, and I will exalt Him. (Exodus 15:2)

Be strong and of good courage, do not fear nor be afraid of them; for the Lord your God, He is the One who goes with you. He will not leave you nor forsake you. (Deuteronomy 31:6)

And the Lord, He is the One who goes before you. He will be with you, He will not leave you nor forsake you; do not fear nor be dismayed. (Deuteronomy 31:8–9)

Have I not commanded you? Be strong and of good courage; do not be afraid, nor be dismayed, for the Lord your God is with you wherever you go. (Joshua 1:9)

But You, O Lord, are a shield for me, my glory and the One who lifts up my head. I cried to the Lord with my voice, and He heard me from His holy hill. I lay down and slept; I awoke, for the Lord sustained me. (Psalm 3:3–5)

And you would be secure, because there is hope; yes, you would dig around you, and take your rest in safety. You would also lie down, and no one would make you afraid; yes, many would court your favor. (Job 11:18–19)

For the needy shall not always be forgotten; the expectation of the poor shall not perish forever. (Psalm 9:18)

Lead me in Your truth and teach me, for You are the God of my salvation; on You I wait all the day. (Psalm 25:5)

The Lord is my light and my salvation; whom shall I fear? The Lord is the strength of my life; of whom shall I be afraid? (Psalm 27:1)

Be of good courage, and He shall strengthen your heart, all you who hope in the Lord. (Psalm 31:24)

The Lord brings the counsel of the nations to nothing; He makes the plans of the peoples of no effect. (Psalm 33:10)

Behold, the eye of the Lord is on those who fear Him, on those who hope in His mercy, to deliver their soul from death, and to keep them alive in famine. (Psalm 33:18–19)

Let Your mercy, O Lord, be upon us, just as we hope in You. (Psalm 33:22)

And now, Lord, what do I wait for? My hope is in You. (Psalm 39:7)

Why are you cast down, O my soul? And why are you disquieted within me? Hope in God; for I shall yet praise Him, the help of my countenance and my God. (Psalm 42:11)

God is our refuge and strength, a very present help in trouble. Therefore we will not fear, even though the earth be removed, and though the mountains be carried into the midst of the sea; though its waters roar and be troubled, though the mountains shake with its swelling. (Psalm 46:1–3)

Behold, God is my helper; the Lord is with those who uphold my life. (Psalm 54:4)

Cast your burden on the Lord, and He shall sustain you; He shall never permit the righteous to be moved. (Psalm 55:22)

No evil shall befall you, nor shall any plague come near your dwelling; for He shall give His angels charge over you, to keep you in all your ways. (Psalm 91:10–11)

Whoever secretly slanders his neighbor, him I will destroy; the one who has a haughty look and a proud heart, him I will not endure. My eyes shall be on the faithful of the land, that they may dwell with me; he who walks in a perfect way, he shall serve me. (Psalm 101:5–6)

I have restrained my feet from every evil way, that I may keep Your word. (Psalm 119:10)

You are my hiding place and my shield; I hope in Your word. (Psalm 119:114)

I wait for the Lord, my soul waits, and in His word I do hope. (Psalm 130:5)

O Israel, hope in the Lord; for with the Lord there is mercy, and with Him is abundant redemption. (Psalm 130:7)

Behold, children are a heritage from the Lord, the fruit of the womb is a reward. Like arrows in the hand of a warrior, so are the children of one's youth. Happy is the man who has his quiver full of them; they shall not be ashamed, but shall speak with their enemies in the gate. (Psalm 127:7–8)

Happy is he who has the God of Jacob for his help, whose hope is in the LORD his God. (Psalm 146:5)

Trust in the LORD with all your heart, And lean not on your own understanding; In all your ways acknowledge Him, And He shall direct your paths. (Proverbs 3:5–6)

In the way of righteousness is life, and in its pathway there is no death. (Proverbs 12:28)

Hope deferred makes the heart sick, but when the desire comes, it is a tree of life. (Proverbs 13:12)

The name of the LORD is a strong tower; the righteous run to it and are safe. (Proverbs 18:10)

Do not let your heart envy sinners, but be zealous for the fear of the LORD all the day; for surely there is a hereafter, and your hope will not be cut off. (Proverbs 23:17–18)

So shall the knowledge of wisdom be to your soul; if you have found it, there is a prospect, and your hope will not be cut off. (Proverbs 24:14)

This I recall to my mind, therefore I have hope. Through the LORD's mercies we are not consumed, because His compassions fail not. They are new every morning; great is Your faithfulness. (Lamentations 3:21–23)

"The LORD is my portion," says my soul, "therefore I hope in Him!" The LORD is good to those who wait for Him, to the soul who seeks Him. It is good that one should hope and wait quietly for the salvation of the LORD. (Lamentations 3:24–26)

Blessed is the man who trusts in the LORD, and whose hope is the LORD. (Jeremiah 17:7)

For I know the thoughts that I think toward you, says the LORD, thoughts of peace and not of evil, to give you a future and a hope. (Jeremiah 29:11)

The LORD also will roar from Zion, and utter His voice from Jerusalem; the heavens and earth will shake;

but the LORD will be a shelter for His people, and the strength of the children of Israel. (Joel 3:16)

Therefore I will look to the LORD; I will wait for the God of my salvation; my God will hear me. (Micah 7:7)

Your ears shall hear a word behind you, saying, "This is the way, walk in it," whenever you turn to the right hand or whenever you turn to the left. (Isaiah 30:21)

He gives power to the weak, and to those who have no might He increases strength. (Isaiah 40:29)

But those who wait on the LORD shall renew their strength; they shall mount up with wings like eagles, they shall run and not be weary, they shall walk and not faint. (Isaiah 40:31)

For I, the LORD your God, will hold your right hand, saying to you, "Fear not, I will help you." (Isaiah 41:13)

The LORD your God in your midst, the Mighty One, will save; He will rejoice over you with gladness, He will quiet you with His love, He will rejoice over you with singing. (Zephaniah 3:17)

Come to Me, all you who labor and are heavy laden, and I will give you rest. Take My yoke upon you and learn from Me, for I am gentle and lowly in heart, and you will find rest for your souls. For My yoke is easy and My burden is light. (Matthew 11:28–30)

Let not your heart be troubled; you believe in God, believe also in Me. In My Father's house are many mansions; if it were not so, I would have told you. I go to prepare a place for you. And if I go and prepare a place for you, I will come again and receive you to Myself; that where I am, there you may be also. (John 14:1–3)

Peace I leave with you, My peace I give to you; not as the world gives do I give to you. Let not your heart be troubled, neither let it be afraid. (John 14:27)

These things I have spoken to you, that in Me you may have peace. In the world you will have tribulation; but be of good cheer, I have overcome the world. (John 16:33)

For I consider that the sufferings of this present time are not worthy to be compared with the glory which shall be revealed in us. For the earnest expectation of the creation eagerly waits for the revealing of the sons of God. (Romans 8:18–25)

Rejoicing in hope, patient in tribulation, continuing steadfastly in prayer. (Romans 12:12)

Now may the God of hope fill you with all joy and peace in believing, that you may abound in hope by the power of the Holy Spirit. (Romans 15:13)

But as it is written: "Eye has not seen, nor ear heard, nor have entered into the heart of man the things which God has prepared for those who love Him." (1 Corinthians 2:9)

And now abide faith, hope, love, these three; but the greatest of these is love. (1 Corinthians 13:13)

For our light affliction, which is but for a moment, is working for us a far more exceeding and eternal weight of glory, while we do not look at the things which are seen, but at the things which are not seen. For the things which are seen are temporary, but the things which are not seen are eternal. (2 Corinthians 4:17–18)

But He said to me, "My grace is sufficient for you, for My strength is made perfect in weakness." Therefore most gladly I will rather boast in my infirmities, that the power of Christ may rest upon me. Therefore I take pleasure in infirmities, in reproaches, in needs, in persecutions, in distresses, for Christ's sake. For when I am weak, then I am strong. (2 Corinthians 12:9–10)

Now to Him who is able to do exceedingly abundantly above all that we ask or think, according to the power that works in us. (Ephesians 3:20)

Being confident of this very thing, that He who has begun a good work in you will complete it until the day of Jesus Christ. (Philippians 1:6)

This hope we have as an anchor of the soul, both sure and steadfast, and which enters the Presence behind the veil. (Hebrews 6:19)

Let us hold fast the confession of our hope without wavering, for He who promised is faithful. (Hebrews 10:23)

Now faith is the substance of things hoped for, the evidence of things not seen. (Hebrews 11:1)

Let your conduct be without covetousness; be content with such things as you have. For He Himself has said, "I will never leave you nor forsake you." So we may boldly say: "The Lord is my helper; I will not fear. What can man do to me?" (Hebrews 13:5–6)

My brethren, count it all joy when you fall into various trials, knowing that the testing of your faith produces patience. But let patience have its perfect work, that you may be perfect and complete, lacking nothing. (James 1:2–4)

Who through Him believe in God, who raised Him from the dead and gave Him glory, so that your faith and hope are in God. (1 Peter 1:21)

Casting all your care upon Him, for He cares for you. (1 Peter 5:7)

May the God of all grace, who called us to His eternal glory by Christ Jesus, after you have suffered a while, perfect, establish, strengthen, and settle you. (1 Peter 5:10)

And God will wipe away every tear from their eyes; there shall be no more death, nor sorrow, nor crying. There shall be no more pain, for the former things have passed away. (Revelation 21:4)

NOTES

1. Matthew 6:11.
2. Psalm 118:24.
3. Romans 2:4.
4. Hebrews 4:16.
5. Ephesians 3:20.
6. Psalm 91:5.
7. 1 Corinthians 13:12.
8. John 10:10.
9. John 8:36.
10. Daniel 3:16–30.
11. Psalm 119:105.
12. Psalm 97:5.
13. Joshua 10:13.
14. Mark 4:39.
15. Matthew 19:26.
16. Revelation 3:7–8.
17. Psalm 23:6.
18. Hebrews 12:15
19. Isaiah 55:8–9.
20. Proverbs 4:23.
21. Philippians 4:8.
22. Philippians 4:7.
23. 2 Kings 6:16.
24. Psalm 91:11.
25. Psalm 46:10.
26. Psalm 56:8.
27. Isaiah 45:2.
28. Joshua 1:9.
29. Philippians 4:13.
30. Psalm 121:1–2.
31. Psalm 139:13–14.
32. Isaiah 61:3.
33. Psalm 23:6.
34. Psalm 18:2.
35. 2 Kings 6:16.
36. Romans 8:28.
37. James 1:2 NASB.
38. Psalm 20:7–8.
39. Isaiah 55:11.
40. Hebrews 12:2.
41. Isaiah 61:3.
42. Psalm 30:11.
43. Genesis 50:20.
44. Isaiah 59:19.
45. Psalm 34:18 CSB.
46. Psalm 68:6.
47. John 15:5.
48. Hebrews 13:8.
49. Numbers 23:19.
50. Matthew 19:26.
51. Daniel 3:25.
52. Isaiah 61:3.

53. Proverbs 13:12.

54. Revelation 21:4.

55. Daniel 3:25.

56. Philippians 1:21.

57. 1 Corinthians 6:20

58. Psalm 46:10.

59. Philippians 1:6.

60. Psalm 139:13.

61. Mark 10:9.

62. 2 Corinthians 12:9.

63. Philippians 4:13.

64. 2 Corinthians 12:9.

65. Isaiah 54:17.

66. Ephesians 6:16 MEV.

67. Hosea 10:12.

68. Revelation 1:18.

69. Romans 10:9.

70. Psalm 118:24.

71. John 14:27.

72. Nehemiah 8:10.

73. Psalm 139:13.

74. Hebrews 13:5.

75. Psalm 51:17.

76. Joel 3:10.

77. Ezekiel 36:26.

78. Hebrews 12:2.

79. Joshua 1:9.

80. 1 Samuel 17:1–58.

81. 1 Samuel 16:7.

82. Galatians 2:20.

83. Psalm 138:8.

84. Psalm 84:11.

85. Proverbs 28:1 AMP.

86. Matthew 8:5–13.

87. Matthew 7:14.

88. Psalm 91:5.

89. Psalm 17:8.

90. Galatians 6:9.

91. Hebrews 4:16.

92. Matthew 26:41.

93. John 8:36.

94. John 10:10.

95. James 4:7.

96. *Strong's Concordance*, "7503. raphah," Bible Hub, accessed February 13, 2025, https://biblehub.com/hebrew/7503.htm.

97. Philippians 4:19.

98. Psalm 50:10.

99. Psalm 84:11.

100. Romans 8:17.

101. Psalm 150:6.

102. Luke 19:40.

103. Luke 22:42.

104. 2 Corinthians 4:8.

105. Psalm 23:5.

106. Psalm 27:13.

107. Lamentations 3:23.

108. Ephesians 2:6.

109. Psalm 91:1.

110. Joshua 24:15.

111. Psalm 127:2.

112. Matthew 6:26.

113. Psalm 34:10.

114. Psalm 23:6.

115. Matthew 6:33 ESV.

116. Psalm 84:11.

117. Revelation 3:7.

118. Isaiah 46:10.

119. Isaiah 54:17.

120. Ephesians 1:5.

121. 1 Corinthians 10:13.

122. Colossians 3:15.

123. Psalm 23:2.

124. Isaiah 55:9 NIV.

125. Isaiah 26:3 NLT.

126. Isaiah 40:31.

127. James 1:17.

128. 2 Timothy 1:7.

129. Jeremiah 29:11.

130. Psalm 139:13.

131. 1 Peter 4:8.

132. Luke 18:27.

133. Joshua 10:1–15.

134. Ephesians 3:20.

135. Revelation 3:7.

136. Hebrews 12:1.

137. Matthew 6:34.

138. James 4:14.

139. Philippians 4:7.

140. Psalm 46:1.

141. John 16:33.

142. Psalm 91:1.

143. Psalm 23:3.

144. Isaiah 40:31.

145. Psalm 18:30.

146. Hebrews 13:8.

147. Psalm 27:4.

148. Deuteronomy 28:12.

149. Matthew 6:10.

150. Revelation 1:8.

151. Romans 5:8.

152. 1 Peter 4:8.

153. Proverbs 18:21.

154. Matthew 12:36.

155. James 1:19.

156. John 12:49.

157. Romans 8:1.

158. Exodus 33:18.

159. John 8:36 NIV.

160. 1 Corinthians 10:13.

161. Jeremiah 29:12.

162. Psalm 84:10.

163. Jeremiah 17:7.

164. Jeremiah 17:8.

165. Hebrews 13:5.

166. Ephesians 6:10–20.

167. Matthew 5:13.

168. Psalm 46:10.

169. Genesis 6:8.

170. Mark 11:23.

171. Mark 9:24.

172. Psalm 23:2.

173. Mark 4:35–41.

174. John 1:5.

175. Romans 8:31.

176. Romans 8:19.

177. Hebrews 11:6.

178. Psalm 139:14.

179. 1 Corinthians 2:16.

180. Psalm 37:4.

181. John 10:27.

182. Malachi 4:2.

183. Hebrews 4:16.

184. James 1:17.

185. Isaiah 40:4.

186. Philippians 2:10–11.

187. 2 Kings 1:10.

188. Psalm 34:8.

189. Proverbs 9:10.

190. Philippians 3:10 NIV.

191. 1 John 4:18.

192. Proverbs 3:5–6.

193. Isaiah 45:2.

194. James 1:5.

195. Psalm 37:23.

196. Isaiah 40:22.

197. Daniel 6:22.

198. Psalm 34:19.

199. Psalm 24:8.

200. 2 Timothy 1:7.

201. Revelation 12:11.

202. Isaiah 42:13 GNT.

203. Hebrews 12:2.

204. Job 42:10.

205. Psalm 23:4.

206. Romans 8:28.

ACKNOWLEDGMENTS

If there is anything I have learned over the years, it's that when God calls you to write a book, it is an invitation to draw near to His heart. It is an offering on the altar to Jesus. It is like breaking at His feet the alabaster box of your heart filled with the costliest oil you own. It is like your heart is the ballpoint of a pen that bleeds love, affection, and gratitude to the Lord. My prayer is that you, too, would experience what I had the privilege to experience with Jesus as we penned the words of this book together to bring you hope, freedom, encouragement, and most of all, an opportunity to experience the everlasting love of God that is found in His Son.

God has graciously placed people in my life who have held my arms high, and the gift of godly friendships is one that I do not take lightly! To my husband, Ryan, you are God's gift of peace to our family every day. Evan, you have lived out your name and are God's grace to us. You've become a young man who speaks truth in the fear of the Lord. We love you deeply, son.

Stephanie Newton, when I look back on my life and remember the people that God sent to believe in me, you are one of them. You are a gift to our family and to the body of Christ. Thank you for believing in me through the years the way that you have. I am forever grateful to you. Kristen Parrish, I thank God for you! I pinch myself sometimes when I think about the friends that the Lord has graciously brought into our lives: Ryan and Kelsey O'Malley, Andrea and Harvey Smith, Karen and Rick Lynch, Laura Hansen, Dr. Roger and Holly Borbon, Troy and April Wiede, Yari Gutierrez, Lloyd and Shayla Brown, Ben and Brenda Peters, Sylvester Starling, Adrian and Sonja Weller, Dean and Amy Deguara, Michelle Fitzhugh, Jeff and Lauren Tharp, Jay and Christy Haizlip, Rick and Belinda Baker, Dr. Darren McGuire, Jose and Ariande Navarro, Tim and Marty Meyer, Fred and Margaret Stunt, Lorraine Coconato, Todd Coconato, Jim and Sharon Hess, Tia Tish, Alan Alfano, Lafe Cook, and Diane Isaacs. Jonathan Lewis, most of this book was written during your worship sets in the prayer room. Thank you for your family; our family is so thankful for yours. Each of you is an expression of the grace of God to us. The midnight-hour prayers, the love, care, and support you have shown our family have been God's kindness to us. We're so thankful for each of you.

ABOUT THE AUTHOR

Cristina Baker is an author and speaker, and her passion is to see people come to know the love and friendship that is found in Jesus Christ through the fellowship with the Holy Spirit. After a ten-year battle with drug addiction, Cristina had a radical encounter with the love and power of God and immediately answered the call on her life to minister the gospel. Cristina and her husband, Ryan, are founders of Power of Hope Ministries, which exists to preach the gospel, share the love of Christ, and teach the power of prayer to bring hope to people of all walks of life. Through media, social media, and itinerant ministry, Cristina's and Ryan's hearts are to serve people, teach sound biblical doctrine, and inspire others to search God's heart through His Word and learn to love the Word of God. Their desire is to fulfill the Great Commission, serve others, and extend the love of God toward people who feel hopeless, rejected, and lost, so that they may find hope in Christ and know they are deeply loved and known by God. Cristina, Ryan, and their son, Evan, live in Dallas, Texas, with their three dogs.

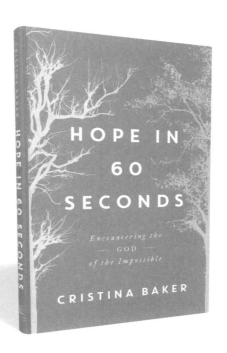

Social media influencer Cristina Baker shares prayers, Bible
teaching, and stories of her miraculous transformation
to help you move from hopeless to hope filled.

ISBN: 978-0-7852-5362-4

Available wherever books are sold.

Rowan Hillson, MD, MRCP is Senior Registrar in Diabetes and Endocrinology at the Radcliffe Infirmary, Oxford. She has completed several research projects in diabetes and is heavily involved in the day to day running of the large diabetic clinics at the John Radcliffe Hospital, also in Oxford. She works in the special adolescent diabetic clinic and has set up a preconception diabetic clinic. Dr Hillson is an enthusiast of outdoor activities and two to four times a year she takes parties of diabetics on Outward Bound courses in the British Lake District. She has a particular interest in helping people with diabetes to learn more about their condition.

DIABETES: A YOUNG PERSON'S GUIDE

ROWAN HILLSON MD MRCP

POSITIVE HEALTH GUIDE

© Rowan Hillson 1988

First published in 1988 by
Macdonald Optima, a division of
Macdonald & Co. (Publishers) Ltd

A member of Maxwell Pergamon Publishing Corporation plc

935476520

British Library Cataloguing in Publication Data
Hillson, Rowan
 Diabetes
 1. Adolescents. Diabetes
 I. Title
 616.4'62'0088055
 ISBN 0-356-15415-7

Macdonald & Co. (Publishers) Ltd
3rd Floor
Greater London House
Hampstead Road
London NW1 7QX

Photoset in 10pt Times by Tek Art Limited, Croydon, Surrey

Printed and bound in Great Britain by
Cambridge University Press, Cambridge

DEDICATION

This book is for Simon, William and Kate.

CONTENTS

ACKNOWLEDGMENTS

This book is the result of talking with hundreds of young people who have diabetes. I would especially like to thank all of them for the lessons they have taught me, and I wish them well for the future.

I am also very grateful to the following for their help: Mrs R. Flinn, North Oxfordshire Careers Service; Harriet Griffey; M. Harris; Mr and Mrs W.R. Hillson; Simon and Kate Hillson; Dr T.D.R. Hockaday; Dr H.H. Jones, Medical Adviser, DVLC; Dr J.I. Mann; the staff of Outward Bound Eskdale (past and present); Dr R. Peveler; Ms E. Snelgrove, Telecom International; Mr A. Taylor, DHSS.

INTRODUCTION

This book is a collection of stories about young people who have diabetes. After each story is an explanation of what was happening and what can be learned from what happened. This book is not intended to include everything there is to know about diabetes. It is not a diabetes textbook: it is a guide to living with diabetes. The stories describe some of the problems that young people may have with their diabetes and some of the things that it is important to think about.

As you read these stories you may think that David, Steven, Lorraine and the others are unusually disaster-prone. You are right! It is uncommon for so much to go wrong for so few people. The majority of young people with diabetes do not have major problems. If you know what can go wrong you can learn how to avoid it. Some of the stories are based on real events but the people in the stories do not exist, and the true stories have been altered to protect the people who told them to me. The book is meant for young people but I hope that their older friends, relatives and colleagues will find it helpful too.

To help you to learn the proper medical words I have used them in the text, with explanations as they appear. There is also a glossary on page 118. At the end of the book you will find pictures illustrating some of the practical aspects of caring for your diabetes. If you do not understand anything in the book, or if you have further questions (and I hope that you will have), please ask your doctor or diabetes nurse. Always ask expert advice about anything you are not sure about.

The aim of this book is to help you to learn how to live with your diabetes without it getting in your way but without losing control of it. Once you have mastered your diabetes you can go out and enjoy life to the full.

1

DAVID AND GARY

The sun streamed in through the classroom window and a large fly buzzed angrily against the glass. The geography teacher was talking about deserts. The Sahara – miles of sand, the relentless sun, no water, no vegetation. David stopped doodling and looked up miserably. His mouth felt like a desert. He was hot and dry and thirsty. The clock seemed to have stopped. He could feel the sand dunes building up on his tongue – he had to have a drink. But Mr Hackshaw never allowed anyone to leave the room in geography lessons. David gazed back at the blackboard. Mr Hackshaw was listing the world's deserts – the Gobi, Tierra del Fuego, the red centre of Australia . . . Despondently David copied them into his note book. Now he needed a pee. His bladder was full again – and he had been to the toilet just before the lesson.

David Pearce was 15. He had always played football and was hoping to be promoted into the school first team this year, but in recent weeks his game had gone off – he just did not seem to have the energy to get from one end of the pitch to the other. In fact, Mr Jobling the sports master told him that if his game did not improve he would have to give up his place on the team altogether. David was getting really miserable and fed up.

At last the bell went, Mr Hackshaw gave a last glare around the classroom and stalked out and David rushed for the toilet. There seemed to be gallons and gallons of urine. He drank three beakers of water but as soon as he got home he was thirsty again. At supper time his elder brother, Stewart, started teasing him about the football. 'Getting lazy, that's your trouble.' 'Stewart's right, you know,' said his dad, 'you spend too much time in front of the television. When I was in the school team I went out training every evening.' David felt a great wave of irritation. Everyone was getting at him. He flung his knife away and jumped up. His chair crashed to the floor. 'Pick your chair up, David,' said his dad. 'Pick it up yourself,' yelled David, 'I've had enough of all your lectures.' 'David!' his mum exclaimed, 'Do as you're told.' 'Oh, get lost!' shouted David, and he rushed upstairs to his room. He would go and

3

see his friend Colin. He took off his school uniform and put on his Levis. They were really loose and he had to tighten the belt another two notches. 'That's odd,' he thought, 'I seem to be losing weight.' He combed his hair and went out.

Next morning everyone started breakfast in stony silence. David munched his cornflakes moodily. 'David,' said his mum, 'were you all right last night? I heard you get up. Is anything the matter?' 'I had to go to the toilet and I was thirsty.' 'So that's where that big bottle of lemonade went to', his mother sighed.

David did not feel very well. He felt really tired, his throat was sore and he felt hot and sweaty. He went to school and bought a bottle of orange pop on the way, but by break he had drunk it all. In the middle of woodwork he suddenly had to rush to the toilet and vomit. 'Now I've been sick I'll feel better', he thought. But he didn't. He ate no lunch and vomited again. Mr Jobling found him in the toilet. 'You look really rough, Pearce,' he said, 'I think you should go home. I'll give you a lift.' The journey home was awful. David just managed not to be sick in Mr Jobling's car. His mum put him to bed. 'I expect it's a bug,' she said, 'or maybe it's all that pop you've been drinking.' David lay in bed staring at the ceiling. He felt so tired and everything seemed a real effort. His throat hurt and his mouth was terribly dry but every time he drank he felt sick. Eventually he went to sleep.

His mother thought it best to let him rest. She was worried about him. He had not been himself for well over a month and she wondered why he was drinking so much. He was losing weight too, and seemed very irritable. And why was he up and down all night? What was worrying him so that he couldn't sleep? A good long rest would help him. But if he was not better perhaps she should call the doctor tomorrow. Dr Linnet was very kind but he was always so busy and she did not like to bother him.

Next morning she and her husband went in to see David. He was still asleep. But he was breathing oddly, great sighing breaths. 'We'd better wake him up and make sure he is all right', said his father. But David would not wake up properly. They shook him and shouted. David's mother was getting more and more scared. He looked awful. His face was pale and dry and his eyes looked sunken. She called the doctor.

Dr Linnet was there in 10 minutes. He telephoned for an ambulance immediately. 'But what on earth is wrong with him?' asked his mother, in tears. 'He's always been so well and strong.' 'I think he may have diabetes,' Dr Linnet replied, 'and I am afraid that he is very ill. Has he been unwell at all recently?' His mother poured out all her anxieties about David's behaviour over the preceding weeks; 'I've been getting more and more worried about him', she said. 'Why didn't you bring him to see me earlier?' asked Dr Linnet. 'I didn't like to bother you', she replied.

David Pearce was seriously ill when he arrived in the accident and emergency department. He was semi-conscious, with the deep

4

sighing breathing which occurs when the body fluids are too acid. He was extremely dehydrated and his blood pressure was low. His throat was inflamed and the glands in his neck were swollen. His blood glucose was 45 mmol/l. He was given seven litres of replacement fluids into his veins that day. His diabetes needed insulin treatment and he was given antibiotics for his throat infection. Every hour nurses checked his blood glucose and monitored his pulse and blood pressure. His treatment was adjusted frequently. He gradually began to wake up, although he was rather muddled for the first few hours.

David woke up to a clattering noise and a loud crash. 'Hooray. That's the dinner lady coming along the corridor and she's dropped the trays again!' said a cheerful voice from the next bed. David looked round and saw a teenager wearing a bright red tee-shirt and a pair of jeans with a large hole in one knee. 'I'm Gary,' he said, 'I got a chest infection and it messed up my diabetes. I didn't need a drip, though. They say I can go home tomorrow. Want to borrow my motor bike magazine? I'm saving up for a motor bike – my dad says he'll help me buy one. Just got to give my insulin.' David watched as Gary pulled up the red tee-shirt and exposed his tummy. He picked

Injecting insulin

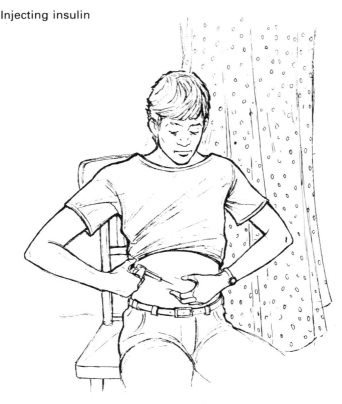

5

up the full syringe from the locker by his bed, casually stuck the needle into his abdomen and pushed down the plunger. He pulled the needle out, put the syringe back on the locker, yanked the shirt down and came over to David with the magazine. 'Here you are,' he said, 'I'm just going to watch TV until the food is handed out.' And he sauntered off down the ward. David watched him go. 'Diabetes', he thought. 'They've told me I've got diabetes.' He looked at the syringe and needle left on the locker. Gary had just stuck it in. He hadn't even winced.

David did not feel much like eating. But he watched Gary wolf his meal and they started to talk. Gary had had diabetes for 10 of his 18 years. He had left school when he was 16. Gary had been fascinated by cars and motor bikes since he was small and had soon found a job in a garage. He wanted to train as a mechanic. His diabetes had been diagnosed while he was staying with his grandparents. Like David, he had been very thirsty and drinking gallons of fluid. His grandmother had diabetes and one day she suggested testing his urine for glucose with her test kit. The urine was loaded with glucose. Eight-year-old Gary was not told this until later and was rather surprised to find himself being taken to the doctor. However, he remembered being very relieved when the doctor told him that insulin treatment would stop the terrible thirst. He was not afraid of having diabetes because he liked his grandmother and her diabetes did not seem to upset her. In fact, it had seemed rather grown-up to have the same condition as grandma.

'But what about AIDS?' asked David. 'In the advertisements it says you mustn't use needles.' 'No,' said Gary, rather offended, 'it says that you mustn't share needles with other people. Those advertisements are to warn drug addicts. Diabetics are definitely not junkies, and you can't catch AIDS by giving yourself insulin with your own personal needles and syringes. I get my syringes from my doctor.'

Next day David felt considerably better. He ate a large breakfast, his drip was taken down and he sat out of bed reading Gary's magazine. That morning, before breakfast, the nurse had helped him give his first insulin injection. He had always hated needles but seeing Gary injecting his insulin so casually gave David the confidence to have a try. To his amazement he just felt a tiny sting. He had privately thought the nurse was talking nonsense when she said it was no more than a gnat bite – but on the whole decided that she was right. His mother came to visit him and together they saw the dietitian and the diabetes sister who were very friendly and spent a long time explaining things. There seemed a great deal to learn, but at least he was feeling more like his old self again.

HOW DID THE DOCTORS KNOW THAT DAVID HAD DIABETES?

David had most of the classical symptoms of diabetes. He was thirsty (the medical word is polydipsia), passed large volumes of urine often (polyuria), lost weight, felt generally off-colour, lacked energy and got irritable. Some new diabetics are constipated, others complain of blurred vision or tingling in their hands or feet, and some have trouble with recurrent skin infections.

What was unusual was that David nearly became unconscious. The state he was in on admission to hospital is called diabetic ketoacidosis and is one form of diabetic coma. Nowadays it is uncommon, but it is something you need to know about so that you can avoid it and it is described on page 9.

Symptoms of diabetes

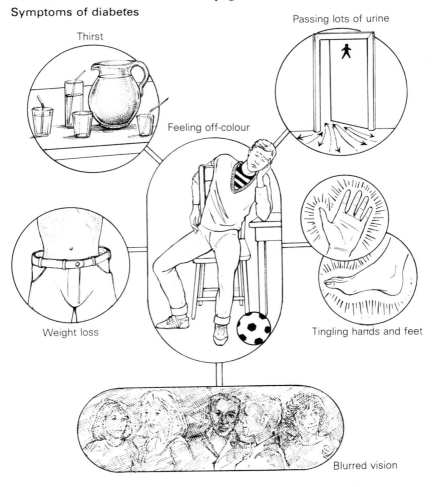

Passing lots of urine

Thirst

Feeling off-colour

Weight loss

Tingling hands and feet

Blurred vision

TESTS FOR DIABETES

Blood test

The test which confirms a diagnosis of diabetes is the blood glucose. When he came into hospital David's blood glucose was 45 mmol/l. That means that in every litre of his blood there were 45 millimols (a unit of measurement) of glucose. The normal blood glucose is 4–8 mmol/l. (In some countries blood glucose is measured in milligrams per decilitre: 1 mmol/l = 18 mg/dl. David's blood level was therefore 810 mg/dl, when it should have been 72–144 mg/dl.) The blood-glucose level can be measured in a sample taken from a vein and sent to the laboratory or in a tiny drop of blood from a finger-prick. People with diabetes can measure their own finger-prick blood glucose (see pages 114–15).

Urine test

Normally there is no glucose in the urine. When someone has diabetes and their blood glucose is so high, glucose overflows into the urine. The syrupy urine draws water out of the body, causing thirst and polyuria. If someone has glucose in their urine, like Gary, this usually means that they have diabetes. Urine-glucose levels are easy to measure but do not give a very accurate idea of what is happening to the blood glucose (see pages 39–40). Some older people like Gary's grandmother still use them as they find finger-prick tests difficult.

WHAT IS DIABETES?

Diabetes mellitus (this means passing a lot of urine which is sweet like honey) is a condition in which the blood glucose is higher than normal.

Why is the blood glucose too high?

The blood glucose rises because it cannot be used properly by the body. Glucose cannot be used unless insulin is present. David and Gary developed diabetes because their bodies stopped making insulin. Insulin is a chemical produced in the pancreas, a gland which lies behind the stomach in the abdomen. It is made in beta cells in tiny clusters called islets of Langerhans. Cells are the microscopic building blocks which make up the whole body. In addition to being building blocks they have many special functions and behave like tiny factories.

What do glucose and insulin do?

Insulin opens passages into cells so that glucose can enter. Starchy or sugary foods are digested in the gut and broken down into simple sugars, of which glucose is the most important. Glucose is used as a fuel to make energy (for example to make muscles move or to make the brain work) or as a storage material called glycogen which is kept until needed by the body. Most of the glycogen is stored in the liver

8

The presence of insulin enables glucose to enter the body's cells

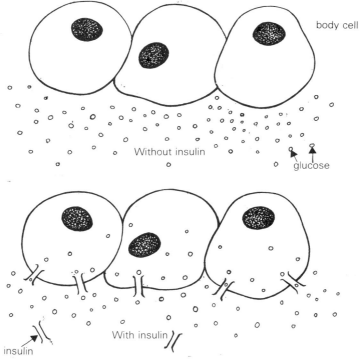

and muscles. Insulin also helps to build up the body's fat stores.

If the beta cells stop making insulin, glucose cannot enter the cells. But glucose is still being absorbed from the gut after every meal, so the glucose builds up in the bloodstream. Even worse, in the absence of insulin the liver breaks down its glycogen stores and releases all the glucose from them into the bloodstream. Body fat is also broken down into fatty acids, which in turn form substances called ketones. In severe insulin deficiency a lot of ketones are made and the blood becomes acid. The person starts overbreathing to try and blow all the acid out of the body (remember David's deep sighing breathing). Ketones smell like rotten apples or pear drops. So the ketones and the acid in the blood explain the name diabetic ketoacidosis.

Insulin is a clear fluid that can be modified chemically in many ways to alter the way it is absorbed or released from the injection site. Fast-acting insulin (which is what the body makes normally) is always clear. Medium- or slow-acting insulins are cloudy because they have been modified. Many companies make insulin – examples of fast-acting insulin are Actrapid, Humulin S (Humulin R in USA) and Velosulin, examples of medium-acting insulin are Humulin I, Insulatard, Protaphane and Semitard, while examples of longer-acting insulins are Humulin Zn, Monotard and Ultratard. Insulin

9

has to be given by injection. It is broken down by digestive juices in the gut if given by mouth.

Why does the pancreas stop making insulin?
The body has a very efficient defence system against germs and other harmful things. In diabetes the body's defence system becomes confused and behaves as if its own beta cells are enemy invaders. Special defence chemicals called antibodies attack the beta cells which become inflamed and die, and once they are destroyed they cannot grow again. The tendency for this 'mistake' to happen in the body can be inherited (remember that Gary's grandmother had diabetes). No-one in David's family had diabetes though. It is thought that the attack on the beta cells is triggered by something, perhaps a virus infection, in people with the genetic predisposition to develop diabetes.

Why was David more ill than Gary when diabetes was diagnosed?
Most people feel quite unwell before their diabetes is discovered, but in the great majority the condition is diagnosed before they become extremely ill. Loss of consciousness is rare in people with a high blood glucose; a very low blood glucose occasionally causes coma (see pages 26–8). Gary was lucky because his family knew about diabetes, but most people go to the doctor because they are thirsty and passing a lot of urine. David was a courageous teenager who did not want to give in and tell his family he felt ill, and David's mother was a very kind woman who did not want to trouble her doctor. But there was another factor.

INFECTION AND DIABETES

David developed a throat infection shortly before his hospital admission. Indeed it was probably the infection that caused his diabetic ketoacidosis. When we have infections the body releases emergency hormones or chemical messengers to help combat the infection. One of their effects is to release glucose from the glucose stores. They counteract the effect of insulin. So as David's throat infection got a grip on him, his blood glucose, which had been rising over the preceding weeks, shot up and his condition deteriorated rapidly. Gary had had a chest infection which caused his blood glucose to rise sufficiently to need a hospital admission to sort it out, but he was already taking some insulin so he was not totally insulin deficient. So, infection usually raises the blood glucose.

WHAT HAPPENS WHEN DIABETES IS DIAGNOSED?

Once the doctor has confirmed the diagnosis with a blood test he will advise insulin treatment. (Older people may not need insulin but it is very rare for people under 30 years of age who develop diabetes to

10

manage without insulin.) Sometimes this is started in hospital: sometimes it is started at home with support from the diabetes sister (who may be called a liaison officer). You will need advice from the dietitian about what is best to eat and help from the doctor about your insulin dose and general health. Most people are followed up in a hospital diabetic clinic, but increasingly family doctors are establishing diabetic mini-clinics. It is important to have regular health checks.

There is a lot to learn to start with, but there is no need to panic. Take it steadily and ask as many questions as you want. There is always help available.

SUMMARY

- Diabetes is a condition in which the blood glucose is higher than normal. People with diabetes may be thirsty, may need to pass large volumes of urine frequently, may lose weight, may be constipated, and may have blurred vision, tingling in the hands or feet and recurrent skin infections.
- The normal blood glucose is 4–8 mmol/l (72–144 mg/dl).
- Diabetes is due to insulin lack. Insulin lack is caused by the death of the insulin-producing beta cells in the islets of Langerhans in the pancreas.
- Severe insulin lack causes ketone formation from fat breakdown.
- Infection usually causes a rise in blood glucose.
- The correct diet and insulin injections return the blood glucose to normal, prevent ketone formation and cure the symptoms of diabetes.

2

LORRAINE

Lorraine had a weight problem. She just loved eating. But now, as she struggled to fasten her blue jeans, she realised that the situation was getting worse. She had bought them only two months ago and now the zip would not do up. She lay down on the floor and wriggled a little further into the jeans. She was wrestling with the zip when her room-mate Lynn walked in. Lynn shrieked with laughter. 'You look like a stranded whale', she grinned. Lorraine was not amused. She wriggled out of the jeans and found a skirt instead. She forced the buttons into the button holes and lit a cigarette irritably.

Lorraine and Lynn were 20. They were both at secretarial college and shared a flat. Lorraine had had diabetes for six years. She was on twice-daily short-acting and long-acting beef insulin. Recently her doses had been going up and up. She attended a diabetic clinic once a year for check-ups.

Lorraine started to cook the supper – beefburgers and chips and a fruit salad. The fruit salad was her concession to her diet. Every time she went to clinic she was handed a pink slip telling her to see the dietitian, but could not face the scolding she thought she would get. She knew she should lose weight, she just had no willpower, that was all. But the stranded whale joke had hurt.

The telephone rang. It was Lynn's mother. Her grandfather had had a heart attack and been rushed to hospital. Lorraine had met the old gentleman. He was a kindly soul who sat in his armchair by the window puffing on a cigarette. He could not walk far because he developed cramping pains in his calves. 'Bad circulation', he had said. 'We'll have our tea and I'll take you to see him', promised Lorraine, who had recently acquired an old car.

Lynn's grandfather was sitting up in bed with ruffled hair and a grin. 'Thought I was a goner there,' he said, 'but it takes more than that to do me in.' It had been only a mild heart attack. The pain had eased and he was now conducting a running battle with the nurses, who refused to allow him to smoke in bed. 'Little chit of a thing in a blue dress and a pinny took my cigarettes away', he said outraged.

He continued to recover and the girls visited him daily. Three days later Lynn's mother came to visit. 'The doctor asked to see me this afternoon when I went to visit dad', she said. 'He says dad must stop smoking. It's the cigarettes that caused the heart attack and his bad circulation, and he says he's got bronchitis as well. That's why he coughs every morning. He says dad's not too good.' In the middle of the night the telephone rang again. Lynn was on the phone for a long time and then she came into Lorraine's room crying. Her grandfather had just had a further massive heart attack and died. Lorraine started crying too and she reached for a cigarette to comfort herself. Then she stopped. They were always telling her to give up smoking at the clinic. Her mouth went dry. Somehow that cigarette did not seem so tempting now.

It was time to go to diabetic clinic again. Lorraine dug out her testing book and inspected it. She had not written anything in it for three months. So she set to work with a black and blue biro and a lot of imagination. It was quite artistic by the time she had finished. She looked at herself in the mirror as she dressed – great rolls of fat everywhere, and there were strange dents in her thighs where she injected her insulin. She had not noticed them before. But then she rarely looked at herself in the mirror – it was too depressing.

She sat in the clinic waiting area and glumly scanned the posters on the wall. When her turn came to be weighed it was a shock – 104 kg (229 pounds or over 16 stones). The doctor sighed as he flipped through her notes. 'Your weight has been going up steadily ever since you developed diabetes.' She nodded in unhappy agreement. Then she handed him her diary, hopefully. Silence. 'How long did it take you to make these results up?' he asked. She was staggered – how did he know? She asked him. 'You've filled in tomorrow's as well', he said, laughing. She had to laugh too. 'I have stopped smoking', she said. 'That's great! Well done,' he replied, 'stopping smoking was the most important step of all.' But he was worried about her insulin dose – it was much too high. Then he examined her. She was embarrassed about her body when she undressed and got on to the couch, quickly clutching the blanket to her chin. He measured her blood pressure. 'Your blood pressure is too high, we must do something about that', he said. He looked at her injection sites. 'That's insulin atrophy', he explained. 'Do you use any other sites?' Lorraine explained that she did not; that part of her thighs was numb, so she liked using it. She was advised to rotate her injection sites to include her abdomen, the upper part of her bottom and her arms. 'Stop using your thighs for the present', he said. The doctor suggested that she should change to human insulin, but Lorraine liked her old insulin and refused to change. The doctor looked at her feet and examined her eyes. Her vision was perfect.

She got dressed and sat down beside the desk again. 'Look,' the doctor said, 'you can't go on like this, can you? You're 5 foot 6 and over 16 stones. Your insulin dose is going up and up. Your blood pressure is high. And you're only 20 years old. We've got to help you do something about your weight.' Lorraine nodded miserably. But at least he had said 'we'. She wasn't on her own. He took her to the dietitian himself. To her surprise she did not get a lecture. The dietitian spent a long time finding out about what she liked to eat, her eating pattern through the day, how she bought her food, who else shared the meals and the cooking. Lorraine told her about sharing with Lynn. 'Would you like me to see both of you together?' asked the dietitian. 'Lynn will be able to help you at home.'

Of course, Lynn helped her. Both of them weighed her every week and wrote the weight down in the diary. Together they went shopping and Lynn helped to distract her when she felt like having an eating binge. She only had one binge – two cream buns in a tea shop – and she felt so guilty while she was eating them she did not enjoy them at all. Gradually her weight started to fall. Both Lorraine and Lynn went to the clinic every month. The dietitian weighed Lorraine and gave her a lot of encouragement. The doctor was pleased too. 'I knew you had the willpower', he said. 'You gave up smoking and now you're steadily winning with the weight.' 'It's not easy', retorted Lorraine. 'I know,' he replied, 'that's why we're all so impressed.' To her relief her blood pressure also returned to normal. She had even been managing to do blood tests several times a week. In fact she had had little option, because her glucose levels fell as she lost weight and she did not want to become hypoglycaemic (to have too low a blood glucose – see pages 26–8). She was able to reduce her insulin dose steadily.

Gradually her new diet became less of a struggle, though it was some time before she really started to enjoy it. A year later she had lost two stones and was feeling much fitter. Lorraine and Lynn moved into a larger flat and redecorated it from top to bottom. The blue jeans were much too loose now, so Lorraine used them for painting in. 'It doesn't matter if I get paint on them,' she thought, 'I'll never wear them again anyway.'

WHAT SHOULD YOU WEIGH?

It was obvious to everyone that Lorraine was overweight. Many people are a little overweight – and most of us think we are too fat in places. When you are in your teens you grow to your full height, and the age at which this growth spurt happens varies, which makes it hard to give guidelines on weight for teenagers. One 15-year-old may not have started his growth spurt, while another may have virtually finished growing. The growth spurt is often earlier in girls than boys. If your blood glucose is high during the time when you should be growing it may stunt your growth, so it is important that you look after your diabetes so you achieve your full height. While you are growing you need to eat plenty. It is as important to eat enough of the right foods at this time as it is to lose weight if you are too fat. It is fashionable to try to lose weight, and some girls think that they are fat when they are not. Look at the chart opposite and see whether

14

Growth chart for teenagers

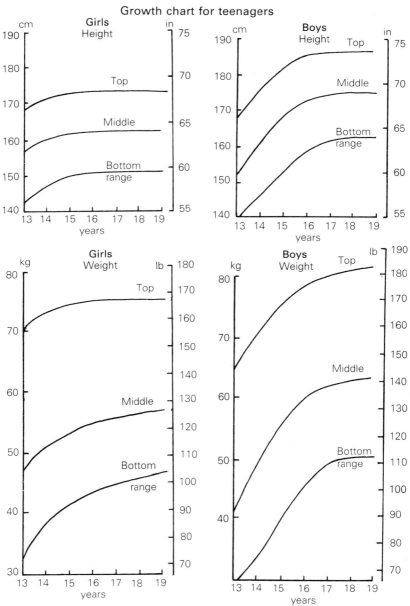

Taken from *Growth and Development Records for Boys* (11A) *and Girls* (12A) aged 0–19 (J.M. Tanner, R.H. Whitehouse and M. Takaishi, *Archives of Diseases in Childhood*, 1966, vol. 41) published by Castlemead Publications, to whom we are grateful for permission to use these records.

you fit into the height and weight range for your age. Your height and weight should be between the two outer lines. The middle lines are those below which the heights and weights of 50 per cent of all teenagers lie. Do not slim unless you need to, and talk to your doctor or dietitian first.

WHAT SHOULD YOU EAT?

Carbohydrates
These are starchy or sugary foods like bread, beans, lentils, spaghetti, potatoes, biscuits, glucose, sugar, chocolates, cakes. They are all digested in the gut into glucose and other simple sugars. Usually, the sweeter a food tastes the faster it is broken down into glucose and absorbed. If you are diabetic your body will find it hard to cope with a lot of glucose arriving suddenly in the bloodstream because you have to wait for the insulin to be absorbed from an injection site. That is why it is not a good idea to eat sugar or chocolates or sweet cakes unless you want a sudden rise in blood glucose in order to fuel exercise or treat a hypoglycaemic attack.

The glucose from high-fibre carbohydrate foods like beans and wholemeal bread is absorbed more slowly and gives the insulin you have injected a chance to cope with it. You should therefore eat plenty of high-fibre carbohydrate foods.

Fats
You should not eat a lot of fatty foods. Diabetes can upset fat chemistry (see pages 17–18, 54) and, furthermore, eating a lot of fatty foods increases your risk of having a heart attack or of your arteries furring up in other parts of your body.

Proteins
These are found in meat, fish, eggs, milk, cheese, as well as in bread, beans and other mainly starchy foods. You must not forget protein foods. If you are still growing you need a good proportion of protein to help build new cells. Try to choose protein foods that are not very fatty – chicken and fish without the skin for example, or cottage cheese, beans, bread, nuts or soya protein if you are vegetarian.

Do not add extra salt to your food at the table. Too much salt may make your blood pressure rise.

'Diabetic' foods
Many manufacturers make food labelled 'diabetic'. Some of these foods, like cereal crunch bars or breakfast cereals, are excellent, but some of them contain large amounts of sorbitol which is a form of carbohydrate. It is not a good idea to eat too much sorbitol. Firstly, it gives you tummy ache and diarrhoea; secondly, such foods are not low in calories (no use for slimming if you are overweight); thirdly, we do not know whether the sorbitol has any long-term bad effects on your body when eaten in large amounts. Other low-calorie diabetic foods are sweetened with aspartame or saccharine; small amounts of such foods are all right but, again, do not overdo it.

Types of food, and the proportions in which they are beneficial to the diabetic's diet.

SMOKING

Cigarette smoking is dangerous. It kills people. This has been proved beyond any doubt. Lynn's grandfather died from the effects of smoking. Smoking had also crippled him – it had furred up the arteries in his legs (a process known as atherosclerosis) so that the muscles did not get enough blood when he walked. This caused the cramping pains in his calves and eventually made him virtually housebound. When the arteries of the heart, the coronary arteries, are furred up (become atherosclerotic) the heart muscle does not get enough blood and this causes pains in the chest on stress or exercise (angina) or, if the blood supply becomes blocked altogether, a heart attack (the proper name is myocardial infarct). This is what killed Lynn's grandfather. The cigarettes also damage the lungs and cause lung cancer. Furthermore, one in four people who are burnt to death die in fires started by cigarettes. So do not smoke. If you do smoke, stop now.

ATHEROSCLEROSIS AND DIABETES

Lynn was risking her life by smoking, but Lorraine was at greater risk. Diabetes and smoking do not mix. Diabetes increases your likelihood of developing atherosclerosis. If you are a diabetic woman you lose your natural protection against heart attacks. (Heart attacks are rare in premenopausal women.) Because people with diabetes have an increased risk of heart attack or poor circulation due to atherosclerotic arteries (in the legs or brain, for example) it is

17

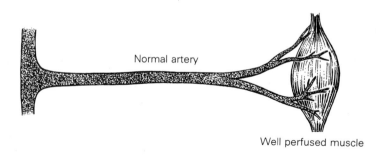

Normal artery

Well perfused muscle

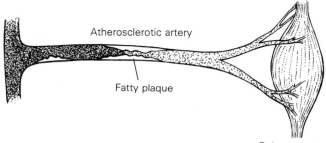

Atherosclerotic artery

Fatty plaque

Dying muscle

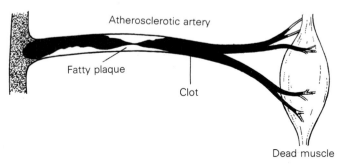

Atherosclerotic artery

Fatty plaque

Clot

Dead muscle

very important to work at reducing other risk factors. And smoking is the most dangerous additional risk factor.

Having high blood-cholesterol levels is another such risk factor. That is why you should eat a diet low in total fats. The fat you do eat should be high in polyunsaturated vegetable fats (sunflower oil, for example) and low in saturated animal fats (like butter, cheese, fatty meat). Other things to watch are high blood pressure and being overweight. Poor Lorraine was a smoking overweight diabetic with high blood pressure – four risk factors for atherosclerosis. With a lot of willpower and a good friend she managed to reduce her risks considerably. She was right to stop smoking first – the risks of smoking are greater than the risks of being overweight.

IMAGINATIVE DIABETIC RECORDS

Lorraine is not alone in making up her blood-glucose results the day before the clinic (or sometimes even in the waiting room). None of us is perfect. But you do not test your blood-glucose for the doctor – you do the tests for yourself. If you do not feel that blood testing is helping you, or you have problems with your tests, then talk with your doctor or diabetes nurse. Blood-glucose tests are not like homework, and a clinic is not a schoolroom. You can discuss whatever you want with your doctor however bad you think it is. He or she is there to help you look after yourself, and if things are not going well then you both need to find out what is going wrong and work towards improvement. Remember it is *your* health that is at stake.

INSULIN AND WEIGHT

If you are fat you need more insulin because it has to work on more cells or bigger cells – this applies whether you have diabetes or not. That is why Lorraine needed so much insulin. As she lost weight her insulin needs fell, which was why she had to start measuring her blood glucose more often – she was afraid that she would become hypoglycaemic. Some fat diabetics use this fear of hypos as an excuse not to try to lose weight, but the solution, as Lorraine showed, is simple. As soon as you start eating less reduce your insulin dose according to your blood-glucose levels.

INSULIN ATROPHY AND HYPERTROPHY

If you inject your insulin into the same area every day it can cause dents or lumps in the fatty tissue under the skin. The dents are called insulin atrophy (which is what Lorraine had) and the lumps are called insulin hypertrophy. These changes are thought to be due to an allergic reaction, and are commoner in people who use beef insulins. If you carry on injecting insulin into an area like this it will not be absorbed properly. This was another reason why Lorraine was needing more and more insulin. In addition, smoking reduces the absorption from the injection site or makes it erratic.

BEEF, PIG AND HUMAN INSULIN

Nowadays, most manufacturers are producing human insulin and are cutting back on their production of pig and beef insulin. Few people take beef insulin. Beef insulins are chemically different from human insulin (more so than pig insulin); the body may even make antibodies to the beef insulin itself and attack it as an invader. This can make the insulin less effective or slower-acting and may cause other problems. Such insulin antibodies are less common with pork insulin. It is simple to change from beef to a more modern insulin.

SUMMARY

- Atherosclerosis is a hardening and furring up of the arteries.
- Diabetes can increase your risk of atherosclerosis.
- The risk of developing atherosclerosis can also be increased by smoking, having a high blood-cholesterol level and being overweight.
- Diabetics must not smoke, and should eat a low-fat diet. They should be neither too fat nor too thin.
- Being an overweight diabetic increases your insulin needs. These needs fall as you lose weight.
- Teenagers who are still growing and developing need plenty of healthy food for growth.
- Injecting insulin in the same place every day can cause dents or lumps in the fatty tissue under the skin. Use as many different injection sites as you can.

3

STEVEN

Steven worked in a bank. He had had diabetes since he was 17. He took his insulin every day, of course, and went to his check-up visits, but never seemed to find the time to check his glucose control. He had learned to test his blood glucose, but he ran out of testing strips and did not bother to get any more. He reckoned he could feel if things were going wrong, and if he felt sugary he just increased his insulin a little for a day or so. Life was fairly steady. He still lived at home – it was convenient and his mother cooked his meals and did his laundry.

He enjoyed his holidays. One year he went to Majorca. Last year three of the other men at the bank approached him to make a foursome. 'We're planning a walking trip', they said. 'Fresh air, plenty of exercise, good company, good beer.' Steven had never been on a walking holiday before, but it sounded fun and he did not fancy a holiday on his own. So he agreed and borrowed some boots and a rucksack from a friend. His spirits rose as they roared up the motorway in Guy's old Renault. They finally arrived at midnight and camped.

Next morning they packed their rucksacks, strapped the tents on top, put on their boots and set off. They planned an ambitious week's backpacking. Guy and Hugh had shared two previous walking holidays, and Mark had been in the Scouts, but for Steven it was all a new experience. They all knew about his diabetes, although they had never seen him take his insulin before and were interested. He let Hugh push down the plunger to inject the insulin before breakfast. Steven realised that the walk was going to be energetic and packed glucose and chocolate bars.

They stopped for a breather by a stream. Steven's little toe was sore and his rucksack was like a ton weight. 'Let's push on to the top for lunch', said Guy, getting up and striding off. Steven hurried off after the others. He had had some biscuits and an apple at an earlier stop but he was looking forward hungrily to his lunch. It started to drizzle and the stones littering the steep path became slippery. He put on his cagoule. The others seemed to be getting further and further ahead. He panted on, the inside of his cagoule like a sauna. His knees felt shaky and he stumbled over a boulder. The rain poured off his forehead and ran down his nose – or was it sweat? His lips tingled. The path seemed to be wavering in front of him and he stopped to look at it. Everything seemed very odd.

Confused

Sweaty

Tingling lips

Heart thumping

Hungry

Wobbly

Stumbling

'Steven. Steven! Are you all right?' The others had come back down hill. 'Steven. What's the matter?' Steven felt very tired. His heart was thumping and the path stopped wavering and came towards him. The others caught him and sat him down. 'What's wrong with you? Steven, can you hear us?' 'Is it his diabetes?' said Hugh. 'Perhaps he needs more insulin,' he said, 'I could give him some, like I did at breakfast. But how much do I give?' Meanwhile Guy was checking Steven's pockets. He found some glucose tablets and Steven's diabetic card. Guy read it carefully. 'It has the dose of insulin here', he said. 'But that's the daily dose, and he's had that', said Hugh looking over his shoulder. 'Well perhaps you need more when you're walking.' Then they turned the card over. 'If I am found ill or fainting, please give me sugar', they read. 'Well, he's certainly

22

ill', said Guy. He got out some glucose tablets and went over to Steven. 'Here you are, eat these', he said and pushed one into Steven's mouth. Steven promptly spat it out. Guy tried again with the same result. He pushed it back in and held Steven's mouth shut. Steven objected. A sticky struggle ensued. Steven hit out at Guy and then at all of them indiscriminately. Eventually they managed to get some of the glucose tablets to stay in his mouth. Gradually he sank down to the ground again. 'Can I have a chocolate bar, please?' he asked. They gave him one and watched anxiously. After 15 minutes Steven was fine again. 'I'll just have to eat more', he explained. They set off again, somewhat shaken.

After lunch it started to rain in earnest. Steven found that his cagoule was not as waterproof as advertised. His little toe was now really sore and his heels were rubbing in the borrowed boots. They plodded on. 'We'll camp by the stream,' said Guy, 'then we'll be ready for the big one tomorrow.' In his tent that night Steven looked dolefully at his blistered feet. His shoulders were sore, too, from the rucksack straps. He slept little. The ground was lumpy and supper had been indigestible because they had not cooked the dehydrated food for long enough. He was hypo again in the night and he ate some biscuits.

When morning came they were all tired and irritable and it took them some time to get up. They ate a hasty breakfast and packed up. Most of the other people camping by the stream had gone off down the valley. 'It looks very misty', said Mark. 'Shouldn't we try a low walk today?' 'No, it'll soon clear', Guy pronounced confidently, and led off. They were heading for Scafell Pike, the highest mountain in England. None of them had ever climbed it. Fortunately the route was well trodden and easy to follow. The mist lifted a little and they caught glimpses of the surrounding mountains from time to time. Steven made sure he had plenty to eat on the way. As the path progressed up the mist thickened. It was cold and there was a steady drizzle. They saw no-one else. It seemed hours before they reached the summit. A buffeting wind blew ribbons of mist and rain across their faces. 'I don't understand why the wind doesn't blow the mist away', said Mark, blowing his nose dejectedly. They had planned to eat their lunch at the top but it was so cold and miserable that they changed their minds and decided to get out of the wind first.

They set off across the strewn boulders. Suddenly a precipice yawned at their feet. 'We must have gone wrong. Let's go further round and try again', said Guy, who was navigating. Steven was cold and miserable; his feet hurt, his shoulders hurt and he wanted to go home. He had put his jumper on under his thin cagoule, but he was still freezing. He stumbled on after the others. 'No, that's not it', said Guy, stopping again. 'Where are we?' asked Hugh. 'Blowed if I know', said Guy. 'Everything looks the same up here.' They reached a narrow and terrifying ridge and slithered down a steep path.

By now they were all cold. Steven was getting left behind again. The stones in the path conspired to trip him up and his rucksack was a millstone pulling him back. He felt inordinately tired and chilled all through. Gradually he ground to a halt. The others stopped and returned to him. 'Are you low again?' asked Hugh. Steven shrugged. He didn't care any more. He was tired and he just wanted to rest. The sweat cooled to a clammy misery against his skin. The others got the glucose out and gave him some. He did not resist this time. It was all too much effort. Guy felt Steven's hands and face. 'He's really cold', he said. 'Perhaps he's suffering from exposure. We can't go on. We'll put a tent up on that flattish ground over there.'

A hour later inside the tent, in his sleeping bag, with some hot sweet tea and some food inside him, Steven started to feel better. He still felt weary but he was gradually warming up. He fell asleep. The stove had warmed the tent and the others had revived too. They talked about what to do next. Every so often one of them peered at Steven in his sleeping bag. He seemed to be improving and felt a little warmer to the touch. But what was happening to his diabetes? Was his glucose going up or coming down? Should they call out the mountain rescue team? But they did not even know where they were, let alone how to reach a telephone. It was getting late in the afternoon. They decided to stay put and found a place to put up the other tent. By suppertime Steven was much better. They ate a huge meal and went to sleep early, exhausted by the perils of the day.

Next morning they woke to a clear day. Glorious views stretched up to the mountains, whose summits towered above them. They broke camp and headed slowly down into the valley. Steven felt good in himself but his little toe was throbbing. They found a path and joined it. At the campsite in the valley Steven inspected his toe. It was red, with pus around the blister.

By the following morning Steven decided that he had had enough. His foot was infected, everything seemed to be going wrong and he was spoiling the holiday for his friends. He made his way to the nearest station and caught the train home. It was another lovely day and he was sad as the beautiful mountain scenery went past. At home his doctor cleaned his toe and gave him a course of antibiotics and it healed rapidly. He had no more trouble with hypos, but he was worried because his diabetes had let him down. Why had everything gone wrong?

DIABETES AND EXERCISE

Glucose provides the muscles with fuel for exercise. At first the glucose is released from stores of glycogen already in the muscles. If you carry on exercising, this glycogen is used up and the muscles have to take in glucose directly from the bloodstream. You need a little insulin to do this. As the blood glucose falls the liver tops it up from its stores. However, if you have a lot of insulin around this blocks the release of glucose from the liver. In such a situation you can top up the blood glucose by eating carbohydrate foods. Steven

Exercise, food and insulin

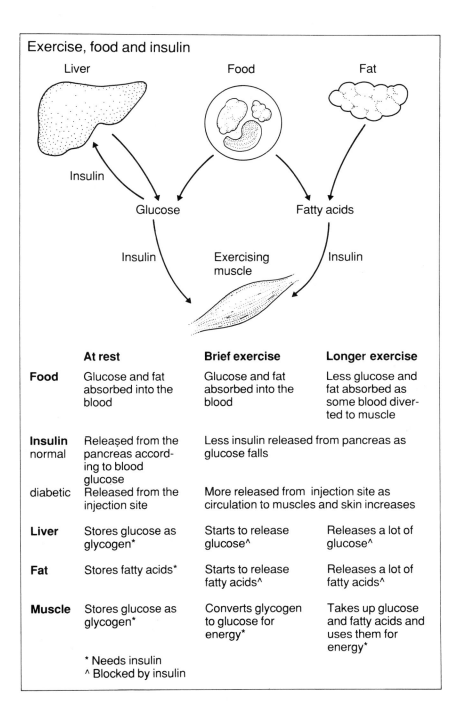

	At rest	Brief exercise	Longer exercise
Food	Glucose and fat absorbed into the blood	Glucose and fat absorbed into the blood	Less glucose and fat absorbed as some blood diverted to muscle
Insulin normal	Released from the pancreas according to blood glucose	Less insulin released from pancreas as glucose falls	
diabetic	Released from the injection site	More released from injection site as circulation to muscles and skin increases	
Liver	Stores glucose as glycogen*	Starts to release glucose^	Releases a lot of glucose^
Fat	Stores fatty acids*	Starts to release fatty acids^	Releases a lot of fatty acids^
Muscle	Stores glucose as glycogen*	Converts glycogen to glucose for energy*	Takes up glucose and fatty acids and uses them for energy*

* Needs insulin
^ Blocked by insulin

was exercising much harder than he had done for years. He had had his usual dose of insulin and had not eaten enough. So when his muscles started using glucose from the bloodstream the blood glucose fell and was not topped up. He became severely hypoglycaemic (low in blood glucose). After exercise the body reorganises its glucose stores. This happened during the night for Steven and, because he had found his supper indigestible and had not eaten enough carbohydrate before he went to bed, he became hypoglycaemic again.

Next day he did not reduce his insulin dose and, although he ate more, it was still not enough to sustain the considerable exertion of ascending 1,700 feet. So he still had too much insulin and not enough food inside him. If he had spent the week walking (or doing any other form of daily exercise) his body would gradually have become more sensitive to insulin; in other words, the same dose of insulin would have produced a greater lowering of his blood glucose. So when you exercise you do not need more insulin as Steven's friends thought – you need less.

If you want to learn more about diabetes and exercise read *Diabetes: A Beyond Basics Guide* by Rowan Hillson.

HYPOGLYCAEMIA

Hypo means low and glycaemia means blood glucose. The body depends on glucose for fuel, just as a car depends on petrol in its petrol tank. The human body can use other forms of fuel in addition to glucose, but the brain depends entirely on glucose. If the blood glucose falls below 4 mmol/l (72 mg/dl) the brain starts to malfunction and, if the blood glucose continues to fall, eventually stops working. At this point the person becomes unconscious. Steven's brain was not working properly when he became hypoglycaemic (most people call it hypo for short) the first time. He was stumbling and slow, everything seemed odd and he fought his friends when they tried to help him. As soon as his blood glucose rose again everything went back to normal.

As the blood glucose falls, the body puts its own rescue system into action. Emergency hormones including adrenaline (epinephrine) are released. They help to raise the blood glucose. But adrenaline has other effects. It is the 'fight, flight and fright' hormone; it makes you sweat and makes your heart beat rapidly. This was happening to Steven – the sweat was literally dripping off him.

Recognising hypoglycaemia
Most people learn to recognise the signs that their blood glucose is falling long before it is obvious to anyone else. Each person has their own pattern of warnings. Steven usually recognised his hypos, so why did he miss them on this occasion?

For Steven, prolonged mountain walking was unusual. It makes

26

everyone sweaty and people who are unfit may feel awful if they attempt something too much for them (remember Steven's very heavy rucksack weighing him down?). He confused the early signs of hypoglycaemia with those of unfamiliar exertion. Then his glucose started falling rapidly, and events overtook him.

Treating hypoglycaemia
If you feel your blood glucose falling eat something sweet. Glucose tablets, drinks (Coca Cola, Pepsi Cola or most non-diet canned drinks contain glucose) or gel (e.g. Hypostop, Glutose) are fastest; sugar lumps, chocolate, candy bars or sweets also work quickly; biscuits, bread and fruit work more slowly. You should tell your family and friends how to recognise hypoglycaemia and explain what to do. Steven's well-meaning friends nearly gave him some more insulin, which would have had a disastrous effect!

If you have a bad hypo and cannot eat, someone can revive you with an injection of glucagon. This is the hormone which has the opposite effect to that of insulin – it raises the blood glucose. Ask your doctor about it – your family and friends can learn how to use it if you keep some in the house or in your pocket.

Recovery position and injecting glucagon

If you are unconscious, helpers should stay calm, turn you on to your side, make sure your airway is clear and telephone a doctor. If they have glucagon they can inject it into your thigh. If they have no glucagon, rubbing small amounts of glucose inside the cheek closest to the ground may help, providing they make sure you cannot choke on it. The main thing is not to be alarmed. It is extremely rare for anyone to be harmed by a hypo – even if it is not treated (for example if it happens while you are asleep at night and does not wake you), the blood glucose will gradually rise as the insulin wears off. But you should be careful not to become hypoglycaemic while you are doing something that could be dangerous if you get confused, for example driving a car or operating machinery.

DIABETIC CARD, WARNING SIGN AND GLUCOSE

Everyone with diabetes on insulin should carry a diabetic card on his or her person *all* the time. Steven's card probably saved his life. Many diabetics wear bracelets or lockets which say that they have diabetes (e.g. Medic-Alert, SOS Talisman). These have the advantage that they do not have to be moved as you change your clothes or bag. With your diabetic card you must carry glucose, as Steven did. There are many convenient forms, e.g. BD glucose tablets, Dextrosol, Lucozade, Boots glucose tablets, Hypostop or Glutose Gel. The gel comes in a waterproof and resilient polythene bottle and is useful in water sports, tucked into a pocket sewn in a swimming costume or tied on a string.

HYPOGLYCAEMIA AND COLD

Steven developed early signs of exposure, but none of the others were that badly affected by the cold. Why? His clothing was not as warm as theirs and was not fully wind- and waterproof, so he was colder than them to start with. If you are hypoglycaemic you cannot regulate your body temperature properly. A hypoglycaemic person who becomes cold cannot shiver to keep warm and just gets colder and colder. Once Steven's friends treated his hypoglycaemia and prevented him from losing more heat by putting him in a sleeping bag in the tent he started to recover. They helped the recovery process by giving him warm sweet drinks and food.

LOOK AFTER YOUR FEET

Steven developed an infected toe because his boots rubbed him. That could have happened to anyone wearing ill-fitting boots or shoes, but infections are more likely in people with diabetes than in non-diabetics. Older diabetics can have more serious foot problems if

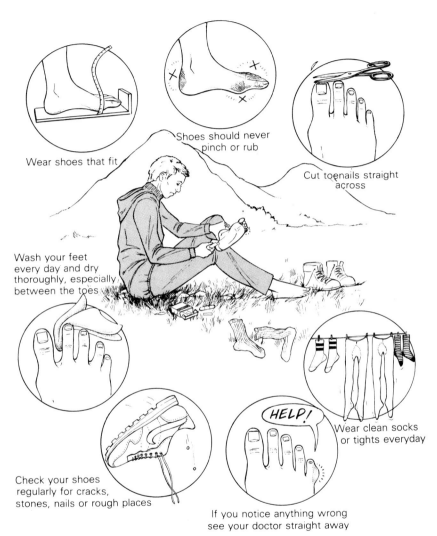

Wear shoes that fit

Shoes should never pinch or rub

Cut toenails straight across

Wash your feet every day and dry thoroughly, especially between the toes

HELP!

Wear clean socks or tights everyday

Check your shoes regularly for cracks, stones, nails or rough places

If you notice anything wrong see your doctor straight away

they have poor circulation or nerve damage (see page 59). Get into the habit of looking after your feet now. Buy shoes which are completely comfortable from the moment you first wear them. They should not pinch or rub anywhere. Check your shoes for nails or cracks which may rub. Do not walk barefoot. Wash your feet every day and dry them carefully, especially between the toes. Cut your toenails straight across. If you have any problems with your feet – a sore place, athlete's foot or any injury, tell your doctor immediately.

Steven was very unhappy about what happened. His diabetes had never spoiled anything for him before and he was deeply ashamed that it had let him down in front of his friends. He asked the doctor about it on his next diabetic clinic visit. The doctor explained about exercise and diabetes. 'It would have been much easier for you if you had been able to measure your blood glucose', he said. 'It would have saved you all a great deal of worry.' The doctor offered Steven some more glucose testing strips and lancets. Steven took them home and put them on the table. He looked at them. He did not like making holes in his fingers but perhaps it would be worth a try. So he started testing again. To his surprise his blood glucose was often 10 mmol/l (180 mg/dl) or more. He thought he had been well controlled. He showed the record to the doctor and between them they adjusted his insulin until most of the values were well under 10 mmol/l (180 mg/dl).

Guy and Mark went to a gym twice a week and they asked Steven if he would like to come. His foot had healed by now and he decided to have a go. He was not sure what to do about his food and insulin at first, so he tested his blood glucose before and after each session. He found that by reducing his short-acting insulin by four units each evening of a gym session and eating a chocolate bar before each session he had no problems with hypos. And before bed he had milk and sandwiches.

A few months later, in a diabetic magazine, he read a feature on Outward Bound courses for people with diabetes. They were held in the mountains. He remembered the stupendous views from the train as he had travelled home last time, so he plucked up his courage and applied for the next course. He was rather nervous when he arrived at the course centre. Supposing last year's disaster was repeated. But at least there was a doctor and nurse here. Most of the others were nervous too. To his surprise he soon discovered that he was fitter than many of them, thanks to his training sessions in the gym. And this year he had borrowed boots from his cousin who had the same size feet as him, and he had had some practice walks in them. He reduced his insulin by 15 per cent on the first day and ate double snacks between meals and before bed. He kept a close check on his blood glucose, but it remained normal with no hypos. He tried rock climbing, canoeing and orienteering. He enjoyed rock climbing immensely. He even braved the high-level-ropes course and led the mountain rescue exercise. The course culminated in a two-day mountain expedition. The expedition was thoroughly planned. As Steven and his group checked the contents of their rucksacks with the safety list, he realised how dangerous his first mountain trip had been.

He was luckier with the weather this time, and after a hard climb stood proudly on the summit cairn surveying the view. It was well worth the effort. He collected his certificate at the end of the course with a feeling of triumph.

SUMMARY

- Exercise uses up glucose. You need less insulin and more food to exercise safely.
- Exercise is good for people with diabetes. It keeps you fit and helps to keep your weight and blood glucose normal.
- People with diabetes can safely enjoy virtually all forms of sport and exercise, from rock climbing to marathon running, if they measure their blood glucose and adjust their food and insulin to prevent hypoglycaemia.
- Hypoglycaemia causes hunger, tingling lips, sweating, fast heart beat, confusion and, rarely, unconsciousness.
- Hypoglycaemia can be cured by glucose or other carbohydrate food.
- Hypoglycaemia makes a cold person colder.
- Hypoglycaemia is avoidable. If you have a hypo, work out why it happened and make sure it does not trouble you again.
- Check with the experts for safety guidelines before trying a new sport or activity.
- Look after your feet.

4

MICHELLE

Michelle sat in the sitting room waiting for the diabetes liaison sister to come and help her with her insulin. She felt very much better than she did a week before. Then she had been desperately thirsty, and had lost count of the number of times a day she had had to pass urine. In fact, she had been feeling generally awful. Her mother had taken her to the doctor, who had diagnosed diabetes and referred her straight to the diabetic clinic. The doctor there had confirmed the diagnosis and spent a long time with Michelle and her parents explaining what it meant and what the treatment entailed. She had given her first injection of insulin there and then in the clinic – she was very proud of that. The diabetes liaison sister – Sister Makepeace – had been very comforting. She had come to the house twice every day to help Michelle learn how to manage her diabetes. The dietitian, Miss Rose, came one morning. Michelle, her mother and Miss Rose had all sat in the kitchen with a cup of tea and worked out Michelle's diet.

Sister Makepeace watched Michelle draw up her insulin and inject it. 'Well done,' she said, 'you've got the hang of it now. I think you can manage on your own tomorrow. But you have my phone number, just in case, haven't you.' The next day Michelle did her injections and all was well. The following day, she had dreadful difficulty getting the air bubbles out, but she started again with a fresh syringe and succeeded. She continued to feel better. She was ravenously hungry and was eating huge meals. Gradually she started to put back some of the weight that she had lost before her diabetes was diagnosed. Ten days after her first clinic visit she was ready to go back to school.

Michelle was 13. Sister Makepeace had given her some information for her teachers to read and, with this, she set off with her mother to see the headmistress. The headmistress was very understanding. 'We have two other diabetic children in school,' she said, 'so we have learned a little about it.' Michelle took a packed lunch every day anyway, so all she had to do was bring some snacks too and her diet would be no problem. The headmistress said that she would tell all Michelle's teachers about the diabetes and her need for snacks and some instant glucose if she became hypoglycaemic. 'I don't know what a hypo feels like,' said Michelle, 'but Sister Makepeace has told me what to look out for.' The games mistress came and joined them and together they discussed the need to eat before and during sports. Both Michelle and the games mistress would carry some glucose in the pocket of their shorts and track-suit.

Michelle settled happily back into her usual routine. Her friends wanted to know what was wrong with her so she told them. The diabetes care fitted in well and she had no real problems with it for several months. But one thing began to worry her. She had had no periods since before the diabetes was diagnosed. She wondered what was wrong with her. What would happen if she did not have a period soon? Was all the blood building up inside her? She was too embarrassed to mention it to the doctor when she went to the diabetic clinic.

It was the evening of the school Christmas party. She was going with Adrian. She had been feeling miserable for the last two days and did not know why. She should have been feeling happy and excited but she was not. Her blood glucose had gone up as well, although she had not eaten anything unusual. She had telephoned Sister Makepeace, who advised her to increase her insulin a little. Her tummy became bloated and uncomfortable. Then, when she was having her shower before dressing for the party, she saw a trickle of blood down her leg. Her period had started, now of all times. Absolutely typical! Fortunately she had some tampons in the cupboard. She still felt uncomfortable and had some low tummy pains, but she was very relieved that her periods had come back. She enjoyed the party.

Three days later she was finishing her last history class before Christmas. It was just before lunch and she was hungry. She began to feel slightly trembly and sweaty and there were prickly feelings around her mouth. This must be a hypo, she thought. She ate some glucose and within a few minutes felt all right again. The same thing happened next day, so she reduced her insulin.

When she next went to diabetic clinic she told the doctor about her hypoglycaemic attacks. 'I don't understand why my glucose went up and down like that', she said. The doctor asked about what she had been eating and sports and exercise but nothing had changed. Then he asked her about her periods. Michelle was surprised and embarrassed. She had never talked about periods with anyone but her mother before. She blushed and then shyly explained about not having periods and then them starting again before the party. The doctor explained that it was common for the glucose to rise around period times. He did not seem at all embarrassed.

Michelle then started writing her period dates in her diabetic diary. Sure enough, every month, her glucose went up just before the period started and went down again a few days later. She learned to adjust her insulin accordingly.

SCHOOL

Most schools will have at least one pupil with diabetes. About one in 1,000 young people have diabetes. If you are the first diabetic student at your school you will need to teach the teachers about diabetes. Most diabetic associations produce a school information pack and the diabetes sister will usually go to your school with you and your parents and explain about your diabetes. There is rarely any problem about having the right food and snacks at school – either take all your food from home, or arrange for proper snacks to be available from the school kitchen. You must always carry glucose and your diabetic card, and it helps if teachers with whom you spend most time, and your games teacher, carry glucose too. Most of the few problems arise from lack of communication – a member of staff who has not been properly briefed about your diabetes or a new person in the kitchen who is not aware of it, for example.

Having diabetes should not stop you from taking part in any of the activities at school, and if you want to go on school trips do so. However, it is important to take plenty of spare food and drink and carry your blood testing kit and insulin with you in case you are delayed on a trip. Make sure that the group leader knows you have diabetes and knows what to do if you do become hypoglycaemic.

PERIODS AND DIABETES

Most women do not have periods every month like clockwork. All sorts of things can upset the pattern of your periods. If you miss periods the blood will *not* build up inside your womb and nothing bad will happen. (However, if have had sexual intercourse recently you should get a pregnancy test straightaway and see your doctor without delay. See page 46 onwards.) Any illness can upset the rhythm of your periods and may delay them for months. This is what happened to Michelle when her diabetes first started. When her diabetes had settled down her body gradually returned to normal and she started having periods again.

Having a period is called menstruation. The hormone changes which cause menstrual bleeding may also upset the blood-glucose balance, as may being less active around period times. The blood-glucose changes commonly follow the same pattern as Michelle, although I have also met women whose insulin needs fall around the start of menstruation – they suddenly have hypoglycaemic attacks. Each woman seems to follow her own pattern of blood-glucose change, if any, at this time. Learn what happens to you so that you are prepared for it and can alter your insulin or your food if necessary.

Sometimes, in younger girls, the development of diabetes will delay the onset of your first period. As your body settles down and the insulin and diet treatment return your body chemistry to normal, your periods will eventually start. However you should see your doctor if you have reached the age of 15 without having any periods at all. Some girls do start later than this, but it is worth having a check-up to make sure all is well.

Having diabetes makes no difference to the way in which you cope with menstrual bleeding. Some girls prefer tampons, others use sanitary pads. Some people use tampons for the heavier days and stick-on pads as the blood flow lessens. If you have not used tampons before and want to try, read the instructions in the box carefully so that you do not make yourself sore. If you have problems, ask your mother to help you. And remember to take out the last tampon at the end of the period.

THRUSH

Occasionally women (and sometimes men) with diabetes develop thrush. This is a fungal condition that is sometimes found in babies' mouths or as a nappy rash and that can also affect adults. It causes a white discharge from the vagina (or penis) and itching and soreness around the vagina (or penis and scrotum). The area may become red and sore and you may see curd-like white bits on the skin. Thrush can be cured with an anti-fungal cream, so go to your doctor immediately to get some. It will soon ease the irritation. Thrush is especially common when your blood glucose is high, so sort out your diabetes if necessary.

SUMMARY

- If you have just developed diabetes make sure that your headmistress or headmaster knows about it and that other teachers understand your needs.
- Having diabetes will not stop you from taking a full part in all school activities.
- If your blood glucose is high, either before your diabetes is diagnosed or for some other reason, it may upset your periods or even delay the onset of your first period. Other illnesses can upset your menstrual rhythm too.
- The hormone changes at period times can upset your blood glucose. It usually rises, but may fall. Test your blood glucose to find out what is going on and adjust your insulin or food if necessary.
- Do not be shy about discussing your periods or any vaginal discharge with your doctor. He or she is used to discussing such things, will not be embarrassed and will be able to help you.

5

WINSTON

Winston sat nervously on the edge of his chair. This was the third job Winston had applied for. He wanted to go into the retail business. One day he would have his own greengrocers shop – high-quality produce only, in a nice neighbourhood. The first job he had applied for had been at the local greengrocers, but they had wanted someone with experience. The second had been in the market, helping the fruit suppliers. They too had wanted someone experienced in the business. But how could you get experience if no-one was prepared to teach you? He was feeling quite despondent.

The door opened and a trim secretary walked in. 'Mr Silcott can see you now', she smiled. He followed her down the corridor. The supermarket head office was vast and everyone else was bustling about importantly. Mr Silcott had Winston's application in front of him. Winston had gone to a lot of trouble with that. He had written out a rough copy first and then typed the top copy on his mother's typewriter. His one-fingered typing had taken ages. 'I see you have six good exam results', commented Mr Silcott. 'Economics and mathematics could be useful in our line of business. Now tell me, why do you want to work at a supermarket?' So Winston told him. He told him everything – all about his Saturday job in the greengrocers near home, his plans for going on a marketing course, his interest in fruit and vegetable selling. Mr Silcott was impressed. The previous candidate for the job had merely answered 'Dunno' to that question! He asked more probing questions and Winston did his best to answer them. At the end he asked if Winston had any health problems. 'It's not a problem,' Winston replied, 'but I do have diabetes. I look after it myself with insulin injections. I adjust the dose depending on my blood tests. I have regular medical checks at the hospital and they told me I was very healthy last time. It has never caused me any difficulties.' 'Well,' said Mr Silcott, 'you look pretty fit to me. We have several diabetics in the company. If you get the job you will have a medical check like everyone else.' He promised to let him know within the next few days and said goodbye.

At last the long-awaited letter arrived. Winston was astonished.

Mr Silcott started by saying that he was very impressed with Winston and that he thought the post he had applied for was not right for him. Instead he was offering him a place on the company's three-year training scheme. This included a day-release course at the local college, practical experience throughout the company, and perhaps management training. Of course Winston accepted.

First he had to see the medical officer. He set off with his diabetic card in his pocket and spare glucose, as always. He took his diabetic record book, his blood-glucose testing kit and his insulin pen, in case the doctor wanted to see them. His clinic doctor had been delighted to hear of his success and had offered to write a report to the company doctor if necessary. Winston met the nurse first. She was very busy. He told her he was diabetic. She weighed him and then asked him for a urine specimen. Winston provided her with one, but warned that he had a low threshold for glucose. But she had already thrust a list of questions into his hand and gone off to test his urine. 'You've got glucose in your urine', she announced a few minutes later. 'You can't be looking after your diabetes very well.' And she bustled him into the next room. The doctor sat him down and started asking him about himself. He too commented on the glucose in the urine, but Winston showed him his excellent glucose record and explained about his renal glycosuria. 'Quite unusual, having that as well as being diabetic', the doctor commented. He asked to see Winston's insulin pen. He had never seen one before. Then he examined him. 'I can see that you're looking after yourself extremely well', he said, 'I'm sure you'll have no problems with your diabetes at work, but if there is any way I can help, please let me know.'

Winston arrived for his first day at work feeling very excited. The first month was called 'orientation'. There were 10 people in his group, and they all looked as nervous as he felt. By lunchtime, however, they were more relaxed. Winston wondered what to do about his insulin. At school he used to give it in front of his friends, but he had known them for years and they all knew about his diabetes. Well, these people were going to be his friends too, and he did not like the idea of concealing his diabetes. So he turned casually to Martin, who was sitting next to him. 'Just got to give my insulin, now. I've got diabetes, you see.' And he took out his pen, lifted up his shirt and injected his insulin. Martin was a little surprised and then tentatively asked if it hurt. 'Hardly at all', replied Winston. 'How often do you have to do that?' Martin asked. So Winston told him. Gradually Martin asked more questions. 'You don't mind my asking, do you?' he said, suddenly. 'Not at all', said Winston.

His first placement was as assistant in the bakery division of one of the supermarket branches. One morning he was helping to restock the shelves when he noticed a customer in difficulties. The woman was not very steady on her feet and he wondered if she was drunk, but as he came up to her he saw that she was sweating and pale. He helped her to sit down. She seemed incapable of answering his questions and he thought she was going to faint. He pushed her head between her knees as his first-aid instructor had taught him and an SOS medallion swung forward. He undid it. She was diabetic! He debated searching her pockets for some glucose, but decided it would be quicker to use his own. Within a few minutes she was sitting up and talking. She apologised to him for being such a nuisance. She had forgotten to put her glucose tablets into her bag when she changed it. 'I always like to have a matching bag', she smiled wanly. After thanking him profusely she finished her shopping and left. Later the manager told Winston that he had had a very complimentary letter from the woman (who was a local councillor) and commended him for his fast thinking.

That was all four years ago. Winston is now assistant manager of one of the supermarket's branches, and it has the best fruit and vegetable selection in town.

PLANNING A CAREER

What do you want to do? This is the most important deciding factor. Some teenagers choose their career early, while some university students still cannot decide what they will do when they graduate. If you are interested in a particular career, talk with people who are doing the job. Learn all you can about it. Will it be right for you? Discuss your plans with your school and college teachers, and with the local careers officer.

And if you still cannot decide? Again, a careers officer can help you. Jobcentres can also advise you. When you have decided what you would like to do, find out what qualifications you need.

APPLYING FOR A JOB

Once you have chosen your career, work as hard as you can to get the best possible entry qualifications. Jobs are scarce and good exam results give you a better chance of being short-listed. When you apply for the job, read the advertisements and application forms very carefully, plan exactly how you are going to complete the form, keep it clean and fill it in with very neat handwriting or, much better, using a typewriter. Check your spelling with a dictionary.

If you are short-listed do some homework on the job. Is there a pre-interview test (e.g. a typing test for a would-be secretary)? If so, what is it? What exactly does the job entail? What does the company make? Talk with people who have been through the course or the job. Have a look around the building, if allowed. What are they likely to ask at interview? Practise answering likely questions. (Winston was asked why he wanted the job – nearly every interviewer asks that. See page 36.) When you attend the interview dress tidily and conform. Interviewers are not likely to appreciate

38

green hair or tattered Levis – this is *not* the time to try and shock the older generation.

A few jobs are not open to insulin-treated diabetics – these include the armed services, the police force, the fire service, and jobs involving driving heavy goods vehicles (HGVs) or passenger service vehicles (PSVs). If you develop diabetes after you have joined a service or company, they will usually try to keep you on, perhaps in a different capacity. Some jobs involve responsibility for other people's safety. If so, you've to ask yourself, if you have a bad hypoglycaemic reaction and become confused, might you harm someone? This is why insulin-treated diabetics are not allowed to fly aeroplanes or hold PSV licences. You should also consider your own safety. You have to be very sure that you will never have a hypo if you want to be an underwater diver, a tightrope walker or a steeplejack, for example.

What should you say about your diabetes on application forms or at interview? Winston was honest and confident about his. It is not a good idea to hide your diabetes – your employer may find out anyway. A young man in our clinic was dismissed when his boss found out that he had not revealed his diabetes – no-one had asked about his health, so he had said nothing. His doctors supported him and he got his job back, but it was a very worrying business. And if you actually lie about your diabetes when you apply for a job, your employer would be within his rights to dismiss you. You may need to explain what diabetes is and how you manage it. The important point is that having diabetes will not stop you doing an excellent job. In fact, diabetics have a better work record than most people. Your diabetic clinic doctor will explain things to your employer if you wish.

THE MEDICAL EXAMINATION

A medical check for a company or college is just like a routine diabetic clinic check-up. As in hospital clinics, staff may be busy, so make sure they hear you if you have something important to tell them. And make sure you understand what hospital staff are saying. Most misunderstandings are due to lack of communication. The company doctor may not have a wide experience of diabetes, so be prepared to explain how you look after yourself. Show that you are in control of your diabetes and well able to handle it. He may have some hints for you about working as a diabetic in that particular organisation.

Some companies have medical schemes or private health care schemes. Discuss such offers with your family doctor.

KIDNEY THRESHOLD AND RENAL GLYCOSURIA

Why did Winston show glucose in his urine if his blood glucose was normal? One explanation could have been that his blood-glucose level varied during the day and that it was higher when the urine was being made and stored in the bladder than it was at the time he did a blood test. However, that was not the case here. Winston has a condition called renal glycosuria. (Renal means kidney and glycosuria is glucose in the urine.)

Urine is made by filtering water and waste products from the blood through special clumps of kidney cells. The body must have a blood-glucose level between 4 and 8 mmol/l (72 and 144 mg/dl) for normal functioning. If the blood-glucose level rises above this, the kidneys allow glucose to leak into the urine. The higher the blood glucose, the more glucose leaks into the urine. But different people have slightly different levels at which this leakage first occurs. Some people, like Winston, allow glucose to leak into the urine at normal blood glucose levels. This is what is called renal glycosuria. It is harmless and can happen in non-diabetics – they keep being told they have diabetes when all they have is slightly leaky kidneys. Other people, for example some elderly men and women, only lose glucose into the urine when the blood glucose is higher, e.g. 13 mmol/l (234 mg/dl) or more.

This means that urine testing is not a very reliable way of monitoring what is happening to your blood glucose. However, if you know at what point you start losing glucose into the urine – and you can find this out by measuring your blood and urine glucose – you can use urine tests to give a general idea of average blood glucose during the time that urine is being made.

INSULIN PENS

Winston injected his fast-acting insulin using a pen. There are several insulin pens on the market. They usually have a cartridge of insulin instead of an ink cartridge and a double-ended needle instead of a nib. They are a very convenient way to carry your insulin around with you. Some people have an injection of long-acting insulin at bedtime and some fast-acting insulin from their pen before each main meal, according to blood-glucose levels.

STARTING A NEW JOB

Everyone is nervous at first. On day one find out where your work area is, where you can put things (e.g. in a desk or locker), where the toilet is, and where the canteen is. Take a note book to write down instructions about how you do your job, the company rules, times of meals, general advice and so on. For some people the level of activity in the new job is no different from that expended at school, but most people will put more energy into something new, and it is hard to predict what will happen to their diabetes at first. A sensible

Differences in renal thresholds

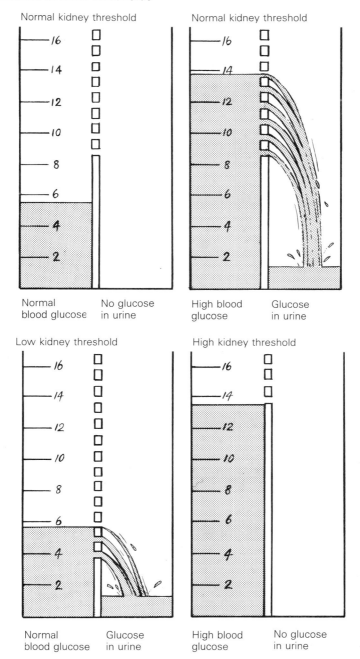

Normal kidney threshold

| 16 |
| 14 |
| 12 |
| 10 |
| 8 |
| 6 |
| 4 |
| 2 |

Normal   No glucose
blood glucose   in urine

Normal kidney threshold

| 16 |
| 14 |
| 12 |
| 10 |
| 8 |
| 6 |
| 4 |
| 2 |

High blood   Glucose
glucose   in urine

Low kidney threshold

| 16 |
| 14 |
| 12 |
| 10 |
| 8 |
| 6 |
| 4 |
| 2 |

Normal   Glucose
blood glucose   in urine

High kidney threshold

| 16 |
| 14 |
| 12 |
| 10 |
| 8 |
| 6 |
| 4 |
| 2 |

High blood   No glucose
glucose   in urine

41

precaution is to reduce your morning short- and medium- or long-acting insulin a little, by 2–4 units for example, and eat a big breakfast. This might make you a little sugary but guards against an embarrassing hypo on your first day. You will also need to know what is happening, which means measuring your blood glucose. Start as you mean to go on.

Being open about your diabetes also means that you do not have to use up a lot of time and effort concealing it. And it means that your workmates can help you if you have a hypo. Tell your close colleagues at work what to expect if you have a hypoglycaemic reaction, and what to do.

If you are doing a very energetic job, you may need to eat extra snacks or bigger meals or to take less insulin on work days. Unless you are trying to lose weight on your doctor's advice, always eat a carbohydrate snack mid-morning and mid-afternoon. If you do not have a proper tea or coffee break, eat something quick and simple. Never let an ignorant employer bully you out of eating your snacks and meals when you need them. Your hospital doctor or family doctor will support you and sort things out if necessary.

Sometimes, your new job is so different from your activity pattern at school or at your previous job that your usual insulin and food pattern just do not work, even if you try adjusting them. You may be sugary all the time or keep having hypos. This can always be sorted out. Everyone's insulin and food needs change from time to time. There may be ways of adjusting your usual treatment that you have not thought of, or you may need a different type of insulin. Tell your diabetic clinic doctor about your difficulties sooner rather than later. It is helpful to discuss your new job before you start, and you should definitely do this if you are planning shift work. Another book in this series, *Diabetes: A Beyond Basics Guide* by Rowan Hillson, may help you.

DIABETES WARNING CARDS, MEDALLIONS OR BRACELETS

Winston was able to help the hypoglycaemic lady in the supermarket not only because he had had first-aid training, but also because she was wearing a medallion which told him that she had diabetes. He was the one person in the shop who instantly knew what was wrong and what to do. If you decide to buy a warning bracelet or medallion choose a stainless steel or pure metal one – gold-plated ones can become corroded if worn by diabetics. At the very least you must carry a diabetic card.

SUMMARY

- When you have decided on your career, go for it. Work as hard as you can to get the best qualifications to enter that career.

- When you apply for jobs, sell yourself. Presentation matters, whether it is a clean, typed, perfectly-spelled application form or tidy clothes at interview.
- Your diabetes bars you from very few jobs. Do not let it hinder you in your choice of career, but be realistic. Will a hypoglycaemic reaction at work harm you or other people? If so, can you guarantee to prevent hypoglycaemia? If not, choose an alternative job.
- Be open about your diabetes. Concealing it rarely pays.
- Be prepared to adjust your insulin and food when you start work. Err on the side of caution to avoid hypoglycaemia for the first few days. Measure your blood glucose at work so that you know what is happening.
- Discuss your job and diabetes with your clinic doctor. Remember he or she is there to support you in whatever way you need. Your doctor will do his or her best to sort things out with your employer if there are any problems related to your diabetes.
- Carry a diabetic card. Consider wearing a warning bracelet or medallion.
- People with diabetes often have a better work record than non-diabetics.

6

SHARON AND JULIA

Sharon tilted her face to the mirror and stroked the eye-liner carefully along her eyelid. Some lipstick, and then she would be ready for the party. She had met Jason at a disco a week ago. He was tall, with a dark beard and brown eyes. She wondered if the black dress would be all right. It had looked very sexy in the shop. The door bell rang. Jason had a huge car! 'Its my father's,' he said, 'I borrow it.' The party was miles away in the next town, and Jason drove very fast.

Sharon did not go to many parties. She was 17 and the second daughter of the managing director of a furniture company. Her mother worked there too, in personnel. Her father was away a lot at meetings. Her sister, Julia, was married and lived a few streets away. Sharon went round whenever she could, but Julia seemed very busy with her husband and friends and work and everything. Both Sharon and Julia had diabetes. Julia had now had diabetes for 10 years, while Sharon had been diabetic for just three years. They both attended the young adult diabetic clinic.

They could hear the party from the other end of the street. The suburban house was crammed with people and music blared out from every window. Jason fought his way to the kitchen and emerged with drinks. There seemed to be a lot of gin and not much tonic. They joined the crush in the sitting room and soon were swaying with the dancers in the smoky din. Jason pulled Sharon closer. He was 19, he told her, and at college studying electrical engineering. The music was deafening and after a while Sharon was content to lean on Jason and dance dreamily.

Gradually the party thinned out and Jason suggested that perhaps it was time to leave. Sharon felt drowsy and comfortable. Jason was so good to be with – her first real boyfriend. They got into the car and Jason drove off. He stopped the car in a layby. 'Come and sit in the back for a while', he said. 'Let's have a bit of peace after all that racket.' They sat and talked. He told her about his plans for when he left college and she told him about herself, her diabetes and her family. He put his arm around her and kissed her gently. She

44

responded eagerly. His tongue started exploring her mouth and a firm hand slid down her black dress. 'You have lovely breasts', he whispered, and caressed her. Sharon's heart was thumping and she felt breathless as he kissed her deeply. He smoothed her bare legs and eased his hand between them. 'It's your first time, isn't it?' he said, and moved his hand further up her legs. Sharon started to feel a little frightened. It was thrilling, but she wasn't ready for all this yet. Everything seemed to be happening so fast. 'Suppose I get pregnant', she said. 'You won't,' replied Jason confidently, 'diabetics don't get pregnant.' Sharon was startled – she had heard rumours in the clinic waiting area, but . . . Suddenly she decided that she really was not ready to go all the way this time. Part of her wanted to, very much, her body was tense with desire, but she was frightened. 'I don't want to,' she whispered, 'not yet. I do like you, honestly, but I want to wait a bit.' Jason took his hand away, gave her another quick kiss and sat up. 'OK,' he said, 'let's go home then.'

Sharon let herself into the house with her feelings in a turmoil. Why had Jason stopped so suddenly? She should have said yes – it had all been so exciting and he was so handsome and all the girls at school had done it and they said it was wonderful. They would think she was a prude. Well she wouldn't tell them. But why couldn't diabetics get pregnant. Poor Julia, did she know? How awful never to have children. Would she see Jason again? She felt rather woozy and wondered if it was the drinks – how many was it? She went to bed and settled into an uneasy sleep. She awoke at 5 am, sweating and shaky and rather unreal. She reached for the glucose tablets on her bedside table and they fell on the floor under the bed. Laboriously she crawled out of bed and picked them up. As she crunched them hungrily the shakiness settled and the world came back to normal. Hypo. But why? She had had a big meal the night before.

After four weeks she finally gave up. Jason was not going to telephone. Every time the phone rang she had rushed to answer. She went to the disco several times with the girls, but never saw Jason there. Life carried on as usual. She had no more hypos. The summer term ended and school finished. She spent part of her holidays with her penfriend Hélène in Paris.

When Sharon returned she visited her sister. Julia's husband was out and the sisters sat drinking tea together. 'I've some wonderful news', said Julia. 'I'm going to have a baby. I did the test myself and it was positive, but the doctor confirmed it this week.' Sharon was pleased, but some of her puzzlement must have been obvious because her sister asked her why she looked so surprised. So Sharon told her about Jason and what he had said. 'Oh Sharon, you must have been miserable', said Julia. 'Of course, diabetics can have children. Michael and I wanted to wait so I used a cap until three months ago. When we first started making love we used a sheath until I went to the family planning clinic. I should have gone to them before we started really. Since we decided to try for a family I've been going to a special clinic at the hospital. I have to keep my glucose between 4 and 8 mmol/l (72–144 mg/dl) all the time. It's been quite hard work. I seem to be forever doing blood tests, but I want my baby to have a proper chance and they said I had to get the glucose normal before I stopped using the cap.'

DIABETIC WOMEN CAN BECOME PREGNANT

Having diabetes does *not* stop you from having a baby. Diabetic women are as fertile as non-diabetic women. So if you do not want to become pregnant you should take precautions.

CONTRACEPTION

There are three main types of contraception – barrier methods, the contraceptive pill and intrauterine contraceptive devices. You need to find the method which suits you and your partner. The best way to do this is to go to a family planning clinic or to your doctor *before* you start having intercourse.

And remember that both partners should think about contraception. It is not just the woman's responsibility – although, of course, it is the woman who ends up carrying the baby!

Barrier methods
The sheath, condom or French letter can be bought in most chemists and should be used in combination with spermicidal (sperm-killing)

Correct way to put on a sheath before intercourse

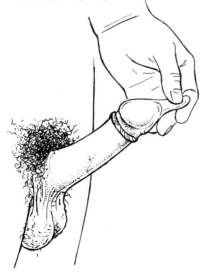
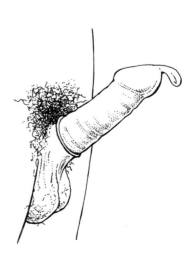

cream, jelly, foam or pessaries. Some condoms are already coated with spermicide. The sheath has to be rolled on to the erect penis. After the ejaculation of sperm, carefully withdraw the penis holding the sheath on firmly. The woman should use the spermicide exactly according to the instructions on the pack.

This method can be used, as Julia and Michael did, if you start having intercourse before seeking family planning advice. It will also help to protect you from AIDS and other diseases passed on by intercourse.

The diaphragm or Dutch cap was the method Julia and her husband chose until they decided to have a baby. The flexible cap is coated with spermicide and slid into the vagina to cover the cervix or neck of the womb before intercourse. It has to be left in place for six hours after intercourse, then it is removed and washed.

Your cap should be the right size for you. Julia's doctor examined her to make sure that her cap would fit perfectly.

The pill
Different contraceptive pills contain variable amounts of the female sex hormone, oestrogen, and another sex hormone called progesterone. These hormones confuse the body so that egg release (ovulation) does not occur, or, if it does, the egg cannot implant itself properly in the womb. All contraceptive pills have some side effects, but if properly used they are the most effective form of birth control. The oestrogen and progesterone can raise the blood glucose, increase blood fats and raise the blood pressure. Diabetes can cause all of these problems, so taking the pill is therefore more risky in someone with diabetes than in a non-diabetic. The pill can also cause blood clots (thromboses). Taking the pill may alter the periods and there can be breakthrough bleeding between periods. The progesterone-only pill may stop periods altogether while you are taking it.

There are no pills for men yet.

Intrauterine contraceptive devices (IUCDs, coils)
These are rarely used in women who have not had children, and the older types of coil did not always seem to work in women with diabetes. There is also a possible risk of infection.

Which method is best?
There is no simple answer to this question. Used carefully, the sheath or the cap are effective contraceptives and have no side effects. However some couples find that they interfere with the spontaneity of love-making, although most become practised at using this method and do not see it as a nuisance. Buy a packet of condoms and some spermicide from a chemist if you do not have time to discuss things. If you cannot be bothered to use barrier methods properly it is probably best to take the pill – and many doctors recommend the progesterone-only pill as the one with fewest side effects.

The important message is that you should think about contraception before starting intercourse. There is no need to be shy. Talk it over with your parents, your doctor or a family planning clinic. If you do go to a separate family planning clinic, tell them that you have diabetes.

THE MORNING AFTER

Suppose you have had unprotected intercourse and are afraid you might become pregnant, but you do not want to have a baby. Go to see your doctor immediately. If he thinks it appropriate he may be able to prescribe a morning-after pill to prevent pregnancy. These contain strong hormones.

Your doctor will then be able to advise you about protecting yourself from pregnancy in the future. Do not repeat your mistake!

THE MONTHS AFTER

Suppose you have missed a period and you are afraid you may be pregnant. Firstly, many women have irregular periods and missed periods do not always mean pregnancy. However, if you have been having intercourse recently it is possible that you are pregnant. If you are pregnant it will eventually become obvious, but you need help now, so do not put things off – go to your doctor immediately. Being pregnant will raise your blood glucose and it is important that you have a medical check. Your doctor will listen sympathetically, will do a pregnancy test and will help you and your partner to decide what to do next.

PLANNING PREGNANCY

If you are a woman with diabetes, like Sharon and Julia, you should plan your family. When you and your partner decide to start a family discuss this with the doctor you see for your diabetes.

You both need to be fit and, as Julia did, you should use contraception until your blood-glucose levels are normal (i.e. 4–8 mmol/l or 72–144 mg/dl). This is because you cannot predict when a baby will be conceived – you only know when it has happened a few weeks after the event. A baby's main body systems develop in the first eight weeks after conception, and if the mother's blood glucose is high during this critical time of development there is an increased risk of the baby being malformed. So, to be certain that your baby has the best possible chance of being completely healthy you must have a normal blood glucose all the time you are trying to conceive. And the blood glucose must continue to be normal throughout pregnancy so that the baby grows properly and you remain healthy.

48

Most hospitals run special clinics for diabetic women who are planning pregnancy or who are pregnant.

Julia had a trouble-free pregnancy. As it progressed she needed more and more insulin (a normal feature of pregnancy in diabetic women) until she was on twice her usual dose of insulin. She had a normal vaginal delivery of a healthy baby boy weighing 8 lb and has called him Harry. Now she is back on her usual dose of insulin but eating more because she is breast-feeding Harry, who is growing rapidly. Harry has a very devoted aunt in Sharon.

WHAT ARE THE RISKS OF YOUR BABY DEVELOPING DIABETES?

Julia and Michael were both worried that their baby might become diabetic. Diabetes does run in families, as Sharon and Julia show. The risk of anyone in the population having insulin-dependent diabetes is 1 in 400, while the risk of the child of a man and woman who both have diabetes becoming diabetic is about 1 in 20. So the risk of Harry developing diabetes is greater than 1 in 400 but not as great as 1 in 20.

ALCOHOL AND DIABETES

Sharon rarely had hypos and was used to dancing for hours, so why did she have a hypo after her evening out with Jason? She was excited and upset but, although in some people this can cause hypoglycaemia, it more often raises the blood glucose. Sharon had had several drinks that evening. She thought they tasted strong and Jason had probably been a little heavy-handed with the gin. Alcohol is a long-term source of calories and should be counted as such in the overall diet. However, alcohol has a more immediate effect on the body. It blocks the release of glucose from the liver's stores. That night Sharon's body needed to replenish her blood-glucose levels after all her dancing but all the gin she had drunk stopped her liver from releasing glucose, so she became hypoglycaemic during the early hours of the morning.

This does not mean that people with diabetes must avoid alcohol, but they should drink in moderation – no more than three small shorts or three half pints of beer or lager a day. Women should drink less than men. Never drink on an empty stomach. And if a drink tastes strong, it probably is!

SUMMARY

- Women with diabetes can become pregnant.

49

- Use effective contraception. Seek advice the morning before, not the morning after!
- If you think you may be pregnant see your doctor immediately, whether the baby is planned or not.
- Plan your pregnancy. The blood glucose must be normal from the first moment of conception until the baby is delivered.
- Alcohol can cause hypoglycaemia.
- Limit your alcohol intake to no more than three small shorts or three half pints of beer or lager a day.

7

ANDREW

Andrew awoke with a start and silenced the alarm clock – 5 am. He got up, threw on some clothes and stumbled downstairs to the yard. He munched a biscuit as he hurried out. Then he trod in a cowpat and swore. The cows' breath steamed in the cold air as Andrew and his father cleaned their udders and attached them to the milking machine. Outside it began to rain. The cows were restless and one of them stood heavily on Andrew's foot. He pushed her off hurriedly. Finally they were all milked and Andrew hobbled back into the farmhouse for a shower. Then he injected his insulin and dressed. He ate a huge breakfast. They had to clear some fallen trees from the lane and he would need plenty of energy.

Andrew was 17. His diabetes had been diagnosed when he was 10 after an attack of 'flu. Andrew soon learned how to manage his insulin injections. The main problem had been the diet. His mother always served big farmhouse meals, with lashings of cream and butter and homemade raspberry jam and cakes. Andrew could get through half a pound of her homemade cheese in a day. His mother was horrified when the dietitian told her that Andrew was eating too much dairy food. 'And what's wrong with that?' she retorted indignantly, 'it's all good wholesome food.' Eventually his mother and the dietitian reached a compromise agreement, much to Andrew's disgust. He had been hoping that his mother would win.

Andrew left school when he was 16 and had been working on his father's farm ever since. While he was at school his job was looking after the chickens and helping with the calves. When he first started working full-time on the farm he had trouble with his diabetes. He had been used to taking his insulin at 7 am when he got up in the morning and having his breakfast about 20 minutes later. When he got home from school at about 5 pm he had his evening injection ready for his main meal. During the first week of farm work he went on taking his insulin as soon as he got up, and then went straight out to the cows. Result? He was hypo every morning! He found that he could manage the morning milking better if he did not take his insulin until afterwards, but he still had hypos during the day and

51

was ravenously hungry every meal time. Gradually he reduced his insulin until he was taking two-thirds of the dose he had been injecting as a schoolboy.

Andrew and his father set out to start work on the trees, but he found his foot had become more painful during breakfast and he could hardly walk. Cows had trodden on his foot before but it had never been as sore as this. A large red and blue bruise was appearing. The swelling increased, so Andrew went to the hospital to have the foot X-rayed. There were no broken bones, it was just badly bruised, but the doctor told him to rest it for a few days. 'Here's a nice quiet job', said his father, and he handed Andrew the year's milk figures to check. Andrew loathed arithmetic. By the second day of enforced rest (and boring arithmetic) Andrew realised that he was feeling very thirsty. He had to keep hobbling to the toilet. His diabetes had not bothered him for some time and he was puzzled. He wondered what his blood glucose was and got the sticks from the cupboard. He had stopped testing because his hands were always so dirty and he was afraid of infection. He was startled to see that his glucose was up to 17 mmol/l (306 mg/dl). He decided to increase his insulin a little. This improved matters, although none of the blood glucose levels he measured while his foot was healing was below 10 mmol/l (180 mg/dl).

Andrew's bruise gradually went down and next week he was able to walk comfortably. He was very relieved to stop the bookwork and go back to the milking. He put his glucose testing strips back in the cupboard. The day of his diabetic clinic appointment arrived. Dr Carberry asked to see his diary. Andrew said he had forgotten it (accidently-on-purpose, he thought guiltily – there was nothing written in it). The doctor checked his feet (which Andrew had washed before he came, at his mother's insistence) and measured his blood pressure. Then he sent him round to the ophthalmologist for an eye check. His visual acuity was excellent, but he had a shock when the doctor looked in his eyes. 'You have some micro-aneurysms,' he said, 'you must look after your diabetes better. Have your eyes checked next time you come.'

Andrew didn't know what microaneurysms were – they sounded rather frightening – but the doctor seemed so busy that he didn't like to ask. He had heard that diabetes could make you go blind.

Over the next few days Andrew thought about what the eye doctor had said. He kept looking across the fields with each eye in turn to prove to himself that he could still see properly. The doctor had said that he must look after his diabetes better. So he got the blood testing strips out of the cupboard again and found his diabetic diary behind the bookcase. He started measuring his blood glucose when he got up in the morning while his hands were still clean and was surprised to see that it was often 11 mmol/l (180 mg/dl). On days when he came into the farmhouse for lunch he checked after he had washed his hands; his blood glucose was usually 4.4–6.7 mmol/l (80–120 mg/dl) and sometimes 2.2 mmol/l (40 mg/dl). Some evenings he checked before supper, when it was usually 4.4–6.7 mmol (80–120 mg/dl), or before bed, when it was often 6.7–9 mmol/l (120–162 mg/dl). These results surprised Andrew – he did not always feel hypoglycaemic when his glucose was 2.2 mmol/l (40 mg/dl) and he had thought that most of his blood-glucose levels would be normal. Why was he so sugary overnight?

To start with Andrew decided to take a bigger snack out with him in the mornings and eat more of it if he was working very hard in the fields. As a result he had no more readings of 2.2 mmol/l (40 mg/dl) before lunch. But what about the evening high glucose levels? Should he eat less for his evening meal? Andrew knew that he was not fat and that he needed plenty to eat because he worked so hard. He was taking Actrapid (fast-acting insulin) with Monotard (slow-acting insulin) in the morning and some Actrapid insulin in the evening. He decided to increase the evening Actrapid insulin. This lowered the before-bed blood-glucose readings but to his disappointment he was still high when he got up. So he increased the evening Actrapid some more – and had a hypoglycaemic attack that evening.

These alterations had taken about six weeks and the bottle of testing strips had run out, so Andrew went to his family doctor to get some more. Andrew had known Dr Bell since he was a small boy. Dr Bell asked him how he was getting on with his diabetes, so Andrew explained what had happened in clinic. 'Am I going to go blind?' he asked, hesitantly. 'Of course not', replied Dr Bell, cheerfully. 'Microaneurysms is just a long-winded word for little red dots. But you were a bit silly about your diabetes, young man. Glad to see you're sorting yourself out.' Andrew explained his difficulty about the night-time glucose levels, and commented that his clinic appointment was not for another two months. 'Sounds as if you should go back sooner', said Dr Bell. 'I'll drop them a note.'

Another appointment came through the post and Andrew returned to the clinic. It was busy as usual, but Dr Carberry spent a lot of time looking at his book and discussing the various options. Eventually they decided to try a small dose of Monotard with the Actrapid before his evening meal. 'Let me know if it doesn't work and we'll try something else', said Dr Carberry. 'You mean write to you?' said Andrew. 'You can if you want,' replied Dr Carberry, 'but why not telephone.' And he gave him the number.

Andrew did as suggested. The morning glucose levels were certainly lower, but he found that he was going hypo while he was milking the cows. So he telephoned the hospital. The switchboard took a long time to answer. Then they said that they would bleep Dr Carberry. He seemed pleased that Andrew had telephoned, but suggested that they meet in clinic to discuss things in more detail. 'I think you need a different insulin', he said. In clinic Dr Carberry changed Andrew's Monotard to a medium-acting insulin. This seemed to resolve Andrew's problems, although it took a few weeks to work out the doses. Next time he went to the hospital the ophthalmologist examined his eyes again. Andrew waited anxiously.

'I can't see any microaneurysms at all', reported the doctor, and Andrew breathed a sigh of relief.

FAT AND DIABETES

In the old days, when insulin was not available, diabetic diets were very low in carbohydrate, in order to try and reduce the blood glucose, and very high in fat and protein, in order to make up the number of calories needed. Even after insulin was discovered it was many years before it was realised that this diet was not good for diabetics (see page 17). Nowadays, everyone, not just people with diabetes, should eat a low-fat diet which contains lots of high-fibre carbohydrate foods (reserving sugary foods for times when you are exercising very hard and need instant energy) and a moderate amount of protein. But why is a high-fat diet bad for you? Fatty foods, like bacon, potato chips and crisps, cream and butter, increase the blood cholesterol. Everyone needs a small amount of cholesterol for body repairs and reserve energy, but one in five people on a Western diet have too much. The excess cholesterol is deposited in layers on the walls of arteries, causing atherosclerosis or furring of the arteries. This process is also related to smoking cigarettes (remember Lynn's grandfather, on page 12). Furred-up arteries (just like furred-up water pipes) eventually clog up, and the tissues they supply, like the heart muscle, die from lack of blood. This is what usually causes heart attacks. Strokes can also be caused by blockage of arteries in the brain, and if the circulation to the legs or feet is blocked gangrene may occur.

To reduce your risk of having atherosclerosis, drink skimmed milk and use polyunsaturated margarine spread thinly on your wholemeal bread. Avoid fried foods. Have fewer chips (baked potato is better) and ration yourself to one or two packs of potato crisps a week rather than several packs a day. Cut all the fat off your meat and choose chicken, turkey or white fish where possible. It is better to grill food than fry it. Eat cottage cheese instead of hard cheese. If you do have hard cheese, some are less fatty than others (e.g. Edam) – ask your dietitian for advice. Avoid cream, and choose low-fat yoghourt instead. Do not eat too many peanuts (choose dry roast rather than the greasy ordinary-roasted peanuts) – most nuts are very fatty. Use low-fat salad creams and dressings.

EARLY-MORNING WORKING

If you are used to getting up at a particular time for school and then start a job which means you have to get up earlier, your diabetes may get in a muddle – just as Andrew's did. Andrew sorted himself out eventually, but it is best to discuss new jobs with your diabetes adviser before you start so as to reduce your risk of hypoglycaemic attacks. Andrew should not have taken his insulin and then started the milking before he had had anything to eat. Of course he became hypoglycaemic! Insulin must always be followed by food.

There are several ways of coping with an early start. One is to have your insulin and a very early breakfast. However if you do this you may need two snacks during the morning to keep going until lunchtime and have to give more long- or medium-acting insulin to last out a long day. Another method is to do as Andrew did and go straight to work, waiting to inject insulin until just before breakfast time. If you do this there has to be a little insulin left over from the evening before to allow your muscles to exercise but not too much insulin or you will become hypoglycaemic.

The sensible thing is to check your blood glucose when you wake up. If it is low, eat something. Be especially careful if you are going out running. You must eat something before this. Do not risk a hypoglycaemic attack running across a road. Always carry glucose with you when you run, and measure your blood glucose when you come back for breakfast to assess what has happened.

CHANGE IN EXERCISE PATTERN

Andrew had enjoyed school sports but had spent much of his time sitting at a desk in class. He was not used to the constant hard work needed on a farm. Because he was now exercising more his insulin requirements fell and he became more sensitive to insulin. But he also needed to eat more to fuel his exercise. When the cow trod on his foot and he had to rest, his food needs fell. However he was probably eating as much as usual and not burning it off with exercise, so he needed to eat a little less and inject more insulin.

There is a constant balance between fuel input (what you eat) and energy output (exercise). To use the fuel you need insulin.
• Too much carbohydrate raises the blood glucose.
  Too little carbohydrate lowers the blood glucose.
• Too much exercise lowers the blood glucose.
  Too little exercise raises the blood glucose.
• Too much insulin lowers the blood glucose.
  Too little insulin raises the blood glucose.
Every diabetic spends his or her life balancing these factors. The important thing to remember is that *you* decide what you want to do and note how much exercise this involves and then eat the right amount to fuel it. The last factor to adjust is the amount of insulin you need to use the food for the day's exercise. People often think that they have to eat and exercise to suit a fixed insulin dose. This is backwards thinking!

BLOOD TESTING IN DIRTY JOBS

Andrew's excuse for not testing his blood was that he was afraid of infection because his hands were always dirty. This was a sensible worry (although I suspect that it was not the only reason for not testing). However, it is extremely rare for anyone to get an infection from a finger prick. All diabetics should make sure that their tetanus immunisation is up to date (ask your family doctor). You should only test your blood glucose on clean hands. This does not mean using antiseptic-impregnated swabs – they will give a false reading if you use them. It means washing the hands thoroughly with soap and warm water and rinsing well. In practice, most people whose hands are reasonably clean do not wash them every time they check their finger-prick glucose, but you must remove obvious dirt. Also clean off any food or sugar – again, this will give a falsely high result.

If you have nowhere to wash your hands try pricking the ear lobe for the blood sample or use urine tests. These will give an indication of a high blood glucose during the time that the urine was being made and was collecting in your bladder. You can find out what sort of urine test results follow particular blood-glucose levels by testing both urine and blood for glucose over a period of several days.

DIABETIC COMPLICATIONS

There are several complications of diabetes. Some, like atherosclerosis, are also found in non-diabetics but are more likely in people who have diabetes. Others occur mainly in diabetes. These changes, which occur after years of diabetes, include damage to small blood vessels and damage to the nerves. This is why you need regular check-ups at a diabetes clinic, even if you think your diabetes is under control.

There are many factors involved in the development of diabetic complications; we do not understand all of them. Large blood-vessel disease or atherosclerosis is more likely if you smoke, if you have a high blood pressure or if you eat too much fat. Small blood-vessel disease and nerve damage is more likely if your blood glucose is above normal for a long time or if you have a high blood pressure. Smoking may also worsen small-vessel disease.

Small blood-vessel damage
Another word for this is microangiopathy (micro = small, angio = blood vessel, pathy = disease). The main parts of the body to be affected are the eyes and the kidneys.

Diabetic eye damage
Andrew had the earliest signs of diabetic eye disease or retinopathy. This affects the blood vessels supplying the back of the eye or retina (this is the part that receives the picture, rather like the film in a camera). A doctor can examine the retina using a magnifying torch

56

called an ophthalmoscope (ophthalmo = to do with the eye, scope = thing for looking with).

In diabetes the retinal vessels may become damaged so that they clog up or, in some instances, leak. They may develop little bulges called microaneurysms which can be seen as tiny red dots when the doctor examines your eye. Later small leaks of blood (haemorrhages) or of fatty fluids (exudates) can be seen. If the damage worsens, areas of the retina may lose their blood supply and release a chemical which encourages the growth of new vessels. However these new vessels, which sound so useful, do not revive the retina but grow forwards into the clear jelly through which we see – the vitreous jelly. They are fragile and can tear, causing a bleed into the jelly – a vibreous haemorrhage – which may cause blindness.

If you develop severe diabetic retinopathy it can be treated by lasers, but it is much better to try to prevent it from starting in the first place. This is why Andrew was told to sort out his diabetes, and one of the main reasons why diabetic doctors make such a fuss about keeping your blood glucose normal.

Diabetic retinopathy

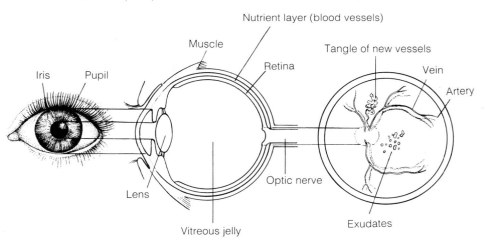

You should have your eyes checked thoroughly every year. This means checking your visual acuity (how well you can see) using charts on the wall or special books with different-sized writing. Then the ophthalmologist (eye specialist) or diabetic doctor will put drops in your eyes to widen the pupil (the black hole in the centre of your eye) so that he can look through it with an ophthalmoscope to see the retina. The effect of these drops soon wears off or can be reversed by other drops.

Cataract

This means deposition of opaque debris in the lens of the eye, causing blurred vision. The lens acts like a camera lens. Cataracts are uncommon in young people but occasionally occur in people whose blood glucose has been very high. Control of the blood glucose may reverse the process; if not the cataracts have to be treated surgically.

DIABETIC KIDNEY DAMAGE

Another name for this is nephropathy (nephros = kidney, pathy = disease). Small blood vessels entering the kidney become damaged and waste substances cannot seep through the vessel walls to form urine. The kidney has a huge reserve capacity but, if the damage continues, wastes will start to accumulate in the body and eventually kidney function will fail altogether. If this happens the person is treated with kidney dialysis or transplant.

Diabetic nephropathy is not common in young diabetics, and once again, you can take steps to prevent it. Keep your blood glucose normal and make sure that your doctor checks your blood pressure regularly. The earliest sign of diabetic kidney damage is protein in the urine. Protein leaks into the urine from damaged blood vessels or kidney tissues. Your doctor can easily test for this using a dipstick similar to the urine-glucose testing system.

Kidney glomerulus where waste products seep through the walls of the blood vessels to form urine

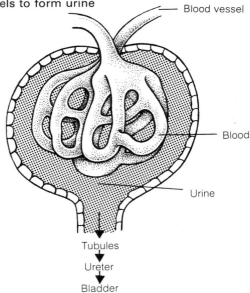

Blood vessel

Blood

Urine

Tubules

Ureter

Bladder

58

Diabetic nerve damage

This is called neuropathy (neuro = to do with nerves, pathy = disease). The nerves are like electric cables carrying signals to and from the brain. The nerves of people with diabetes can be damaged in several ways – abnormal sugars can build up in them, their blood supply can be damaged and they can lose their insulating sheath. All these factors can alter the way in which they conduct signals. This may mean that the wrong signals are conducted – or nothing is conducted at all – rather like a faulty electric cable.

The commonest form of diabetic neuropathy is numbness or tingling of the feet. This is one reason why you should look after your feet very carefully (see pages 28–9). Again, this condition is more likely in people who have had high blood-glucose levels.

DON'T PANIC!

Diabetes can cause damage, but there is a lot you can do to prevent the damage. Do not smoke. Do not eat too much fatty food. Keep your blood glucose normal. Ask your doctor to watch your blood pressure. If you do develop diabetic complications they can be treated, so attend your check-ups – you should expect a thorough eye examination, a urine test for protein (or blood tests for kidney function) and tests of sensation. Andrew had a bad fright, but he did something about it and the early signs of eye damage disappeared.

COMMUNICATION

Andrew was very worried after his check-up. He was too shy to ask the doctors at the hospital what was wrong with his eyes and waited six weeks before asking his family doctor – six weeks of anxiety.

One of the problems of coming to a large hospital diabetic clinic is that it can be rather scary and off-putting. The doctor may be very busy and you may be shy, as Andrew was, about asking him or her questions. But you have to remember that the hospital staff are there to help you. It is their job. You have gone to the trouble of getting to the hospital, and perhaps waited a long time before seeing the doctor, so make sure that you get the most from the consultation.

You and the diabetic clinic staff are part of a team working to keep you healthy. This means that everyone needs to know exactly what is going on. You need to be straight with them and they need to be straight with you. If you do not understand something – ask. The father of one of my patients used to tell his son 'No question is ever stupid if it has to be a question.' Do not be ashamed to admit that you have forgotten something you think you should know. It is especially important to ask about things that are worrying you – make a list before the clinic if necessary. And never leave the clinic confused – keep asking until you understand. Doctors are so used to

Diabetic diary

Diabetic Diary

Date / Time	Urine Glucose				Urine Ketones				Blood Glucose am		pm		MT = Monotard AR = Actrapid Insulin Dose		AR	Remarks: — Hypos., Body Weight, Medications, Exercise, Colds, etc.
									5	12	6	10	MT	AR	AR	
Mon 10									9	2.2	11	6.7	24	10	8	Loading trailer am Hypo lunchtime
Tue 11									11	6.7	4.4	6.7	24	10	8	2 extra biscuits morning snack
Wed 12									11	4.4	6.7	4.4	24	10	8	High morning glucose
Thu 13									11	6.7	4.4	2.2	24	10	12	Increased evening insulin too much Hypo
Fri 14									9	4.4	6.7	4.4	24	10	10	
Sat 15									9	6.7	4.4	6.7	24	10	10	
Sun 16									9	6.7	9	9	24	10	10	Big Sunday lunch Lazy afternoon

Blood Glucose Chart

Date	Mon 10	Tue 11	Wed 12	Thu 13	Fri 14	Sat 15	Sun 16

Time

Blood Glucose mmol/l: > 20, 20, 15, 10, 5

HYPO   HYPO

Comments:

High glucose every morning but can't increase evening insulin too much because that causes bed time hypos

phone clinic on Monday

60

speaking about diabetes that they may not realise that you have not understood. It is harder to understand things when you are nervous.

TROUBLE-SHOOTING

No diabetic ever has normal blood-glucose levels all day, every day. If you have problems with your blood glucose, as Andrew did, it is helpful to have a plan for sorting things out.

- Keep a diary. In this troublesome phase test your blood glucose four times a day for a week, at least. This will allow you to pinpoint the times at which the problem occurs. If you are waking up with very high or very low blood-glucose levels, measure your glucose at night, say at 2 am (use an alarm clock to wake you up). Jot down what you were doing each day and note any missed or unusual meals or snacks.
- When you have pinpointed the troublesome times, look at what you were doing in terms of exercise and what you were eating beforehand. Thus if you have low blood-glucose levels before lunch consider your morning exercise, your breakfast and your mid-morning snack. Is there something you could alter to improve things?
- Look at your insulin dose affecting that time of day. For the before-lunch example it would be the pre-breakfast short-acting insulin. Is it too much or too little for your needs?
- If you cannot solve the problem easily yourself, get help. Also get help if you feel ill at any stage or if your blood-glucose levels are very high or persistently or often hypoglycaemic. If in doubt seek help early.
- Who do you ask for help? Your family doctor or your diabetes adviser? If you do not know who to contact, find out *now*. You need an emergency telephone number day and night for 365 days a year. Some diabetic clinic doctors are happy to discuss things on the telephone, others prefer you to see your family doctor first. Never be afraid to ask for an earlier appointment at the diabetic clinic if you are worried. Do not be put off by appointments clerks or receptionists – they are not doctors and cannot stop you from seeing your doctor.

SUMMARY

- Exercise, food and insulin all alter the blood glucose.
- A change in job or hobbies can change exercise and eating patterns. Your insulin injection pattern may change too. Discuss your new job or hobby with your diabetes adviser.
- Diabetes can cause damage all over the body. This damage can be largely prevented. Do not smoke, reduce your intake of fatty

foods, keep your blood glucose as close to normal for as much of the time as possible, ask your doctor to monitor your blood pressure.

- Diabetic tissue damage can be treated. Attend your check-ups so that early changes can be detected in time to prevent them worsening.
- Make sure that you and your diabetes team understand each other. Never be afraid to ask questions.
- If you have problems with your diabetes, start the trouble-shooting procedure, but ask for help if you feel at all unwell or your blood-glucose levels are very high or very low.
- If in doubt ask for help.

8

SANDRA

Sandra hated revising. She sat in her room gazing at the heap of heavy textbooks in front of her. She could hear the television downstairs. Physics, chemistry and biology. Hundreds of pages to be memorised. She was fed up with it all.

Sandra had wanted to be a biochemist since her first hospital admission with diabetes. She had been fascinated by all the things the doctors could find out from such a small amount of her blood. She had asked so many questions about the tests that the doctor had taken her to see the laboratories. She later discovered that a school-friend's father worked in the biochemistry department and discussions with him had increased her interest. Now she was in her last year at school and the exams loomed ahead. Her future depended on them.

During the previous year she had looked at university prospectuses from all around the country. Then there was the difficult business of applying, but eventually the form was filled in and sent back to the clearing house. Several universities had interviewed her.

The first was in a northern town. She travelled the 200 miles by train, the first time she had been so far by herself. The interview panel sat formally around a vast polished table. 'Why do you want to be a biochemist?' asked the professor, so Sandra explained about the diabetes and going into hospital and how she had been fascinated by the work of the laboratory. The professor explained that science was a very demanding profession. 'Do you think that you will be able to cope with your diabetes and all the hard work and long hours?' he asked. 'Yes', said Sandra, quietly and confidently. 'That was the right answer', smiled a tall man opposite her. 'I have diabetes. I've had to keep a good eye on it and it has been difficult at times, but my diabetes has never stopped me from doing what I wanted to.'

The second university was closer to home. The interview there was less formal, and they asked her a lot about her interests. Then they asked her for her views on the 'potential conflict between the needs of industry and those of pure scientific research, especially in the current financial situation'. She did not quite understand what they

63

wanted so she politely asked them to explain the question in a little more detail. It still seemed rather beyond her but she did her best. When she got home her father told her that there had been articles about this in the newspaper recently. 'They were testing your general knowledge', he said. Both universities offered her a place – providing her exam results were good enough.

Sandra had had few problems with her diabetes over the years. She attended the children's clinic. She used twice-daily short- and medium-acting insulin and sometimes adjusted the doses herself if her blood glucose was too high. It was rarely too low. She tested once every few days at different times, checking the results in a meter. During the weeks of revising she started to feel increasingly thirsty and had to keep interrupting her work to pass urine. She measured her blood glucose and found that it was rarely below 10 mmol/l (180 mg/dl) these days, so she kept increasing her insulin.

The first exam paper was chemistry. She woke up that morning with her heart thumping. She gave her insulin but by breakfast time she felt sick. She managed to force down some wholemeal toast and coffee. Her teachers were well used to her needs and did not mind her taking glucose tablets, glucose sweets and a drink into the exam room. She checked her blood glucose beforehand, sure it would be low. It was 13 mmol/l (234 mg/dl). As usual the paper looked terrible at first glance. However, as she worked through it she realised that she did know most of the answers. Halfway through the exam she had to go to the toilet escorted by a teacher. Bother.

The rest of the exams came and went. She had increased her morning and evening insulin dose and her blood glucose was between 4 and 10 mmol/l (72 and 180 mg/dl). She did not have to leave the exam room again, but she always checked her glucose before each exam, just in case she was low. It was important that her brain was working at its best.

She went to stay with her grandparents after the exams. Her blood-glucose levels steadied and her insulin dose came down to her usual level. She came home two days before the results were to be announced. When the envelope came she rushed upstairs to her room with it and shut the door. She tore it open. She had done it. She had the grades she needed. Sandra cried with relief.

She started at university that autumn. Her father and mother drove north with her and helped her unload her luggage into the bare room in the university hall. She waved them goodbye and started to unpack. She felt very lonely. There was a knock on her door. 'Hello, I'm your new neighbour – have you found the kitchen yet? I'm gasping for a cup of tea!' During the next few weeks Sandra made a lot of new friends. She joined several societies. The course was hectic. Lectures, practicals and tutorials. One morning the first practical session overran and she had to rush across the campus to her tutorial. Her tutor's question seemed to come from a long way away. Kreb's cycle? She struggled to think. The rest of the group were staring at her. Sandra started sweating with embarrassment.

No, not just embarrassment. She got her glucose out of her pocket and ate some. The tutor moved on to her neighbour and soon the whole group were discussing the oxidation of carbohydrates. At the end of the session the tutor quietly asked Sandra if she was all right now. She explained that she had missed her snack. 'Why not carry some biscuits around with you?' he suggested. 'I'm afraid life is going to get more hectic as you go on.' So Sandra bought a bigger briefcase and kept some food and a little carton of fruit juice in it.

This solved the snack problem, but her glucose seemed to be going up and down erratically. She had never had so much difficulty with it. The adjustments that had worked so well at home just did not seem to be right here. One day her glucose would be 10 mmol/l (180 mg/dl), another it would be 2 mmol/l (36 mg/dl). She decided that she needed help. But who could help her? The children's clinic was 200 miles away. Her doctor had given her the name of the local diabetes consultant and had written to him explaining the situation. He had told Sandra to make an appointment for the new clinic, but she had been so busy with her new life at university that she had forgotten. And she had felt shy about going to a different clinic. He had also suggested that she contact the student health service, but she had not got around to that either.

Eventually Sandra plucked up her courage and telephoned the hospital. After a long wait she spoke to the appointments clerk. 'Are you a new patient?' the voice asked. Sandra did not think so – she had had diabetes for years. However, after lengthy discussion it appeared that she was a new patient because she had never seen Dr Smith before. 'In that case, you must have a referral from your doctor', said the voice firmly. 'But I need help now', she pleaded. 'Sorry, Dr Smith is a very busy man you know,' the voice replied, 'go and see your family doctor.' He was 200 miles away too. So Sandra booked an appointment with the student health service.

The student health service building was on the far side of the campus. It looked very new and clinical compared with her friendly family doctor's cluttered surgery in the old corner house. Everything seemed very business-like – she was asked all sorts of questions and the answers were entered on a computer. By the time she saw the doctor she was quite nervous. But she need not have been. Dr Bowden was a kindly young man with large glasses and they were soon chatting about her home town and what she was doing at university. He went through her diabetic diary carefully and agreed with her that something needed to be done. So he telephoned Dr Smith there and then and arranged an appointment for the next morning. Dr Bowden told her exactly how to contact him if she needed help and asked to see her again in a few days. 'We are always here if you need us', smiled the nurse as she showed Sandra out.

Dr Smith's clinic was much bigger than the one she was used to – all the chairs were occupied and people were standing in the corridor. She missed the motherly children's nurse, even if it had been a little embarrassing having to wait with the little children playing with their toys. Today she waited for an hour before her name was called. The doctor said he was not Dr Smith but his registrar – Dr Northcote. He listened to her story. Then he asked her a lot of rapid questions – previous history, family history, insulin dose, testing routine, driving, smoking, what she ate, what medicines she was taking. He finished the questions, looked at her diary with her and then checked her injection sites, her feet, her blood pressure and her eyes. When he had finished he said, 'Now, what do you think we should do about your diabetes?' Sandra had never been asked this before. At home, when she had a problem, the doctor told her what changes to make and she did what he said. 'I don't know', she said miserably.

'Look,' Dr Northcote said, 'a lot of people get into a bit of a muddle with their diabetes when they go to college or university. You and I can work out how to sort things out but you have not really been measuring your blood glucose often enough to find out what is going wrong.' And then together they worked out how to reduce the risk of hypoglycaemia while she was sorting things out.

She went to the tea shop on the way out. As she sipped her tea a young man came over. She recognised him, he lived on the top floor of her hall at university. He asked if he might join her. 'I saw you in the queue at the clinic', he said. 'I've been going there for two years.' 'You mean you have diabetes too?' asked Sandra. 'Oh yes,' he replied, 'I know four other people at university with it', and they began to compare notes. Neil had been to a children's clinic like Sandra's at first – not just for diabetics but all mixed in with asthmatics and children with coeliac disease. When his family moved house he went to a hospital that had a special children's diabetic clinic. There he had helped with a study of a new sort of insulin pen; 'it was quite fun being a guinea-pig', he said. At the end of the study they had offered everyone their pen to keep and he was still using his. He showed it to her.

By the time of his next house move he was 15, and he went to an ordinary diabetic clinic rather like Dr Smith's. 'Are diabetic clinics always as busy as today's?' asked Sandra. 'Oh, yes!' he replied, 'and some are even more hectic than Dr Smith's.' When Neil moved again his new doctor referred him to a young adult diabetic clinic. 'Everyone was about my age and I didn't have to sit with the little kids like at the children's clinics, nor among the old ladies like today.' Sandra was curious. She had never heard of such a clinic. 'They asked us what we wanted', continued Neil. 'We had a separate waiting room and the nurse used to bring a stereo cassette player and we all brought tapes. They used to treat us as if our point of view mattered. And they let us talk about anything we wanted – like sex and girlfriends and getting drunk and things. They kept on about getting the blood glucose normal but at least they made sure we understood why.'

Sandra measured her blood glucose four times a day for a while.

66

Her friends were curious about the blood testing at first, but after a while they just took it for granted. She met Neil again and he asked her out to a dinner. He told her all about his geology course and his field trips abroad. They had a wonderful evening and soon they were going out regularly.

When she took her blood-glucose results back to Dr Northcote they went through them carefully together and realised that there was a pattern to them. It was always higher on Wednesdays because she had lectures in the morning and afternoon and spent all day sitting down. It was lower on Thursday lunchtime because the practical tended to run late so lunch was late too. And so on, through the week. Between them they worked out a pattern of snacks and slight insulin changes. After a little trial and error Sandra managed to sort things out.

She was sad when term ended and it was time to go home. She was really enjoying university life.

QUALIFICATIONS

People with diabetes do as well as, or better than, non-diabetics at school. In an analysis of the achievements of people with diabetes attending one young adult diabetic clinic 73 per cent had passed one or more exams, compared to 66 per cent of the non-diabetic population in the same age range.

You must get as many qualifications as you can at school – jobs are scarce nowadays and the more qualifications you have, the more jobs will be open to you. Start thinking about your career early, well before your GCSE exams. What you decide may affect how you spend the rest of your life. There are some subjects on every school curriculum that everyone has to do, but where there is a choice, think carefully. It is easier to work at subjects you enjoy, but they may not always be the ones you need for a particular career. However to do nothing but subjects that lead to a career may mean that your life is not as rich and varied as it could be. One of my patients suggested that all diabetics should do human biology at school, and I am inclined to agree with him – if you get to know your body better it will be easier to look after yourself.

REVISING

Very few people actually enjoy revising. Trying to cram more and more facts into an already-crowded brain can be really tedious. But it is extremely rare to do well in an exam without some prior revision, however brilliant you are. There are all sorts of ways of making revision more interesting. Buy some coloured pens, cheerful note-books, rainbow erasers. Give yourself little rewards – 'If I finish this chapter I can have some coffee', 'If I get this right I can go for a short walk', but not 'If I get this right I can have a chocolate!' Some people find that music helps.

Whatever tactics you employ to improve your revision, the essentials are plenty of time, a quiet, reasonably warm room and no interruptions. Then just sit down and get on with it.

STRESSES AND STRAINS

Everyone worries about exams and assessments. You have to learn how to handle the stress. Certainly if you want to go on to university or college, you must be able to do exams. If you are not worried about your assessments you will not get down to your revision in time, and a little adrenaline on the day sharpens your wits. But if you find yourself so overcome with terror and worry that you cannot revise or even go into the exam room, you must sort yourself out right now. Very few people are in this situation, but if you do get really worked up about exams, discuss it with your teachers, parents and, if necessary, your doctor or student health service.

Stress has an unpredictable effect on diabetes. Logically it ought to put the blood glucose up, because that is what adrenaline does. This is what happened to Sandra. However, there are a few people in whom stress has the opposite effect – one teenager I knew used to become suddenly hypoglycaemic every time he got excited. Check your blood glucose more often when you are worried or frightened so that you know what is going on.

THE EXAM ITSELF

On the day of the assessment, eat a proper breakfast (or lunch if it is an afternoon exam), even if you have to force it down. No-one thinks well on an empty stomach. If your glucose has risen during the revision period you will already have either reduced your meals or increased your insulin. Check your blood glucose before breakfast and before lunch. Aim to enter the exam room with a blood glucose of between 6 and 10 mmol/l (108–180 mg/dl). Measure your blood glucose (not in the hand you write with) just before the assessment to make certain you are not hypoglycaemic. Take a can or carton of drink, some glucose tablets or candy, some biscuits, your diabetic card and, if it is a long exam, your blood-testing kit into the exam with you. Make sure that you have told the examination authority that you have diabetes and that you have obtained clearance from them to bring these things in with you. This needs to be done well in advance with external examination bodies; with exams at school it can be done nearer the time.

It is very unusual for anyone's diabetes to cause problems during an assessment. I have, however, met a few diabetic teenagers who have (either consciously or subconsciously) tried to avoid doing

68

exams by letting their diabetes get into such a muddle that they have had to come into hospital. The only person this sort of behaviour harms is themselves. In every case we sorted out the diabetes and arranged for them to do the exam anyway. Do not use your diabetes as a smokescreen for your worries about something else in your life. Recognise your worries and discuss them with your parents, friends, teachers, tutors or your doctor.

GOING TO COLLEGE OR UNIVERSITY

When you leave school your lifestyle will change. If you go to a university or college away from home you may move into student accommodation or into digs or a flat on your own. You may have to cater for yourself or eat in canteens or cafeterias which do not understand the needs of someone with diabetes. You will have to organise your academic work with less formal structuring of your day. It may be your first time away from home and everyone gets a little homesick at first. That is why it is often helpful to go away on holidays or courses away from your family before you leave school so that you start to become used to doing things on your own.

Diabetes should not stop you from succeeding in any college or univeristy course. In *Diabetes: A Beyond Basics Guide* I told the sad story of Anna who gave up her university place because she was afraid she could not cope with her diabetes at university. She would have managed well if only she had had the self-confidence to have a go. However, as Sandra found, the change in lifestyle can occasion-ally upset your diabetes to start with. That is why you need to keep an eye on your diabetes with blood-glucose testing. You also need a new doctor if you are studying away from home, and a link with the local diabetic clinic. As soon as your place at college or university is confirmed, find out if they have a student health service. If they do, ask your doctor at home to write a letter to the health service, introducing you and your diabetes and any other medical problems. If there is no student health service ask your doctor to contact a temporary doctor near your new home. Tell your diabetic clinic that you will be moving and ask them to write to the diabetic clinic in your new town requesting an appointment during your first term. Then you can get to know the new clinic staff and the system before you need them in an emergency.

CLINIC CARE FOR PEOPLE WITH DIABETES

Hospital clinics
As Neil and Sandra discovered, there are many ways of providing hospital-based care for people with diabetes. Diabetes is quite uncommon in little children, so it is unusual to have a separate children's diabetic clinic. More often children are seen by a general paediatrician (children's doctor) who may or may not have a special

69

interest in diabetes. But no-one is a child forever. Some people are ready to move on sooner than others, and the time you change clinics must be right for you. Discuss this with your doctor.

Diabetes is a medical disorder rather than a surgical one, so adults with diabetes are looked after by general physicians. They are always called Dr. (Surgeons are called Mr.) General physicians usually have a special interest, like heart disease or chest disease or diabetes. In small towns people with diabetes may be seen by a general physician who has not specialised in diabetes, because small hospitals cannot afford to have a doctor in every specialty. However, most large towns or cities should have a physician with a special interest in diabetes. Such diabetes specialists are called diabetologists. The sorts of clinics run by diabetologists vary. Some have one clinic for everyone; some have separate clinics for new and follow-up patients; some have a clinic for people with a lot of problems and another for routine check-ups. Some run separate clinics for pregnant diabetics or pre-pregnant diabetics (usually jointly with an obstetrician – a doctor who looks after pregnant women), or for diabetics with foot problems or only for diabetics who are taking insulin, with another clinic for non-insulin treated patients. And some run clinics for teenage and young adult patients.

Young adult diabetic clinics may be run jointly with a paediatrician. They act as a link between children's clinics and adult clinics and as a referral centre for teenagers with newly-diagnosed diabetes. They are usually run by doctors who are used to getting on with teenagers and young people and who are well aware of the sorts of problems that they have. You will not be treated like a child but it will not be automatically assumed that you are fully ready to take on all the responsibilities of being grown up either – unless of course you are.

Hospital doctors
Most of the doctors you see in hospital clinics also work on the wards. The consultant will have junior doctors working on his team, called senior registrars, registrars, senior house officers and house officers. They are often extremely busy and may have been up all night looking after ill patients. But that will not stop them from giving you the time and sympathy you need in clinic.

In a large clinic there may be a lot of doctors – one clinic rota I used to organise needed seven doctors per clinic out of a pool of nearly 20 doctors who were available on different days. Some clinics see 120 patients a week. This may mean that it is difficult to ensure that a patient sees the same doctor every time. However, if you want to see a particular doctor, learn his or her name and ask to be put on his or her list every time. Ask to see that doctor when you arrive in clinic. Find out who the appointments clerk, clinic nurse and consultant's secretary are – it is helpful to know people's names. Learn how your diabetic clinic works – it can make life easier.

70

Diabetic centres
A diabetic centre is a building or group of rooms, usually in or near a hospital, and used specifically for people with diabetes. The centre's main aim is diabetes education, but often you will also see the doctor, nurse, dietitian or chiropodist there instead of in the hospital clinic. Such centres are often open all week to help any diabetic who is in difficulties, either in person or on the phone. There will be evening meetings and the building is often used by the local diabetes association.

General practitioners
More and more family doctors are running diabetic mini-clinics or seeing their own diabetic patients. They will often work in hospital diabetic clinics as well and will have had training in diabetes care. This means that you should not necessarily expect to be referred to a hospital clinic for your diabetes supervision. It can be very helpful seeing the same doctor for all your problems – he or she knows all about you and you do not have to keep explaining what has happened before.

COMMUNICATIONS BETWEEN HOSPITAL AND GENERAL PRACTICE

It is extremely important that all the doctors who look after you know what is going on. The hospital will write to your family doctor every time they see you. If your diabetic clinic doctor asks you to see your family doctor, please do so, and make sure you know why. If a doctor gives you a note for another doctor, please pass it on as requested – it is to help you. It is always useful to take your insulin (or diabetic card) and any other pills or medicines you are taking with you every time you see any doctor so that they know exactly what you are taking and do not prescribe something that may not agree with your existing treatment.

SUMMARY

- People with diabetes do as well as, or better than, non-diabetics at school.
- Consider your career options early. Once you have decided, obtain the best qualifications you possibly can.
- Learn to cope with the stresses of doing exams and assessments so that you can take them in your stride. Keep a close eye on your blood glucose at such times. It will usually go up, but falls in a few people.
- Tell the examiners you have diabetes well in advance.
- Measure your blood glucose immediately before the exam. Take glucose, food and drink into the exam with you.

- If your teachers advise you to opt for a college or university course, consider it carefully. Your diabetes will not stand in your way.
- When you move, organise a new doctor and diabetic clinic in your new town before you go.
- Keep a close eye on your diabetes for the first few weeks at college or university. Your new lifestyle may need different amounts of food at different times, and a different insulin pattern.
- There are many types of diabetic clinic. Ask if there is a young adult clinic near you. Whatever clinic you go to, ensure that you learn who is who and how the system works.

9

KEVIN

Kevin was on his way to Rome. He had never been abroad before and was travelling with his friend Adam Miller and Adam's parents.

When Kevin rushed home with news of the invitation, his mother had said no at first. 'How will you manage your diabetes?' she said. 'It'll all be foreign food and the hotel won't cook you special meals like I do and you won't have the right portions and I know you won't do your tests properly without me to keep an eye on you and supposing you have a hypo?' She went on and on. Kevin's mother always worried about him. It was only recently that she had allowed him to inject his insulin on his own. Kevin's parents had become divorced seven years ago. Kevin, like Adam, was an only child. He was getting really fed up with all the nagging. After all, he was 14 now and he had had diabetes for six years.

Kevin's mother had cried when the doctor told her he had diabetes. The nurse took him outside to play but he heard his mother's voice rising hysterically and the doctor talking soothingly. He started his insulin treatment at home and the diabetes nurse came twice a day for the first week. The dietitian visited too and his mother followed every recipe exactly. She looked very tired those first few weeks and kept asking him if he was all right. He felt fine within three days of starting the insulin. She never let him go on school trips 'in case anything happens to your diabetes'. They had their holidays at a hotel by the sea that catered for diabetics.

Kevin longed to go to Rome. He told Adam's parents what his mother had said and they went to see her. Mrs Miller had been a nurse before Adam was born and she persuaded Kevin's mother to ask the diabetic clinic staff about the holiday. In the clinic the doctor asked Kevin how he was getting on. 'He's doing very well, doctor', answered Kevin's mother, who always came in with him. 'Can I see your glucose diary?' asked the doctor. 'Here it is', replied his mother, reaching across Kevin to put it on the desk. 'He's going a little low in the evenings, what do you think I should do about that?' The doctor looked at Kevin 'What do you think about it, Kevin?' he asked. 'I'd like to eat a bit more in the evening', Kevin replied. 'Oh no, dear,'

73

his mother interrupted, 'you already have exactly what's on your diet sheet.' But the doctor agreed with Kevin. 'Teenagers need plenty of food to help them grow,' he said, 'and you must be prepared to increase his diet if necessary. Kevin certainly isn't overweight at present.' The consultation continued. Kevin's mother did all the talking as always. Kevin felt rather left out.

Finally he could bear it no longer. 'I want to ask something', he said breathlessly. And he asked about the holiday. The doctor thought it was a wonderful idea and they spent the rest of the time discussing how to manage the travelling and cope with different sorts of foods and variable meals. Kevin and his doctor finally persuaded Kevin's mother that the holiday would be possible. Afterwards they had a chat with the diabetic nurse and the dietitian who gave them some helpful advice. Kevin rushed home to tell Adam that he could come after all.

Adam's father had driven to the airport. They checked their suitcases in and went up to the departure lounge. Kevin had his passport and ticket all ready. They each had to put their hand luggage through the X-ray scanner. The security man made Kevin open his briefcase. Kevin was carrying all his diabetic kit with him on the plane so that it did not get lost. The man asked him about the syringes and Kevin showed him his diabetic card which he had kept with his passport. Mrs Miller was carrying his spare insulin and syringes in her makeup bag and the man made her open that too. She explained, and he was quite satisfied. The plane took off on time. Kevin and Adam were thoroughly enjoying the flight. Soon the stewardess brought meals round for them, all neatly set out in small dishes. Kevin looked at it. He knew he should not eat the little sweets, and the pudding looked very sugary, but he was very hungry and he thought his glucose was getting low. He was still looking dubiously at his tray when the stewardess came back. 'Is everything all right, sir?' she asked. Kevin blushed. 'I'm diabetic,' he said quietly, 'and I'm not sure whether I can eat this.' 'You should have told us,' she said, 'but don't worry, one of our passengers requested a diabetic meal but had to take a later flight. I've still got it in the galley.' And she quickly changed his tray. Kevin ate it all.

Soon they had flown over the Alps and the shining sea and landed in Italy. Kevin stayed close to the Millers as they reclaimed their baggage and started walking out. Then a moustachioed officer stopped them. He seemed to want to look at their luggage. Kevin couldn't understand a word he said. They all undid their suitcases and the officer went through each one. In Kevin's he found some syringes (Kevin's mother had insisted he took plenty of spares). He took them out and waved them around and all the other officers came to look. They were doing a lot of talking. 'It's all right,' he said, 'I'm diabetic', and he showed them his card. But they did not understand. They seemed to be getting very excited. Then another man with gold braid all over his uniform appeared. 'Ah, diabetico', he said. 'Mio bambino e diabetico.' And he silenced the other officers. He gave Kevin a piece of paper with an explanation written in Italian in case he needed it another time and sent them on their way. Kevin was very relieved to be sitting safely in the taxi *en route* to the hotel.

Kevin and Adam's hotel window looked over the roofs to the dome of St Peter's. As soon as they had unpacked the four set out to explore. Kevin and Adam had studied Roman history at school last year and were looking forward to seeing the real thing. They soon found themselves in the Forum. It was larger and more ruined than Kevin had expected. Kevin started to feel hungry, but he had a chocolate bar in his pocket and ate that. Eventually it was time for the evening meal. They stopped at a cafe. Kevin knew that pasta was spaghetti so he ordered that. A huge plateful arrived. He ate the lot. There were some delicious looking peaches for afterwards, and Mrs Miller told him to peel his ('they don't always wash fruit in foreign countries', she whispered).

The next day they had decided to visit St Peter's. They walked there through the market and across the River Tiber. The square in front of St Peter's was vast. He saw a Swiss guard in his medieval costume. (Wouldn't catch *me* wearing striped bloomers and tights, he thought.) They wanted to see everything. The basilica was magnificent. Kevin had saved a breakfast apple for his snack but by midday he was tired and hot and ravenously hungry. They started to look for somewhere to eat but there did not seem to be any cafes nearby. Keven knew he was going hypo. Everything started to go wobbly and he began to sweat. Then he saw an ice-cream van. Mrs Miller brought him and Adam an ice-cream each. It was delicious and soon Kevin was himself again.

They walked a little further and found a grocer's shop. Mrs Miller bought a picnic and some extra packets of biscuits and canned drinks for Kevin. 'I think we need some emergency rations', she said. Kevin was rather worried about the different food. 'Don't be silly,' said Mrs Miller, 'you need more energy while you're sightseeing.' He enjoyed the bread with cheese and salami, and the little cakes, washed down with fruit juice.

Next day they walked to the Colosseum. It looked just like the pictures. Kevin and Adam had great fun running up and down the different levels and looking out of the top windows across the city. The underground chambers were eerie. They saw themselves as gladiators and had a battle. However, by lunchtime Kevin was hungry and low again, despite the biscuits he had had for a snack. Quickly they found a cafe and ordered a meal. They could see the food being cooked in the kitchen but it seemed to take forever to arrive. Eventually Kevin had to eat some of his emergency glucose to stop a bad hypoglycaemic attack. Afterwards Mr Miller wanted to look at some nearby churches.

Kevin wondered if he should alter his insulin. He had never done it on his own and even his mother telephoned the diabetes nurse before adjusting it. He remembered that the doctor had said he might need less insulin and decided to reduce next morning's dose.

Kevin reduced both his short- and his medium-acting morning insulin and had no more hypoglycaemic attacks. He was rather pleased with himself. He experimented with some of the exciting-looking dishes in cafes. He had a weakness for the wonderful ice-creams. They found an ice-cream shop by the Trevi fountain not far from the hotel and he had mango-flavoured and even prickly pear ice-cream. But he checked his blood glucose after one ice-cream session and found it was 17 mmol/l (306 mg/dl), so he reluctantly reduced his ice-cream intake to just one a day instead of pudding.

Then one night he woke up feeling awful. He was very sick and had diarrhoea. Mrs Miller was worried about his blood glucose, but they measured it and it was 10 mmol/l (180mg/dl). He spent the rest of the night feeling very miserable and kept vomiting. Mrs Miller opened a can of Coca Cola and he sipped that. By morning he felt weak but better. His glucose was 6 mmol/l (108 mg/dl). He had his insulin, followed by some dry toast and another can of Coca Cola. They spent a gentle morning looking at the Pantheon. By afternoon he felt all right again.

The holiday rushed past. They visited all the famous buildings and even took a train trip out to Ostia Antica to lie in the sun on the beach. All too soon it was time to come home. Guiltily Kevin realised that he had forgotten to send his mother a postcard. He bought one and posted it hurriedly. They arrived at the airport a little early, booked in and then settled themselves with books in the departure lounge. It was an evening flight. The time passed and it became obvious that the flight was going to be delayed. They waited another two hours. Mr Miller went to the information desk. Apparently there was a fault in the engine and they were waiting for a replacement part to arrive from Milan. Kevin had been relying on the meal on the plane, but he had some biscuits and ate them and drank a can of fruit juice. Four hours after the scheduled departure time there was an announcement. Due to a power cut there would be further delays. Mr Miller looked around the airport for a restaurant. They were all closed but he managed to buy some chocolate. Kevin was getting very hungry. He had eaten all his biscuits. He started on the chocolate. Soon that had all gone too. He was just finishing the last of his emergency glucose when their flight was called, seven hours after they were due to take off. As soon as they arrived home safely, Mr Miller telephoned Kevin's mother to explain about the delay.

Kevin's mother burst into tears when he arrived home. 'Are you all right? I was so worried, I thought the plane had crashed, I kept listening to the radio. Why didn't you send me a card? Did you manage your diabetes? What about all that foreign food? You've caught the sun. You haven't got sunburned have you? You know your skin is very sensitive.' Finally Kevin managed to get a word in. 'I had a fabulous holiday, mum', he said.

OVER-PROTECTIVE PARENTS

Parents are always very shocked when their child is diagnosed diabetic. Every mother and father wants their children to be perfectly healthy for ever. They find it hard to adjust to the fact that their little boy or little girl has a life-long condition which will always need treatment. And they want to make sure that they look after the diabetes as well as possible. Parents are very reassured when their child bounces back to health, but they still have nagging anxieties. Most parents hide much of their anxiety from their children. Obviously when children are small their parents have to manage their diabetes, but as they grow towards their teens most children should gradually be taking over their diabetes management themselves. Every fledgling has to leave the nest sometime. And the only way to become confident in managing diabetes is to do it yourself. Start with small changes in food and insulin and check with your parents or diabetes nurse that you have got it right. Gradually you will have the confidence and the knowledge to adjust your treatment yourself.

Kevin's mother was on her own and Kevin was all she had. She had been very hurt when her husband had left her to live with another woman. She felt very lonely, and concentrated all her energies on Kevin. She was so used to doing things for him that she forgot that he was developing his own point of view. She had become over-protective and found it hard to realise that he was growing up. It had taken a lot of courage on her part to let him go abroad.

After his holiday in Rome, Kevin decided that he wanted to see the clinic doctor on his own in future. His mother was very upset, so the doctor said his mother could join them after Kevin had discussed things. Kevin gradually started doing more things on his own after school and, following his successful Rome trip, his mother allowed him to join school excursions. Kevin joined a youth club run by the man who owned the do-it-yourself shop. He became interested in carpentry and had soon made a set of book shelves and a coffee table. Eventually Kevin took over many of the repairs in the house. Both Kevin and his mother began to understand each other better.

It can be hard for parents to find the middle road, especially when you become a teenager and start developing independence. If they remind you about your blood test or carrying glucose or coming home in time for a meal you accuse them of fussing. If they say nothing you accuse them of not caring. Be patient with your parents!

TRAVELLING WITH DIABETES

People with diabetes can do as much travelling as they want (or as they can afford). If you take a few simple precautions your diabetes should not cause problems or get in your way. Many of these precautions apply to any trip, whether at home or abroad.

PLAN AHEAD

Where and when
Make sure you know where you are going, when and for how long. This means getting a written plan from the school or the group leaders if you are going on a group trip. A map is helpful. Gain a general idea of what sort of holiday it is going to be and how active it will be.

Phrase book
Try to learn something about the foreign countries you will be visiting and get a phrase book which includes lists of foods. Go through the food list and mark those which will definitely be suitable for a diabetic diet, those which are moderately suitable, and those for special occasions (your dietitian can help you with this). Learn a few key phrases, including 'Please can I have some sugar', 'Where is the nearest restaurant/food shop?', 'Where is the men's/women's toilet?', 'I have diabetes' or 'I am diabetic' and 'I am ill, please call a doctor'.

The following are some translations of 'I am a diabetic on insulin. If I am found ill, please give me two teaspoons of sugar in a small amount of water or three of the glucose tablets which I am carrying. If I fail to recover in 10 minutes, please call an ambulance.' And make sure you *are* carrying glucose tablets.

- **France** Je suis un(e) diabétique sur insuline. Si on me trouve malade, donnez-moi s'il vous plait, deux cuillères à thé de sucre dans un peu d'eau ou trois des comprimés de glucose que j'ai sur moi. Si au bout de dix minutes je ne reviens pas à moi, appelez une ambulance.

- **Germany** Ich bin Diabetiker und brauche täglich Insulin. Finden Sie mich krank, geben Sie mir bitte zwei Esslöffel Zucker in Wasser aufgelöst. Der Zucker befindet sich in meiner Tasche oder Handtasche. Finden Sie mich ohmachtig, rufen Sie bitte einen Artz oder einen Krankenwagen.
- **Italy** Sono un diabetico e sono attualmente sottoposto a trattamento con insulina. Se fossi colto da malore, per favore datemi due cucchiai di zucchero in una piccola quantità di acqua o tre delle pastiglie di glucosio che porto con me. Se non mi reprendo entro dieci minuti, per favore chiamate un ámbulanza.
- **Norway** Jeg har sukkersyke og bruker daglig insulin. Hvis jeg blir funnet syk, vennligst gi meg to spiseskjeer sukker rørti vann. Det er sukker i min lomme eller min veske. Hvis jeg er bevisstløs eller ikke våkner, vennlist tilkall lege eller sykebill.
- **Portugal** Sou um doente Diabético usando diairamente insulina. Se me encontrar doente deem-me faz favor duas colheres de sopa de açúcr em agua. Encontrarao açúcar no men bolso ou saco. Se me encontrar inconsciente sem recuperar, faz favor de chamar um medico ou uma ambulancia.
- **Spain** Soy diabético(a) y tomo insulina. Si usted me encuentra enfermo(a) tenga la bondad de darme dos cucharillas de azúcar en un poquito de agua o tres de los comprimidos de glucosa que llevo encima. Si no me recupero dentro de diez minutos, tenga la bondad de llamar un ambulancia.
- **Sweden** Jag är diabetiker med dagliga insulininjektioner. Om Ni finner mig omtöcknad, var snäll och ge mig två teskedar med socker, gärna upplost i vatten. Det skall finnas socker i min ficka eller väska. Om jar är medvetslos eller ej svarar på tilltal kallapå en doktor eller ambulans.
- **Yugoslavia** Ja sam dijabeticar i dnevno uzimam insulin. Ako me nadjete bolesnog, molim vad dajte mi 2 supene kasike secera rastopljenog u vodi. Secer se nalazi u mom dzepu ili torbi. Ako sam i nesvijesti i ne osvijestim ne, molim vas zovite doktora ili prvu pomoc.

Money
Get some foreign currency from a bank, including small change, so that you can buy food or pay for transport if necessary.

Insurance
Make sure that you have full medical insurance that will not only cover the cost of treatment in a foreign country, but also pay to fly you home if necessary. Also insure against cancellation or delays because of illness as soon as you have booked your holiday.

Foreign health hazards
Ask your family doctor if you need any special inoculations or malarial preventives. If you are going to some exotic countries you may need to know about poisonous animals or plants so that you can avoid them or deal with their consequences.

Luggage

Find out about the climate of the place you are visiting and take sufficient clothing to keep you warm and dry if appropriate. Several thin layers give you more choice of outfits and can be worn on top of each other if you get cold. Take sunscreen cream or lotion if you are going to a hot country.

Your shoes are very important – they must be completely comfortable and not rub anywhere, especially when your feet are hot, swollen and sweaty. Do not burden yourself with more clothes than you need. Vanity is all very well but you don't want to exhaust yourself teetering around in high heels with an enormous suitcase.

Take a day case/handbag/rucksack/bum bag in which to carry personal items and spare food while exploring. Something with a shoulder or waist strap is usually more convenient – it leaves your hands free. Keep this with you all the time and carry your medical survival kit in it. Luggage you entrust to someone else (e.g. an airline or porter) could get lost.

MEDICAL SUPPLIES

Take at least two bottles of each sort of insulin and at least twice the number of disposable syringes and needles that you would expect to need. Include your needle clipper and take some antiseptic swabs. Do not forget your blood- and urine-glucose testing kit and plenty of paper tissues. Include an up-to-date diabetic card and some emergency glucose. If you travel frequently a ready-to-go diabetes travel pack or survival kit containing all these items is useful (see *Diabetes: A Beyond Basics Guide* by the same author in the same series). Try to cut down on weight – a heavy meter or box may not be necessary.

As Kevin found, a card explaining about diabetes in the language of the country which you are visiting is very helpful. Telephone your diabetic association or the tourist information office or consulate for a translation if necessary.

RATIONS

Other towns or countries may have different early-closing days and holy days from your home town, and cafe and restaurant opening hours vary widely. For example, Mediterranean countries have an afternoon siesta; shops and other establishments may not be open on Friday afternoon or Saturday in a Jewish community, or on Thursday afternoon or Friday in a Islamic community. It may be difficult to find food or snacks in an unfamiliar place. Variable exercise, foods and meal times may increase your risk of becoming hypoglycaemic, as Kevin found.

Kevin did not take nearly enough spare food with him. Take nonperishable food that is easy to carry and will not spread itself about on your clothes or make them smell. I carry individually-wrapped high-fibre bars or biscuits with me when I go abroad, with some small cartons of fruit juice. (Check that the country you are visiting does not forbid certain food imports.) I also carry apples in a polythene bag in my briefcase to eat on the journey. Mini-chocolate or candy bars are good in a cool country but melt in a hot one, where boiled sweets or candy may fare better. Take enough food for several days' snacks. Do not forget your glucose tablets, Hypostop or Glutose gel.

THE JOURNEY

If your journey can be delayed, it will be. This may be an unduly pessimistic view, but if you travel prepared for delays and missed meals you will be always be able to survive the journey and arrive ready for fun, not exhausted and starving. Carry a book or lightweight game to prevent boredom. More important, carry enough food and drink to feed you for twice as long as you expect to be travelling. This is in addition to your rations for snacks during your first few days' holiday. If travelling by air, ask the airline to book diabetic meals for you when you buy your ticket.

If you find a restaurant *en route*, eat something – it is better to travel with a slightly higher glucose than normal in case of delays or unexpected exercise (for example carrying your suitcase for miles because there is no bus). It is also worth using toilets whether you think you need to or not – they may be hard to find later.

More detailed suggestions for insulin adjustment are available in *Diabetes: A Beyond Basics Guide* by Rowan Hillson, in the same series. In general, reduce your insulin dose by about 10 per cent of your usual total daily dose – say 6 per cent off the morning dose and 4 per cent off the evening dose – on the day you leave home. (If you are travelling by night reduce the evening dose by 10 per cent.) Keep measuring your blood glucose – it is not always easy to tell if you are just tired, hot, sweaty and hungry or in fact hypoglycaemic. Keep to a reduced insulin dose while away unless your blood-glucose measurements suggest that you need more insulin. If you are driving and are not used to covering long distances, have a moderate meal before you set off and stop every hour for a stretch and walk around. Eat something every two hours or, if necessary, every hour, and check your blood glucose often. Write down blood-glucose results – the information will help you to plan your next journey (see page 60).

FUNNY FOREIGN FOOD

Do not be afraid to experiment with unfamiliar dishes. Do not worry too much if you cannot work out the carbohydrate content – eat well to avoid hypoglycaemia. You can always measure your blood glucose to see how it has been affected by an unfamiliar food and have a little more insulin if necessary. If, like Kevin and his ice-creams, you have overdone it, have less of that food next time or avoid it and try something else. Every country has a staple food which is mainly starchy carbohydrate, for example bread, maize (corn), nan, pitta, pasta, rice, potato, beans, chapatti. Use this for your basic carbohydrate needs.

People are sometimes afraid to try strange foods in case they upset their stomachs. While some foods can cause indigestion in some people, and different foods or drinks can alter your bowel habit, it is rarely the food itself which upsets you, but usually its cleanliness. Never drink local water unless you know it is clean – just because it comes out of a tap do not assume it is safe to drink. Take water purifying tablets with you. Most cafes serves bottled mineral water or canned drinks – and insist on opening the bottle or can yourself. Avoid ice in your drinks, and do not eat ice-cream or water-ices unless they come from a reputable source. (It may have been Kevin's fondness for gelati that was his undoing.) Always wash fruit or salad thoroughly – use bottled mineral water if the drinking water is unsafe. An alternative is to peel fruit or vegetables if you can. Be especially wary of seafood and salads, and only eat thoroughly cooked meat, especially poultry. Choose a clean eating place if possible.

Every country has its own range of alcoholic drinks, but they may have different laws about selling to teenagers than your home country. Moslem countries allow no alcohol at all. Don't break the law. If you are above age, there are all sorts of interesting beverages to try, but be wary – they may be very much stronger than you think. Do not risk hypoglycaemia later (see page 49).

EXPLORING

This is what travelling is all about. With comfortable clothes, to protect against excess sun, cold or rain as appropriate, and – most important – comfortable shoes, some rations and diabetic travel kit in your day bag, some well-guarded money, a map and a phrase book you can explore for as long as you like. Sunburn hurts – treat the sun with respect unless you are well used to it. Equally, remember the hazards of getting very cold and hypoglycaemic (see page 28).

Many people do more walking on holiday than they are used to, so eat more or reduce your insulin further if you become hypoglycaemic or have blood-glucose measurements under 4.4 mmol/l (80 mg/dl).

TRAVEL SICKNESS AND TRAVELLERS' TUMMY

Most people do not suffer from travel sickness but a few are unlucky enough to be sensitive to unusual movements. If you suffer from travel sickness it is worth considering a proprietary motion-sickness preventive – ask your doctor what he recommends. Never take travel-sickness pills if you are driving. If you bring up your breakfast, check your blood glucose. If your blood glucose is low or you feel hypoglycaemic, sip a glucose drink (Coco Cola or Pepsi Cola or other canned drinks can usually be bought) or suck glucose tablets. Even if you vomit again, some glucose will be absorbed from your mouth. You will soon be better once you have arrived at your destination.

If, like poor Kevin, you have food poisoning, your glucose will probably rise in response to the infection (see page 10) rather than fall, even though you are vomiting and have diarrhoea. But the only way to make sure is to measure your blood glucose frequently – at least every four hours until you are better. It is worth taking a proprietary glucose and electrolyte solution – Diorylate is one – and some kaolin-containing medication with you. Discuss this with your doctor. If these are not available, try canned drinks again – Coca Cola or Pepsi Cola, for example. Keep sipping and try to replace the fluid you have lost. Stay in bed until you feel better – you may find the fluid loss has made you feel dizzy. If you are very ill or it does not settle within 48 hours, find a local doctor.

SUMMARY

- Be patient with your parents. They should try to see your point of view but you should also try to see theirs.
- Be prepared when travelling. Plan ahead.
- Where are you going? When? For how long? Climate? Language? Currency? Local health hazards?
- Take out medical and travel insurance.
- Take twice as many medical supplies as you think you will need.
- Keep your diabetic travel survival kit with you always.
- Take plenty of rations to cover the journey and the first few days' snacks.
- Take comfortable clothes and your most comfortable shoes.
- Never run the risk of becoming hypoglycaemic while travelling.
- Enjoy exploring foreign food, but use some common sense about food hygiene.
- Enjoy your holiday.

10

BEN

Ben was really fed up. He lay on his bed and lit another cigarette. He turned up the volume of his stereo cassette player and the room vibrated to the beat. He heard his mother calling to him to turn it down. 'No-one understands what I'm feeling', he muttered and flung himself back on to the bed. The cigarette fell out of his hand on to his duvet cover. A little flame appeared and he hastily poured his Diet Coke on to it. He threw the wet cigarette away and inspected the damage. There was a little round hole in the material and his duvet was soaked. His mother called up the stairs again. 'Turn that noise off, it'll soon be supper time.' Supper time. He ought to have his injection. He looked at the bottle on the shelf. Why did he have to stick needles in himself every day. It wasn't fair. All his friends at school could do whatever they wanted and he had to keep sticking needles in himself. He picked up the syringe, turned it in his hand and then threw it across the room. He was fed up with having to stick to the rules. He went downstairs to supper.

Ben was 15. He had had diabetes for two years. When the doctor first told him he was diabetic he had not really understood what that meant. He had thought that it was like having 'flu and he would get better. And within a couple of months that was what seemed to be happening. He had started to have a lot of hypos and his insulin dose had been reduced and reduced until he was taking a tiny amount. So he was obviously getting better. The doctors were wrong and he was right. He left off his insulin several times and nothing seemed to go wrong. Then, about 10 months later he became thirsty and started peeing a lot and his insulin dose gradually rose. Ben had been bitterly disappointed. The first time the insulin was increased he had gone home from clinic and shut himself in his room and cried. Of course, he wasn't going to let anyone see that he was upset. When he went to clinic he just sat there and said 'Yes' and 'No'. They could do what they liked with the diabetes. He didn't care anymore.

Nothing much seemed to happen when he left off his insulin that evening. He felt a bit thirsty and had to go to the toilet in the night – that was all. So Ben didn't have his morning insulin either. By mid-afternoon he was really thirsty so he had a bit of insulin when he got home. Then he went out with his friends. They went to a hamburger bar. Ben had two beefburgers and three portions of chips. 'I thought you had to watch your diet', said Ian. 'Not any more', replied Ben.

Over the next few weeks Ben decided to forget about his diabetes. He gave himself some insulin when he felt really thirsty but he stopped bothering to measure it. He ate what he wanted – although he still ate his diabetic diet at home. His mother noticed that he was thirsty. She asked him if his diabetes was all right. 'Yeah, of course,' said Ben. 'Are you doing your blood tests?' his mother persisted. 'Yes,' lied Ben. 'Well, what do they show?' she asked. 'They're all right. Now stop pestering me', said Ben and ran up to his room and shut the door. But his mother was still worried and she telephoned the diabetes liaison sister, who came the next evening.

'How are you getting on, Ben?' she asked. 'OK', he shrugged. 'Are you sure everything's all right?' 'I'm OK,' he said. She insisted on checking his blood glucose. It was 22 mmol/l (396 mg/dl). 'This is very high, Ben', she said. 'How much insulin are you taking at present?' He told her the dose written on his diabetic card and she advised an increase. Three days later he was surprised to receive an early clinic appointment in the post. When the date came his mother reminded him that he was due in clinic that afternoon. He went to school with a note explaining about the clinic visit, but when afternoon came he decided he wasn't going to go. He went into town instead and spent the afternoon and all his pocket money on the fruit machines in the amusement arcade. When his mother asked him what the doctor had said in clinic he told her that his diabetes was fine now. 'He said there was no problem.' The diabetes sister came round again. Ben saw her car coming up the road and slipped out of the back door.

This went on for two months. Ben managed to evade the diabetes sister and tore up the next diabetic clinic appointment before his parents saw it. His parents became more and more worried. His father tried to talk to him, but he refused to listen. What did they know about what he was feeling? They didn't have diabetes, and anyway they were too old to understand. During this time he had very little insulin and got used to feeling thirsty. If he felt really thirsty he had some insulin, but otherwise he stopped bothering. He went into the supermarket to buy sweets on most days now. He liked the girl on the till. She had red-gold hair and green eyes and sometimes their hands met over the change. One day he finally plucked up the courage to ask her out. She accepted and they went to the cinema together. They had a really good evening and agreed to meet at the same place next week to see the next feature. They began going out more often. He had never told Nicola about his diabetes, but one evening while they were sitting alone in her parents' house watching a video she asked him why he had to drink so much. So he explained about the diabetes – 'But it's no problem', he said.

One day they took Nicola's little brother to the fair for a treat. The child had a streaming cold and a few days later so did Ben. He started to feel distinctly off colour. He went round to see Nicola. By now he was feeling very sick and he had to keep going to the toilet to pee. Nicola asked him if he was all right but everything seemed to be hazy and he felt awful. She put her duvet over him on the sofa and phoned her parents, who were out with friends. They came back straight away and telephoned for an ambulance. Ben did not remember much about the rest of that night. He awoke next morning in hospital to find Nicola sitting beside his bed holding his hand. A nurse came in with two cups of tea. 'She's been there all night, you know. You're a lucky lad to have such a devoted girlfriend.'

When the nurse had gone, Nicola looked at Ben and started to cry. 'I thought you were going to die', she wept. 'Oh Ben, I do love you.' She kissed him gently. 'I was there when they talked to your parents. The doctor said it was because you weren't looking after yourself. Ben, what's the matter? Please let me help you.' And suddenly Ben found himself crying. He just couldn't stop himself. He told her about the diabetes getting better to start with and then how it got worse again and how he hated it and he admitted that he had not been to clinic and not taken his insulin. Everything that had all been bottled up inside him for months and months just came pouring out. He talked until he was exhausted, and Nicola calmed him gently to sleep.

He was in hospital for three days and Nicola came to see him for several hours every day. His parents came too. His mother looked awful. Her face was grey, with bags under her eyes. When they allowed him home he spent a few days off school. He talked to his mother as he sat on the kitchen stool and watched her doing the cooking.

If this was a fairy story they would all have lived happily ever after, but real life is not quite like that. Ben did start giving his insulin twice a day again and felt better, but he still hated his diabetes. He asked Nicola to go with him to the diabetic clinic. Nicola had insisted that he tell the doctor what he felt about his diabetes. It was very difficult admitting all the things he had done and not done, but to his surprise he did not get the telling off he had anticipated. The doctor listened for a long time and then said 'I'm sorry you've had such a rough time. You're not alone, you know. Lots of diabetics hate their diabetes. Shall we see what we can do to sort things out?'

There were ups and downs over the next two years. Once Ben ended up in hospital with ketoacidosis again when he had a sore throat. By now he had left school and was working as an apprentice in a builder's yard. He found that he could not manage the heavy work as well as the others when he was sugary so he began to look after his diabetes better.

He and Nicola decided to get married and went to the registry office on his eighteenth birthday. They set up house in a small flat

86

near the supermarket and were soon expecting their first child. Nicola made Ben stop smoking so that it would not harm their baby and he found it easier to give up than he expected. Ben had great fun looking in the toy shops and planning what sort of nursery furniture they would buy. He decided that he had better look after his diabetes now that he had a family to support.

HAVING DIABETES

No-one likes having diabetes. People react to the diagnosis in different ways. Most people find it hard to believe to start with – they are shocked that this has happened to them. Why me? What have I done to deserve this? The answer is nothing. It is not your fault that you have diabetes, it is just something that has happened. Indeed, you were probably born with the tendency to develop diabetes at some stage. It is a part of you and you have to learn to live with it. But nobody says that comes easily.

Some people react to having diabetes by being angry. Some become very depressed. Some act like an ostrich – 'If I pretend it isn't there it will go away.' Ben had a mixture of these feelings. Some people become obsessional – 'I've got to get it right or something awful will happen.' There is nothing wrong or wicked about having any of these reactions. Everyone copes in their own way. The vast majority of people with diabetes gradually get used to having it and devote enough time to their diabetes care to ensure that their diabetes does not cause them any trouble. At the same time they do not let it interfere with their enjoyment of life. But each person takes a different route to acceptance of their diabetes over a different time span and everyone has times of feeling sad or frustrated or rebellious or worried.

Ben had a very bad time. He was not sure how to cope and he felt unable to ask anyone for help. He started by deluding himself into thinking that his diabetes had gone away (the ostrich approach) and then when it did not he felt very depressed. Then he got angry and rebelled against his diabetes. But all the time he was hurting inside. He kept all his feelings bottled up. It was not until Nicola told him how worried she had been and encouraged him to talk that he was able to release all his worries.

IT HELPS TO TALK

'A trouble shared is a trouble halved.' Not always true, but it often helps to talk about things that are worrying you with someone you trust who is a good listener. You can always trust your family doctor or diabetic clinic doctor – they cannot break your confidences. Your doctor is not just there to distribute pills and repeat insulin prescriptions. However, if you do not find it easy to talk to your doctor perhaps you can talk with the diabetes nurse – you may know her better if she has visited you at home.

The staff at the diabetic clinic had realised what Ben was doing and had tried very hard to see him so that they could help. Diabetic clinic staff are well experienced in the sorts of difficulties people have in coming to terms with their illness, as well as with the practical problems they may have in managing it. Every diabetic clinic knows people like Ben. The diabetic clinic is always there and never gives up on anyone. No matter what you have done or said, the clinic staff will see you and try to help you sort things out.

And your parents care very much about what happens to you. Ben's mother was nearly ill with worry about him, but did not know how to help him. He found that he could talk about his diabetes with her after he came home from hospital. Like Ben, you may have a girlfriend, or boyfriend, you can confide in; sometimes friends from school or work are good listeners. Some schools, colleges or universities have tutors or counsellors whose job it is to help you through difficult situations. Student health services contain good listeners. Some diabetic clinics even have groups of young diabetics who have been through what you are going through and will gladly help you over a difficult patch. If you really feel that you do not want to talk to anyone you know you can always telephone the Samaritans anonymously – their number is in the telephone book.

BE KIND TO YOURSELF

Most people are their own harshest critic. However, no-one can be brave and strong all the time: everyone needs comfort occasionally. No-one can know all there is to know about diabetes. Doctors and nurses know quite a lot. People with diabetes know quite a lot, but it takes time to learn. Do not expect to learn everything all at once. Some knowledge comes with experience and much can be learned from talking with experts and reading. The more you know about your diabetes the better you can look after yourself, but take it steadily and do not be too hard on yourself. Nobody copes perfectly every minute of their life. Everyone makes mistakes. Learn from them. Share tips with other diabetics. Read diabetic magazines and books.

And remember, the important thing is to enjoy life. Sort out your diabetes, give it the attention it needs to keep it under control and then and go out and have fun.

HONEYMOON PERIOD

Ben thought his diabetes was disappearing two months after it was diagnosed. Why was this?

Many people experience this honeymoon period after the diagnosis of diabetes. Diabetes is due to the destruction of insulin-producing beta cells because they become inflamed (see page 10). When diabetes is diagnosed there may still be a few surviving cells in the pancreas, but they are so inflamed that they cannot make insulin. As the diabetes is treated this inflammation lessens temporarily and these cells make a little insulin. This lessens the need for insulin given by injection, but eventually these cells die too and you become totally dependent on the insulin you give by injection. It is a pity that Ben did not discuss this in more detail at the clinic when he was in the honeymoon period – it might have lessened his disappointment when it ended. The honeymoon period varies in length from a few weeks to over a year, and not everyone has such a honeymoon period.

SUMMARY

- Having diabetes can cause many emotions – you may feel sad, angry, frustrated, rebellious, frightened, obsessional.
- It takes time to adjust to having diabetes, and everyone has their ups and downs.
- Do not be surprised if your diabetes goes into a honeymoon period, and do not be disappointed when the honeymoon period inevitably ends.
- Learn as much as you can about diabetes in general and your diabetes in particular. Once you have learned how to manage it you can control it.
- Share your worries with a good listener whom you trust.
- Be kind to yourself.
- Put your diabetes in its place and go out and enjoy life.

11

TRACEY

Tracey opened her seventeenth birthday presents. A new hair dryer, some patterned tights, two new tapes and an envelope from her parents. Inside was a card entitling her to three driving lessons. She imagined herself, hair blowing, in a red open-topped sports car racing down the road.

She came to earth with a bump. First she had to get a provisional driving licence. She got the form from the post office. There were a lot of questions. It asked about her eyesight; that was all right – at her last clinic check she had easily read the smallest letters on the chart. Then there was a section about health. 'Have you now or have you ever had epilepsy or fits or sudden attacks of disabling giddiness or fainting?' She thought back. There was the evening that she had missed the bus home after the school hockey match and had to wait an hour for the next one. She had eaten her snack and her sugar lumps hours previously. She woke up in hospital with a sore tongue and bruises all over. They said she had blacked out and had a fit because she was hypoglycaemic. The doctors had injected glucose into a vein to revive her. So the answer was yes. (She always left biscuits in her locker now, in case she needed them.)

'Have you now or have you ever had any other disability or medical condition which could affect your fitness as a driver either now or in the future?' Again the answer was yes – diabetes.

Her father wrote to his car insurance company, told them she had diabetes and asked if she could drive his car. They sent him a form for Tracey's doctor to fill in. The driving licence authority sent her a form seeking her consent for them to obtain details about her condition from her doctor. All these forms. It all seemed to be taking ages. Tracey was longing to get behind the wheel. Next time she went to clinic Dr Grant told her that he had been asked to send a report about her to the driving licence doctors. He asked if she had had any recent hypoglycaemic attacks. There had been two slight ones before lunch but she had had good warning and eaten some glucose tablets. Dr Grant said that there should be no problem about her licence but he warned her never to drive if there was any possibility of a

90

Application form for a driving licence

hypoglycaemic attack, and gave her a sheet to read about driving and diabetes.

Eventually everything was sorted out. Her driving instructor was tall and good-looking. Tracey really looked forward to her lessons. One Saturday morning Tracey was waiting for him to arrive for her 10.30 lesson. She was just about to have her snack when the phone rang. It was her boyfriend Richard. She was still talking when the door-bell rang. She rushed out for her lesson. They drove around the town centre for a while and then headed on to the dual carriageway. Tracey was starting to feel hungry. Still it would soon be lunch time. Then she began to sweat and everything went blurry. There was a layby ahead. Shakily she signalled left and pulled in carefully. 'What are you doing?' asked her instructor. She couldn't answer. She pulled out the ignition keys and reached across her instructor for the biscuits in the glove compartment. 'What's going on? Are you all right?' he asked, worried. She stuffed the biscuits into her mouth, choking on the crumbs. After a few minutes the world came back to normal. She explained what had happened and the instructor drove her home. When they got there he stopped outside and turned to her. 'Are you OK now?' he asked. She was. 'Right,' he said, 'don't you ever do that again. I'm not going to risk my neck with some stupid girl who can't be bothered to look after herself.' Tracey burst into tears and ran into the house.

She wasn't too sure how she would get on next time, but her instructor did not mention to her hypoglycaemic episode and the driving lesson passed uneventfully. She had several more lessons. She was very nervous before the driving test and was quite convinced she would fail. But she passed.

DIABETES AND DRIVING

Most insulin-treated diabetics drive cars, but you must obey the law and, more importantly, you must make certain that you are safe to drive. Tracey was very upset when her driving instructor told her off, but when she thought about it he was right. She had been stupid. She hadn't had her snack and she knew that her rare hypoglycaemic attacks tended to be before lunch. Supposing she had lost control of the car – she might have killed them both, and other people.

There are no half measures. If you drive you must *never* allow yourself to become hypoglycaemic behind the wheel.

THE LAW

Everyone who drives a car must have a current driving licence *and* be insured to drive that car.

You must state that you have diabetes on the licence application form. If you withhold information about your medical condition you can be prosecuted. If you have blacked out because of hypogly-caemic attacks (or for any other reason) you must say so. If you have been disabled by hypoglycaemia you must say so. Disability in this context means losing control of yourself in any way, including being confused. If you have had a hypoglycaemic episode which had to be treated by someone else you must say so. If you have diabetic retinopathy, cataracts or other eye problems, if you cannot feel your hands or feet because of diabetic nerve damage or if you have other disabilities, you must say so. (If you have temporary blurring of vision while your diabetes is coming under control do not drive until you can see properly. This rarely lasts more than a week or so. Check with your doctor.)

You may think that these regulations are very strict. They are, with good reason. In addition to accidents caused by diabetics who have blacked out at the wheel, the driving licence authority receive notification of many accidents due to insulin-treated diabetics driving while in a state of altered awareness due to hypoglycaemia.

When the authority receives your driving licence form they send it to one of their medical advisers. This doctor will then ask for your written consent to your doctor(s) releasing information about your health to the authority. It may help if you send a covering letter with your licence application. For example, Tracey could have written:

                                              Tracey Smith
                                              36 Greenwood Road
                                              Whiteford

Medical Adviser
DVLC
Swansea
SA6 7JL

Dear Sir

I enclose a completed application form for a provisional driving licence.
I have had diabetes mellitus since June 1980. My diabetes is treated with
a diet and twice-daily insulin injections. I check my blood glucose balance
with finger prick testing. My blood glucose level is usually between 4
and 10 mmol/l. Four years ago I had a hypoglycaemic attack during which
I had a fit. Since then I have had no further fits or blackouts of any
kind. I have had no other severe hypoglycaemic attacks.

My GP is Dr Green, The Surgery, Whiteford. The doctor who usually treats
my diabetes is Dr Grant, Diabetic Clinic, St Gloria's Hospital, Bampton.
I go to clinic about every four months.

Yours faithfully

Tracey Smith

With your consent the medical adviser sends a form to your doctor asking how long you have been diabetic, whether you attend a diabetic clinic regularly, whether you keep your glucose balance stable, whether you have had any severe hypoglycaemic attacks and whether you have any complications of diabetes. If your family doctor does not manage your diabetes or you have complicated problems, they will also ask your diabetic clinic doctor for a report.

The things which may stop you getting a driving licence are frequent or bad hypoglycaemic attacks, having no warning of hypoglycaemic attacks, blacking out or being confused from hypo-glycaemia, not being able to treat your hypoglycaemia quickly or being careless with your diabetes – for example, not carrying glucose, or not bothering to eat meals so that you become hypoglycaemic, or never bothering to go to clinic. (If you do not attend for check-ups your doctor has to say that he or she never sees you and so cannot give a report. You would then be asked to see a doctor for a special check.) Severe diabetic eye damage or nerve damage may also stop you from driving.

When you do get a licence it is usually reviewed every three years, but if you do not attend your diabetic clinic or doctor regularly, or if the driving licence centre considers that you are the sort of person who does not look after yourself properly or who has unstable diabetes, you may have to get a new licence each year.

CAR INSURANCE

You also have to tell your insurance company that you have diabetes.. If you do not they will not cover you in the event of any accident (whether it was your fault or not). And if you have not told the driving licence authority that you have diabetes your insurance will not cover you.

The attitudes of insurance companies vary, so shop around. A registered insurance broker can help you with this. One study found that the premium for insuring the same person with diabetes for the same type of motor policy could cost up to twice as much with some companies as with others. Your local diabetes association or their head offices may be able to help. The insurance company will (with your consent) ask your doctor or hospital consultant for a report.

SAFE MOTORING

Prevention of hypoglycaemia
When you first start driving as an insulin-treated diabetic, drive after a meal or have a snack, and check your blood glucose before you set off. On long journeys stop and have a snack every hour, or check your glucose to see if you need a snack. As you get used to driving you will not need to measure your glucose before most journeys, but

still check it if anything unusual has happened, i.e. more exercise than usual, less food than usual, different insulin dose, timing or method of injecting it – examples would be playing in a football match, playing squash, going to a disco and dancing a lot, missing a meal, changing to a new insulin. Never drive when your blood-glucose control is in a very unstable phase.

Be especially careful when driving before meals (remember what happened to Tracey). This particularly applies to driving home from work in the evening and driving back from sports or exercise sessions (again remember Tracey's hypoglycaemic attack after her hockey match – fortunately she was not driving). Be especially careful if you are in a hurry. It is never worth missing a snack or a meal because you are late – 'Better a few minutes late in this world than a few years early in the next!'

And never drink and drive. This means no alcohol at all if you are driving. Alcohol impairs your concentration and coordination, whether you are diabetic or not, but if you are an insulin-treated diabetic it can cause or worsen hypoglycaemia (see page 49).

Treatment
Always carry food in the car. You may be late for a meal or snack (for example, stuck in a traffic jam) but if you have food readily to hand you can deal with hypoglycaemic symptoms immediately. The food should include glucose or sweets, biscuits and a drink – canned or boxed drinks with glucose in them. If you drive another car, transfer your food box to it.

At the *very first* suspicion of a hypoglycaemic attack you should:

- decide where you are going to stop, i.e. the nearest safe place – beside the kerb if there is no layby or parking place visible;
- check the rear-view mirror;
- signal;
- slow down gently;
- when it is safe to do so, carefully pull into the kerb or off the road and stop;
- turn off the engine and take the keys out of the ignition;
- switch on the hazard-warning lights if appropriate;
- eat some glucose immediately.

Remember that your concentration and coordination will be slow and poor if you are hypoglycaemic, although you may not realise this. Some diabetics actually have a compulsion to keep driving as they become more and more hypoglycaemic, even though another part of their brain is telling them to stop. This is why it is vital that you stop the car at the *very first* suspicion that you might be hypoglycaemic.

After you have eaten some glucose move into the passenger seat to rest if you can. Do not get out of the car, as you may be unsteady and could be killed or injured by passing traffic. Eat plenty (for example, glucose tablets followed by several biscuits washed down by a

96

glucose drink), wait *at least* 20 minutes and when you feel completely normal (or preferably when your blood glucose is 6 mmol/l (108 mg/dl) or more) continue your journey. Only move off if you are sure that you are in complete control of yourself and you are not at risk of becoming hypoglycaemic again. If you are in any doubt you must not drive.

These are just suggestions. It is *your* responsibility to make sure that you are a safe driver. Discuss the situation with your diabetic adviser.

PUBLIC SERVICE AND HEAVY GOODS VEHICLE LICENCES

It is very unlikely that an insulin-treated diabetic will be granted a PSV (public service vehicle) or HGV (heavy goods vehicle) licence. People on insulin who control their blood glucose meticulously, never have hypoglycaemic attacks and have no tissue damage, are sometimes allowed to hold PSV or HGV licences if they need them to continue their job. Examples are a mechanic who repairs public service or heavy goods vehicles, or a driving instructor for such vehicles.

ADVANCED MOTORING

Once you have passed your driving test it is possible to have advanced motoring lessons. These are exciting and can enable you to pass the advanced driving test. Some insurance companies offer a reduced premium for people who have passed this test. It should also help to make you a safer driver.

SUMMARY

- By law, every driver must have a current driving licence and motor insurance.
- Report your diabetes to the DVLC (the licensing authority).
- Tell your car insurance company that you have diabetes.
- Only drive if it is safe for you to do so.
- Never drive if you feel hypoglycaemic or there is a risk of your becoming hypoglycaemic while you are driving.
- Check your blood glucose to make sure you are safe to drive.
- Eat before you drive if possible.
- Never drink alcohol and drive.
- Always carry food and glucose in the car.
- If you do feel at all hypoglycaemic while driving, stop immediately it is safe to do so and eat glucose. Do not resume your journey until you are 100 per cent normal again and there is no further risk of hypoglycaemia.
- Happy motoring.

12

PETER

Peter was 16. He had always liked helping his father with electrical repairs in the house. When he left school with five O levels he applied to work with a telecommunications company as a trainee technician apprentice. He was accepted. The first month was to be spent on an introductory training course at their regional engineering training centre 50 miles away. He was given a room in a house shared by four other trainees, with a shared kitchen and bathroom. The course began and he rapidly realised that he had found the right subject. He enjoyed the classes, especially the practical sessions.

Living away from home came as a bit of a shock, though. It was very different from living at home, where he had taken the regular appearance of delicious meals for granted. Do-it-yourself catering was not nearly so appetising as mum's cooking. He wished he had taken a little more interest in what went on in the kitchen. One evening he decided to make a beef casserole. He was not sure what sort of meat to buy and it looked very fatty when he got it home. The meat took ages to cut into cubes with the blunt kitchen knife. He put it into the dish. Then he went to work on the onions. A few minutes later he was blundering about the room, tears streaming from his eyes, trying to find his handkerchief. He put the onions into cooking oil in the frying pan and left them to cook. Then another student came in. Would Peter come and help him with a circuit diagram? They solved the problem together and he returned to the kitchen. A terrible smell of burnt onions and some ominous black smoke filled the room. Nothing was left of the onions but some malodorous cinders. He threw them away, opened the windows and started again. This time he put the onions straight into the dish with the meat, scraped the carrots and threw them in, poured on some water, dropped a stock cube in and put the lot into the oven. Then he peeled some potatoes and put them on to boil.

He was getting hungrier and hungrier. When should he have his injection? Well, it would not take very long for the meal to cook now. So he gave his insulin and sat down with a manual on telephone wiring. Half an hour later, he was feeling slightly hypoglycaemic and decided that he would have to eat. The potatoes were cooked. The stew had virtually dried out. He hadn't put enough water in – or were you meant to cover it? He dumped the unappetising mess on to a plate and chewed . . . and chewed . . . and chewed. In the end he ate the potatoes and the carrots and threw the rest into the bin. Then he went out to the chip shop round the corner.

Every lunch time he ate in the centre canteen. The food there was plentiful but fried food and chips figured heavily on the menu. His breakfast was all right, providing he remembered to sniff the milk before he poured it on to his muesli – it seemed to go off so fast without a fridge. He filled the gaps with bread and marmalade or Marmite. But the main problem was in the evening. He learned how to cook baked beans and tinned stews, but it was so much easier to pop round the corner to the chip shop. He got so hungry that he bought chocolate bars at the newsagents. He had been keeping an eye on his blood glucose and noticed that it was gradually creeping higher. 'Not surprising, really,' he thought; 'I'm not sticking to my diet at all.' So he increased his insulin. As the weeks passed he found that his trousers felt tighter – he had to loosen the belt.

When the course came to an end Peter found he had come first in the final assessments. He returned home and started work with an engineer, helping to install telephones in houses. He spent two days each week at the local college on a day-release course. His diabetes was no trouble – he took his snacks and meals with him in a small rucksack. He was enjoying his food now that he was home again.

Three weeks after his return he went to the diabetic clinic. He told his doctor all about the telecommunications course. Then with a grin he described his dietary adventures. Together Peter and Dr Osgood looked at his diabetic diary. Then they inspected his weight chart. 'Dietitian?' asked Peter, ruefully. 'Straightaway', smiled Dr Osgood. The dietitian laughed when Peter told her about his culinary disasters. 'Next time you go away you'd better buy a cookbook.' She advised him about reducing his total calorie intake and explained which foods to cut down on for a time. Then she arranged to see him in a month.

A week later Peter had a letter from Dr Osgood. In it he said that Peter's glycated haemoglobin was 14 per cent. 'This confirms your high blood-glucose readings. I am afraid your problems with your diet while you were away really upset your diabetes. Please work hard at losing that extra weight. Remember that you may need to reduce your insulin as you lose weight.' Peter stuck to his diet; gradually the excess weight disappeared, and he was able to reduce his insulin back to his old dose.

His apprenticeship lasted three years in all, and included training in every aspect of telecommunications engineering. His work included muddy days down holes in the road, climbing telephone posts, hours in the basements of telephone exchanges, installation and maintenance of systems in large factories and small houses, computer work – the list was endless. He had shown particular aptitude in the complex field of satellite links and was offered a job away from home as a technical officer working with satellite communication. It was a wonderful opportunity to work with advanced technology.

When Peter moved his parents loaded the car with food and furniture – even a small fridge that his mother no longer needed. He had found two books (one for diabetics) about cooking for one. His parents left and he unpacked. He felt rather isolated in this vast city. He knew no-one. Then he remembered that the landlady had told him the other lodgers were students about his age, so he went round all the other rooms and invited everyone round for a cup of coffee. Soon they were on first-name terms – Narayan and Aaron were trainee accountants, Janet was a textile design student.

His new job was demanding and very exciting but living away from home was much more expensive than he had anticipated. By the time he had paid the rent and travel, and fed the electricity meter in his room, there were only a few pounds left for food. He was obviously not going to live on chips and take-aways again. Even tinned foods were expensive. He discussed the food problem with the others. Narayan was a vegetarian and he offered to teach Peter some recipes. Peter found that he could buy dried beans, lentils and peas cheaply, and even though they took a long time to soak and he had to be careful boiling them for the right length of time, they were filling. Narayan also showed him how to use spices to make them more interesting. They went shopping together in the market. He began to use vegetables more, and cooked some vegetarian dishes, and he also learned how to use vegetables to make meat and fish go further in stews and soups. Porridge made a good start to the day.

His diabetes care had been transferred to a large local diabetic clinic and he had a new doctor whose surgery was at the end of the road. His blood-glucose balance had been reasonable during the past few years, but improved on his new diet. His diabetic clinic doctor told him that his glycated haemoglobin was down 8.5 per cent. He had a full check-up, and there were no signs of diabetic complications.

COOKING FOR YOURSELF

Every one should know how to cook, whether they are a man or a woman. And I don't mean *Cordon Bleu* or *Cuisine Minceur* – you can move on to that later. I mean survival cookery. Do you know how to make a cup of tea? Boil an egg? Make stew? Cook potatoes? Boil rice? If you cannot cook, then start learning. Ask your mother. Write down the recipes as you learn them, even for simple things. There is a whole range of cookery books for beginners or for one person – buy one. Books in this series include *The Diabetics' Diet Book* by Dr Jim Mann and the Oxford Dietetic Group, *The Diabetics' Cookbook* by Roberta Longstaff and Professor Jim

100

Mann, and *The High-fibre Cookbook* by Pamela Westland. Start practising. If there are cookery classes at school, go to them. It is particularly important for people with diabetes to be able to cook. That way you can ensure that you eat the right foods. Learn which foods are high in fibre, and how to prepare them. Learn how to cut down on fats. Learn how to use artificial sweeteners if you have a sweet tooth or, better still, how to manage without them in your cooking.

Although the chip shop, pizza bar, burger bar or take-away is a tempting and convenient option, most of the foods sold in such places are quite fatty. And they are also an expensive way of eating – although often less so than a restaurant. Use them only occasionally. Try to get out of the habit of dropping into the take-away on the way home.

BUDGETING

Peter found that it can be much more expensive living on your own than you realise. When you are part of a family, living at home, your parents pay the heating bills, the mortgage, the rates, the electricity and gas bills, the house maintenance costs. They buy the food. Ask your parents about what things cost – you need to have some idea of the cost of living for when you start paying the bills.

SHOPPING FOR YOURSELF

Similarly, everyone should know how to buy food. Most people need to watch how much they spend each week – you do not want to waste your money. Go shopping with your parents and watch how they choose food. Learn how to tell when different sorts of fruit and vegetables are ripe. Learn how to choose meat and fish. Start reading the contents lists on foods. What do they really contain? What are you actually buying? When you start living on your own, get to know the local shops and the best places to buy what you want at the best prices.

A diabetic diet need not be any more expensive than any other diet – in fact it is the same diet that everyone who wants to stay healthy should eat. However, to keep it cheap you do need to learn how to cook the basic foods, because made-up dishes – tinned or packaged meals, for example – are more expensive. Bulk-buying of foods which you use often, and which keep, is cheaper. As Narayan taught Peter, pulses (beans, lentils, peas etc.) are cheap and filling, but they must be cooked properly – always read the instructions. Beans must be boiled thoroughly for at least 10 minutes before further cooking until soft. Cereals (try making your own muesli) and bread are cheap and filling. There is a wide range of meat and fish to choose from. Some of this may be very expensive, while very cheap cuts are often fatty or gristly. Shop around. Peter found that he could use vegetables in casseroles to make meat go further. Vegetables vary in price considerably. It is nearly always cheaper to choose your own and have them weighed and priced than to buy pre-packed vegetables in a supermarket. But do not forget that fruit and vegetables go off – do not buy too much.

Your dietitian will be able to help you. She may also know which local shops have the best choice of foods suitable for diabetics. It is sometimes possible to obtain a government allowance for special diets – ask about this if you are having great difficulty financially.

ASSESSMENT OF BLOOD-GLUCOSE BALANCE – GLYCATED HAEMOGLOBIN

Remember Steven? He thought that he could tell what his blood glucose was by how he felt (see page 21). Some people with diabetes can do this, but most cannot. The only way to be sure what is happening is to measure the blood glucose itself (see pages 56, 106–108 and 114–15). This is an instant measure – it tells you what your blood glucose is now. However it does not tell you what it was half an hour ago or yesterday or last month. But glycated protein measurements can give you this information.

The body contains hundreds of different proteins, all doing different jobs. Some act as building blocks, some are important in chemical processes, some in healing, some in fighting off bacteria, and so on. In a sugary environment, many of these proteins can become glycated – glucose can be incorporated into them. It is thought that this process may play a part in the development of diabetic complications. But we can use glycation (glycosylation is another way of describing the process) to measure how much above normal the blood glucose has been at the time when that protein was being formed. Haemoglobin (the red protein which carries oxygen around in the blood and makes it red) can be glycated. This is what Dr Osgood measured in Peter's blood. Peter's first level was 14 per cent, whereas the normal level in most laboratories is less than 8 per cent.

SUMMARY

- People with diabetes need to know what sort of foods they should eat.
- Everyone should know how to cook.
- Everyone should know how to shop for food.
- Living on your own is more expensive than living at home. Start learning how to budget now, before you move out.

13

SARAH AND NAIMA

Sarah and Naima both work for a multinational pharmaceutical company. Sarah developed diabetes when she was 13. She was 22 when she joined the company as a medical representative. Then the company bought a firm which manufactured and supplied medical equipment, mainly for people with diabetes. Because Sarah had diabetes she was asked if she would like to take a special interest in these diabetic products. She thought this was an excellent idea, and it seemed an even better idea when her manager told her that she could go to some of the international diabetes meetings to learn about advances in diabetes care.

Naima's diabetes had been diagnosed when she was five years old. She was 21 now and worked in the computer department of the company. She met Sarah at an evening project meeting. There was a buffet meal and Sarah had sat down in a corner, quietly taken out her insulin, and injected her evening dose into her abdomen. Naima was probably the only person who had noticed. 'I'm diabetic too,' she said, 'but I have a pump.' And she simply pressed a button on a small box at her waist. Sarah was fascinated. She had heard about pumps, but had never seen one. The pump was about the size of two matchboxes and had a fine tube from the human insulin vial inside to the needle under the skin of Naima's abdomen. Naima explained that she set a continuous basal rate for the whole 24 hours and gave herself extra boosts of insulin before each meal. 'Do you have to wear it all the time?' asked Sarah. 'What happens when you have a bath or go swimming?' 'I just disconnect the machine, put a bung in the end of the tubing and cover the lot with tape,' Naima replied, 'and then reconnect it again when I'm dry. I'm quite pleased with the pump, even if it does mean I have to do three or four finger-prick glucose levels every day. I've kept my blood glucose between 4 and 8 (72 and 144) for months now.' Sarah went away wondering if she would like one. She could see the pump hanging off Naima's belt. What would it be like to have something like that with you for most of every day?

She thought of Naima when she went to her first diabetes meeting.

To her disappointment it was not abroad, but it was about insulin pumps – CSII, continuous subcutaneous insulin infusion. She saw some very sophisticated pumps. One was half the size of Naima's, with a microcomputer that allowed you to programme in all sorts of variations in insulin dose. She took an extra copy of the literature to show Naima even though it cost over £1,000 (US $1,800). Several of the companies represented at the meeting had started by making heart pacemakers and had now extended the technology to insulin pumps. She learned about the different safety systems – warnings of motor failure, insulin lack, kinked tubing, prevention of pump runaway. She also learned about the work which had gone into ensuring that the fast-acting insulin in the pump was stable at body temperature and did not clog the tubing. Sarah was particularly interested in an implantable pump which had a rubber reservoir into which insulin could be injected through the skin. The insulin was pumped directly into a tube in a vein. The batteries would probably last for 10 years, although this device had not been in use for that long and was still mainly experimental. Another pumped the insulin into the peritoneal cavity (the cavity which contains the abdominal organs). Several teams were working on a needle glucose sensor which would measure the amount of glucose in the tissues and feed this information back to an insulin pump which would then release the right amount of insulin – in other words, an artificial pancreas.

When she came back from the meeting Sarah asked some of the doctors at the hospitals she visited about their views on CSII. Two of the large teaching hospitals in her area each had about 10 patients using CSII. The doctors there felt that despite the considerable effort needed by patients and staff to look after the pumps, such patients had no better blood-glucose levels than those taking twice- or thrice-daily insulin injections and who used careful monitoring and treatment adjustment. In the third centre there were more people using pumps. The diabetes unit there had done a CSII research project and many of the participants had opted to continue CSII after the study had finished, and there was a separate clinic for the pump patients. There were few pump patients in any of the other hospitals.

Sarah had not met Naima for some weeks. One day she saw her sitting in the dining room and went to join her. Naima was looking worried. 'I'm terribly sugary', she said. 'I just don't understand why. My pump is running, I've checked. I've had 20 boosts so far today and my glucose keeps going up.' 'Have you any ordinary insulin?' asked Sarah. 'Yes,' replied Naima, 'but it's at home and I don't have a car and I feel awful.' So Sarah took her home. Naima found her ordinary fast-acting insulin and gave herself 10 units immediately. Then they had another look at the pump. Eventually they found the problem. Virtually the whole of the tubing leading from the insulin vial in the pump to Naima's abdomen was full of air, not insulin. The air would do no harm under the skin but Naima had not had insulin for hours. She primed some new tubing with insulin, resited the needle and reset the pump. But Sarah was still worried about Naima. Although she looked a little better, her glucose was over 22 mmol/l (396 mg/dl). So Sarah encouraged Naima to contact the diabetes nurse, who came to see her straightaway.

Sarah and Naima became friends after this. When Sarah was invited to attend a meeting about computers in diabetes care she asked Naima to come with her. Naima's boss agreed. Most of the computer systems described at the meeting were designed to help run diabetic clinics. Some of the systems stored the patients' details – name, address, annual physical examination and so on – so that the record could be built up over the years, like the hospital notes, but much tidier. Other systems included programmes for organising outpatient appointments, recalling people who missed appointments and planning check-ups. Some systems stored a diabetic register – a list of the names and addresses of all the people with diabetes known to a diabetes unit covering a particular area. The register could then be used to ensure that everyone is seen regularly and to help plan diabetes care for the community.

In addition to these systems were several computers which analysed blood-glucose results from finger-prick tests people had done at home. The blood-glucose meters had memories which could be interrogated by a master computer in the clinic. One hand-held computer even calculated each day's insulin doses after analysing blood-glucose levels, planned food and exercise.

There were several teaching computers. Sarah and Naima both tried some of them. They both thought they knew quite a lot about diabetes, but were somewhat shocked to discover that they got some answers wrong. But the programme provided the right answers and the explanations. They enjoyed a brightly-coloured cartoon game designed to help diabetic children learn about their condition.

Six months after the start of Sarah's new role in the company she went to a major international medical meeting in Salzburg. When she arrived she was overwhelmed. There were 4,000 doctors and scientists from all over the world, all there to learn about new research and advances in treatment and to share ideas. There were literally hundreds of scientific and medical presentations. Her job was to go round all the trade stands looking at equipment for people with diabetes and to attend the presentations that related to these devices.

She started with blood-glucose testing. There were strips in round bottles, flat rectangular packs, wrapped in foil, and they turned blue/beige/green, or yellow/green/orange, or grey/purple with glucose. New blood testing meters were smaller and lighter than the ones Sarah had seen in hospital. There was a meter for every type of strip and one even read half-strips. Different meters could be calibrated by entering a number or a code strip or by drops of standard solutions. One was supposed to be virtually unbreakable – the representative dropped it to prove the point. They had different timing devices and beeps and buzzers. There were some with special offers of reduced prices. The simplest meter was a slim pen-like one; you simply put a drop of blood on to the disposable tip at the end and 30 seconds later the blood-glucose concentration appeared in a digital read-out on the pen.

The pump manufacturers were there in force, but even if she decided she would like a pump she knew she could not afford it just yet. However she could afford an insulin pen, and there were several of these on display. They had an insulin vial instead of an ink cartridge (the older models had an actual insulin syringe), a needle instead of a nib, a push-button or dial to inject the correct amount of insulin and a cover for the needle. She put all the literature together to discuss with her diabetic clinic doctor when she got home. She also found an injection aid which hid the needle and syringe inside a tube so that you could not see it going in when you injected. She had never worried about needles herself but thought the device might help people who were scared of them.

After three days her feet were aching, but she had the information she needed for her report. She decided she had earned a day off and toured the city. She even mounted the steep slope up to the castle. That evening she went to a performance of Mozart's *Magic Flute*.

EQUIPMENT USED IN DIABETES CARE

The basic equipment for an insulin-treated diabetic is:

- bottle(s) of insulin;
- syringe and needle;
- needle clipper/disposal container;
- bottle of blood-glucose testing strips;
- finger-pricking lancet/needle;
- watch with second hand.

Other things you must have are:

- glucose tablets/glucose gel/sugar lumps/sweets;
- diabetic card.

Nowadays diabetes care is big business, and there are a lot of devices to make life easier or to help improve blood glucose control. Will they help you? How do you choose?

BLOOD-GLUCOSE TESTING

See pages 114–15.

Strips
BM-Test-Glycaemie (Chemstrip bG) and Glucostix are the strips which are most commonly used in the UK, although other companies in different countries manufacture strips too. Your clinic may only

106

supply one type of strip, in which case the decision has been made for you. If not, consider which colours you find easier to see. Remember you will be looking for subtle changes. Nowadays there is no need to use a strip which needs cleaning with water before reading. With modern strips you either wipe the blood off (BM/Chemstrips bG) or blot it off (Glucostix). Some people find wiping easier, some prefer blotting. Try it and see.

Whichever strips you use, read the instructions very carefully, several times. Follow the instructions exactly, to the second. Keep the top firmly on, never let them get wet, excessively hot or frozen. Check the expiry date. Put the right amount of blood on and clean it off thoroughly before allowing the colour to develop before reading.

Finger pricking

You can prick your finger simply using a sterile needle or lancet, but there are now many devices on the market which do it for you – all you need to do is activate the device. Look at several devices before you choose. The simpler the device, the more reliable it is. Some devices come with different ends to press on your finger. These determine how deep the prick is – if you cannot make a hole you need a thinner stage or stop, if you bleed all over the place you need a thicker one.

Blood-glucose meters

Many people become very skilled at reading their glucose strips by eye – almost as accurate as the laboratory – but it is often helpful for a machine to read the result for you, especially if you are looking for subtle colour changes over a narrow range, from 4–6 mmol/l (72–108 mg/dl) for example. However a meter is only as good as the person doing the test; it will only give you the right result if you calibrate it properly, put the right amount of blood on the right strips (which are in-date and properly stored) and time the test properly. I have seen a result of 4 mmol/l (72mg/dl) obtained in someone whose blood glucose was 17 mmol/l (306 mg/dl), simply because the test was done wrongly. I have also seen a meter result of 22 mmol/l (396 mg/dl) in someone whose blood glucose was less than 1 mmol/l (mg/dl). The patient had sticky, sugary fingers which had contaminated the test strip.

How do you know if a meter would help you? Well, do you have problems reading your strips? Have you discussed these problems at your diabetic clinic and still not solved them? Are you colour blind or partially sighted? Do you want more accurate results than you are obtaining at present? If the answer is yes, then see if you can borrow a meter from your clinic or local diabetic association. Try it for a week or so and see if it is easy to use. Two of the most popular meters are Reflolux (Accu-chek, uses BM/Chemstrips bG) and Glucometer (uses Glucostix). There are many others.

When choosing a meter, consider how easy it is for *you* to obtain accurate results with that meter, its size and robustness, the ease of calibration, the ease of operating it (are the steps simple?), how portable it is, what sort of batteries it needs and how easy they are to buy or recharge, the ease of cleaning the entry port for the strip, its guarantee, who is going to repair it and who can help you if you have problems with the meter. Ask your diabetic clinic staff for advice.

INSULIN INJECTIONS

Most people simply use a disposable insulin syringe and needle. You do not need to clean your skin with a medicated swab (unless your skin has become very dirty): simply stick the needle in at right angles and inject the insulin. If you are slim you may need to pinch up the skin with its fatty tissue underneath before injecting into it. If

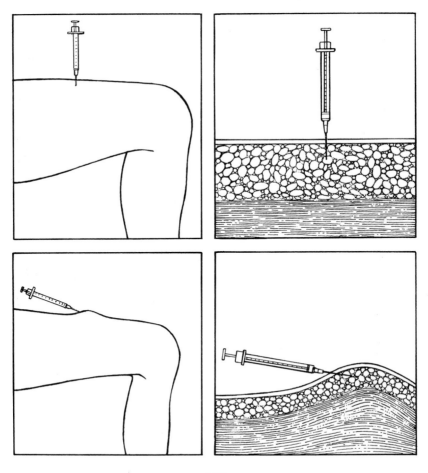

you are very slim, pinch up the skin with what fatty tissue you have and inject at an angle so that the needle does not penetrate the muscle underneath (the insulin would be absorbed too fast if that happened).

Indwelling needles
There are several systems which allow you to slide a needle under the skin and tape it into position for a day or two. These either have a button or bung just above the needle, through which you inject the insulin, or a tube leading to the needle. Few people use them, but it does mean only one needle prick every day or two rather than four or more.

Insulin injection pens
These are a relatively cheap simple way of carrying your fast-acting insulin around with you (pens are being made for longer-acting insulin too). Pens are usually used in a flexible insulin regimen in which background insulin is supplied by a very long-acting injection in the evening (Ultratard or Humulin Zn, for example) and fast-acting insulin is given from the pen before breakfast and the evening meal, and sometimes before lunch. This has the advantage of allowing you to eat more or less when you want. If your timetable, meal or exercise pattern is very varied or you travel a lot it is well worth considering a pen.

One of the earlier models was called Penject. This used an ordinary insulin syringe inside a plastic tube. The modern equivalents such as Novopen, Insuject and Accupen, use insulin cartridges made specifically for pens. They are quick to load and very simple to use. One insulin cartridge lasts for days, depending on how much insulin you need (Actrapid Penfills hold 150 units of insulin).

If you would like to try a pen discuss it with your diabetic clinic doctor. Many clinics have pens which they lend out for a few weeks so that people can decide if they want to buy one. They cost under £20 each and should only be ordered after discussion with your doctor. Again, when buying a pen consider how easy it is for *you* to use, whether you like pushing a button or twisting the top, whether you want to know how much insulin you have used each day or in total from that cartridge, and how easy it is to change the cartridge and needle.

Insulin pumps
Naima's story gives an example of the benefits of CSII (normal blood-glucose levels) and one of the hazards (rapid rise of blood glucose if the insulin delivery stops). Pump patients are at risk of developing ketoacidosis because all the insulin is fast-acting and only tiny amounts are being infused. If no more insulin is infused because the tube is full of air or kinked, for example, the tiny quantity of insulin in the infusion site is soon used up and the blood glucose rises. Used properly CSII can normalise the blood glucose; it means fewer insulin injections and a more natural pattern of insulin delivery. (A

non-diabetic's pancreas produces a trickle of insulin all the time, to cope with body 'housekeeping' needs, and bursts of insulin to cope with snacks and meals.) But it is also possible to normalise the blood glucose using carefully-monitored injection therapy – using a pen for example. Pump therapy requires frequent monitoring, and access to instant expert medical advice. (Naima should have contacted the hospital earlier instead of struggling on by herself.)

I have looked after patients in whom CSII has revolutionised their diabetes care, and they are very pleased with their pumps. However I have also cared for patients who hated CSII. The treatment of your diabetes must be right for you. The answer is not always new equipment but new thinking – if you really work at sorting out your diabetes you can achieve normal blood-glucose levels without fancy equipment.

OTHER ADVANCES

Groups interested in the inheritance of diabetes are studying the genes linked with the later development of diabetes. It seems that the difference between the genes of a family member who develops diabetes and those of the family members who do not become diabetic might be the presence or absence of just one amino-acid (the simple chemicals that build up proteins) in a particular place on one gene, i.e. this amino acid protects against diabetes. Work with strains of mice certain to become diabetic has shown that it is possible to introduce 'non-diabetic' genes into some of the mouse embryos, which then grow up without diabetes.

Once someone has started to develop the inflammation of the islet cells which leads to diabetes, it should theoretically be possible to treat the inflammation before damage is done. This inflammatory reaction is due to the immune defence system, getting confused and attacking the islet cells as if they were invaders from outside. Several studies have given immunosuppressive treatment to people with early inflammation of islet cells and in this way have delayed the onset of diabetes. However the side effects of such immunosuppressive treatment are potentially worrying and no-one knows how long treatment would need to continue. Investigators are also studying the trigger for this inflammatory response and why the inflammation mainly attacks insulin-producing cells in the islets of Langerhans and not, for example, the glucagon-producing cells next door to them.

There is continuous research into different preparations of insulin. Insulin manufacture was the first commercial use of genetic engineering. A human insulin-producing gene is inserted into the genetic material of bacteria called *Escherichia coli* (E. coli), which are then grown in large vats. Then the bacteria are killed and the insulin that they have produced is purified; the first insulin produced in this way was called Humulin insulin. This now means that insulin manufacturers no longer have to rely on animal pancreases.

Different ways of prolonging the action of insulin by adding zinc or protamine are also being explored. Insulin made in the body is released as a compound called proinsulin which is broken up to form insulin and a fragment called C-peptide. We can use C-peptide measurement to see if someone with diabetes who injects insulin is making any of their own insulin. Doctors have used proinsulin to treat diabetes.

For years scientists have been searching for a preparation of insulin that does not have to be injected. Insulin is a protein, like meat, and is digested after eating, so it is no use swallowing insulin. However some researchers have tried wrapping the insulin in fatty globules which are not digested but absorbed whole. Another approach is insulin which is blown up the nose. This is how anti-diuretic hormone replacement for diabetes insipidus is given. (Diabetes insipidus is similar to diabetes mellitus in causing thirst and polyuria, but it is a totally separate and much rarer condition due to a pituitary hormone lack.) The problem with giving insulin by mouth or through the nose is knowing how much of the dose has been absorbed.

It would obviously be better if one did not need to give insulin from outside at all. Pancreas transplantation has been used in a few selected patients – usually people who also need a kidney transplant because of very severe diabetic nephropathy. There are probably under a hundred long-term survivors with functioning pancreas transplants worldwide. The problem with transplanting the pancreas is that it makes strong digestive juices, in addition to hormones like insulin and glucagon. Before it can be transplanted some way has to be found to prevent these juices leaking out, for example surgeons can block the duct through which these juices drain. However, the transplanted pancreas seems to produce insulin better if its digestive juice production continues. Now surgeons often connect the duct into a loop of bowel at operation. Whole pancreas transplant is not, at present, a practical way of curing diabetes.

However diabetics do not need the whole pancreas, just the islet cells, so other research groups are working on islet-cell transplant. The problem is keeping the islet cells alive after transplant and stopping the body from recognising them as foreign and destroying them. Islet cells are so small that the scavenging white blood cells can easily gobble them up. Tiny cages have now been devised which protect the islet cells from the white blood cells but allow the insulin to seep out. Techniques for harvesting and culturing islets cells are improving.

Literally millions of pounds and dollars have been poured into the treatment of diabetes and its complications by compounds other than insulin. One approach is to reduce the amount of glucose absorbed from food, or at least to slow down its absorption. Guar gum is a soluble fibre (rather like that found in baked beans, for example) which can be added to meals to slow down its absorption, and it is sometimes used in the treatment of diabetics. Another compound, an alpha glucosidase inhibitor, blocks the enzymes which break down carbohydrates, especially sucrose (sugar). The glucose these carbohydrates contain cannot then be absorbed. The danger of this sort of compound is that it will cause malnutrition by blocking glucose absorption too effectively. This does not seem to be a problem so far, and the compound seems promising, particularly for people who do not stick to their diets. But both guar and enzyme blockers can cause indigestion and embarrassing wind in some people.

Diabetic complications seem to have complex causes. One theory is that there is an accumulation of abnormal sugars and a lack of other essential sugars, for example in nerves. One of these abnormal sugars is called sorbitol. Drugs called aldose reductase inhibitors block this accumulation of sorbitol, and it is hoped that these aldose reductase inhibitors may prevent or treat diabetic neuropathy or retinopathy. Many other compounds have also been considered in the treatment of diabetic complications, including oil of evening primrose. Other research projects are looking at prevention of glycation of proteins (see page 102).

The momentum of diabetes research is accelerating and the future has never looked more exciting. Young people with diabetes today have some exciting advances to look forward to.

SUMMARY

- There is a wide range of diabetes care equipment to choose from.
- Much of it is expensive. Think carefully before spending your money and discuss any new purchase with your diabetes adviser first.
- Consider carefully whether a new device will help you and your diabetes. Do you really need it?
- Keep up to date with advances in diabetes care. Read all you can about them. Many of the advances in years to come will help you with your diabetes.
- Remember that it is the person with diabetes who determines what happens to them, not the equipment.
- Look after your diabetes and look forward to an exciting future.

STANDARD DIABETIC PROCEDURES

Urine-glucose testing

or

Dip stick into urine

Hold stick in urine stream

Time according to instructions

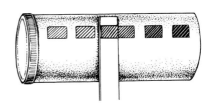

Compare colour with chart

Blood-glucose testing

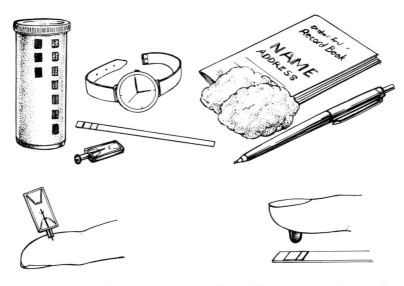

Prick clean warm finger
to obtain a big drop of blood

Drop blood onto stick covering
test pad completely. Do not
rub or smudge

Leave drop on test pad for
specified time (check
manufacturer's instructions)

Clean blood from test pad and
wait extra time (check
manufacturer's instructions)

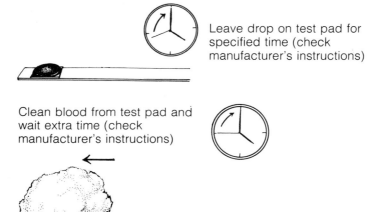

Wipe e.g. BM-test – Glycemie,
Chemstrips bG

Wash e.g. Dextrostix

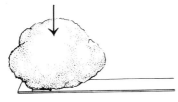

Blot e.g. Glucostix, Visidex

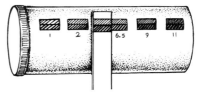

Check result and write it down e.g.
4 p.m. blood glucose 6.5 mmol/l

Insulin injection sites

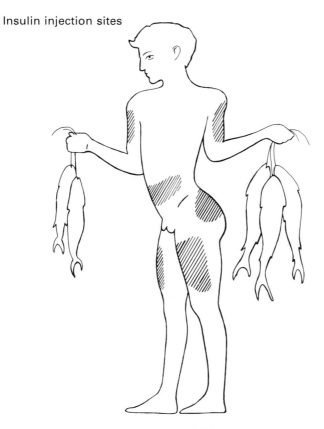

115

Drawing up and mixing insulin

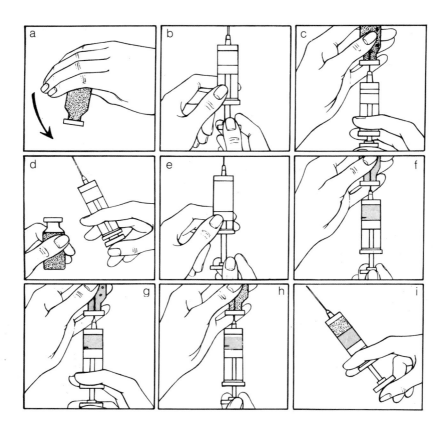

a) Gently rotate bottle to mix insulin
b) Draw up air
c) Inject air into cloudy insulin bottle
d) Put cloudy insulin down
e) Draw up air
f) Inject air into clear insulin bottle. Draw up clear insulin
g) Express air bubbles and check you have drawn up correct dose of clear insulin
h) Draw up correct dose of cloudy insulin
i) Ready for injection

Injecting insulin

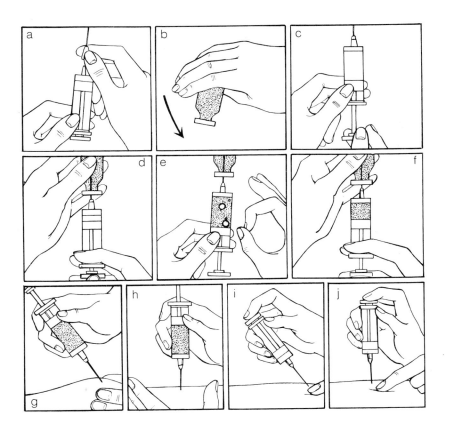

a) Attach needle to syringe if necessary
b) Gently rotate bottle to mix insulin
c) Draw up air and inject into the insulin bottle
d) Draw up insulin
e) Clear air bubbles
f) Check syringe contains correct insulin dose
g & h) Inject insulin into fatty layer under skin
    i) Withdraw needle
    j) Press on the hole

GLOSSARY

abdomen Part of the body between the chest and the pelvis. The belly or tummy.

acidosis Condition in which the blood is more acid than normal.

adipose tissue Body fat.

adrenal gland Gland found above the kidney which makes adrenaline (epinephrine) and steroid hormones.

adrenaline (American name **epinephrine**) Flight, fright and fight hormone produced by the adrenal gland under stress.

antibody The body's defence chemicals. They are programmed to attack specific invaders.

arteriopathy Abnormality of an artery or arteries.

artery Vessel which carries blood from the heart to other parts of the body.

arthropathy Abnormality of joint.

atherosclerosis Hardening and furring up of the arteries.

atrophy Shrinkage, wasting away of muscles.

autonomic nervous system Nerves controlling body functions such as heartbeat, blood pressure and bowel movement.

autonomic neuropathy Abnormality of the nerves controlling body functions.

background retinopathy The common form of diabetic retino-pathy, with microaneurysms, dot-and-blot haemorrhages and exudates.

balanitis Inflammation of the penis.

barrier contraception Prevention of pregnancy by putting a barrier between the sperm and the cervix (e.g. condom, cap).

beta cells Insulin-producing cells in the islets of Langerhans in the pancreas.

bladder Usually means urinary bladder. Bag in the pelvis where the urine collects before urination.

blood pressure BP. Pressure at which blood circulates in the arteries.

bloodstream The blood which flows around the body in the arteries and veins.

carbohydrate CHO. Sugary or starchy food which is digested in the gut to produce simple sugars like glucose. Carbohydrate foods include candy or sweets, cakes, biscuits, soda pop, bread, rice, pasta, oats, beans, lentils.

cataract Lens opacity.

cells The tiny building blocks from which the human body is made. Cell constituents are contained in a membrane.

Charcot joints Damaged joints in areas of neuropathy (rare).

cheiroarthropathy Stiffening of the hands.

chiropodist (also podiatrist) Someone who prevents and treats foot disorders.

chiropody (also podiatry) Treatment and prevention of foot disorders.

cholesterol A fat which circulates in the blood and is obtained from animal fats in food. If present in excess it can cause atherosclerosis.

clinic Place where patients are seen. Usually implies medical staff with a particular interest in a condition or conditions seeing patients with those conditions.

continuous subcutaneous insulin infusion CSII. A system for the constant pumping of insulin through a fine needle left under the skin all the time. Also known as an insulin pump.

creatinine Chemical produced by breakdown of protein in the body and passed through the kidneys into the urine. A measure of kidney function.

cystitis Inflammation of the urinary bladder.

dehydrated Dried out, deprived of water.

diabetes insipidus Condition in which the lack of the water-conserving anti-diuretic hormone causes the passage of large volumes (diabetes = a siphon) of tasteless urine (in = not, sipidus = well-tasting). Diabetes insipidus is nothing to do with diabetes mellitus.

diabetes mellitus Condition in which the blood-glucose concentration is above normal, causing passage of large volumes (diabetes = a siphon) of sweet urine (mellitus = sweet, like honey).

diabetic amyotrophy A form of diabetic nerve damage which causes weak muscles, usually in the legs.

diabetic complications Damage done to parts of the body or tissue by diabetes (e.g. retinopathy, neuropathy, nephropathy, atherosclerosis). Also called diabetic tissue damage.

diabetologist Doctor who specialises in the management of diabetes. Called Dr.

dialysis Artificial filtration of fluid and waste products which would normally be excreted in the urine by the kidneys.

diastolic blood pressure Blood pressure between heartbeats.

diet What you eat.

dietitian Someone who promotes a healthy diet and recommends dietary treatments.

digestion Process by which the food we eat is broken down in the body.

dot-and-blot haemorrhage Tiny bleeds into the retina in diabetic retinopathy.
drip Infusion of fluid into the body, usually into a vein. See intravenous infusion.
Dupuytren's contracture Tightening of the ligaments in the palm of the hand or fingers.
dysmenorrhoea Period pains.
dysuria Pain or discomfort on passing urine.
electrolytes Blood chemicals such as sodium and potassium.
enzyme Body chemical which facilitates other chemical processes.
epinephrine See **adrenaline**.
essential hypertension High blood pressure for which no specific cause can be found.
exudate Fatty deposit on the retina in retinopathy.
fat Greasy or oily substance. Fatty foods include butter, margarine, cheese, cooking oil, fried foods.
fibre Roughage in food. Found in beans, lentils, peas, bran, wholemeal flour, potatoes, etc.
fit Convulsions. People who are severely hypoglycaemic occasionally have a fit. They can be cured by glucose.
fluoroscein angiogram Picture of fluoroscein dye passing through the bood vessels in the eye.
gangrene Death of a part of the body because it has lost its blood supply. Gangrenous tissue usually goes black.
gene Piece of genetic material found in the chromosomes. The chromosomes are the proteins which transmit inherited information from parent to child.
genetic Inherited, passed on from parent to child.
glomeruli Tangles of tiny blood vessels in the kidneys from which urine filters into the urinary drainage system.
glucose A simple sugar obtained from carbohydrates in food. Glucose circulates in the bloodstream and is one of the body's main energy sources or fuels. The brain must have glucose to function normally.
glycaemia Glucose in the blood.
glycated haemoglobin Haemoglobin (the oxygen-carrying chemical in the red blood cells) to which glucose has become attached. A long-term measure of blood-glucose concentration.
glycation Process in which glucose is added to proteins, e.g. glycated haemoglobin.
glycogen The form in which glucose is stored in liver and muscles.
glycosuria Glucose in the urine.
glycosylated haemoglobin See **glycated haemoglobin**.
guar gum A substance which slows the absorption of carbohydrate from the gut.
haemoglobin Al$_c$ See glycated haemoglobin.
haemorrhage Bleed.
honeymoon period of diabetes The reduction of insulin needs shortly after diagnosis, thought to be due to temporary production of

insulin from the last few islet cells.

hormone A chemical made in one part of the body and acting in another part of the body. A chemical messenger.

hyper- High, above normal, over.

hyperglycaemia High blood-glucose concentration (i.e. above normal).

hypertension High blood pressure.

hypertrophy Enlargement, increase above normal dimensions.

hypo- Low, below normal.

'hypo' Abbreviation for hypoglycaemic attack.

hypoglycaemia Low blood-glucose concentration (i.e. below normal).

hypotension Low blood pressure

hypothermia Low or subnormal body temperature.

immune system The body's defence mechanism which recognises alien chemicals, bacteria, viruses, etc., and destroys them. Antibodies and some white blood cells are part of the immune system.

infusion Continuous flow of a drug or fluid into the body.

insulin A hormone produced in cells of the islets of Langerhans in the pancreas. Essential for the entry of glucose into the body's cells.

insulin-dependent diabetes IDD. See Type I diabetes.

insulin receptor Site on the cell surface where insulin acts.

intermittent claudication The intermittent limping caused by insufficient blood supply to the leg muscles.

intravenous Injected into a vein.

intravenous infusion Continuous flow of fluid or a drug into a vein.

islet cells Cells which produce insulin. Also called beta cells.

islets of Langerhans Clusters of cells in the pancreas. One form of islet cells produces insulin.

juvenile onset diabetes Diabetes starting in youth. This term implies a need for insulin treatment. Type I diabetes.

ketoacidosis A state of severe insulin deficiency causing fat breakdown, ketone formation and acidification of the blood.

ketones Fat breakdown products which smell of acetone or pear drops and make the blood acid.

kilocalories Cals or kcals. A measure of energy, for example in food or used up in exercise.

kilojoules Another measure of energy: 1 kilocalorie = 4.2 kilojoules.

lens The part of the eye responsible for focusing (like the lens of a camera).

lipid General name for fats found in the body.

liver Large organ in upper right abdomen which acts as an energy store, chemical factory and detoxifying unit and produces bile.

macroangiopathy See **macrovascular disease**.

macrovascular disease Disease of large blood vessels such as those supplying the legs.

malaise Feeling vaguely unwell or uncomfortable.

maturity onset diabetes Diabetes starting over the age of 30. This term usually implies that the person is not completely insulin deficient, at least initially. Non-insulin-dependent diabetes, Type II diabetes.

menstrual bleeding or flow   Blood loss at menstruation.

menstruation   Monthly periods.

metabolism   The chemical processing of substances in the body.

microalbuminuria   The presence of tiny quantities of protein in the urine.

microaneurysm   Tiny blow-out in the wall of a capillary in the retina of the eye.

microangiopathy or microvascular disease   Disease of small blood vessels such as those supplying the eyes or kidney.

milligrams per decilitre (mg/dl)   Unit of measurement of body chemicals; mg/dl has now been replaced by mmol/l in much of Europe (see below). However mg/dl are still used in America. 1 mmol/l = 18 mg/dl.

millimoles per litre (mmol/l)   Unit of measurement of body chemicals. If the blood glucose is 10 mmol/l it means that there are 10 millimoles of glucose for every litre of blood.

myocardium   Heart muscle.

necrobiosis lipoidica diabeticorum   Diabetic skin lesion (rare).

nephropathy   Abnormality of the kidney.

nerve   Cable carrying signals to or from the brain and spinal cord.

neuropathy   Abnormality of the nerves.

nocturia   Passing urine at night.

non-insulin-dependent diabetes   NIDD. Type of diabetes in which insulin treatment is not essential initially. See **Type II diabetes**.

nutritionist   Someone who studies diets. Nutritionists may be dietitians and vice versa.

obese   Overweight, fat.

obesity   Condition of being overweight or fat.

obstetrician   Doctor who specialises in the management of pregnant women. Called Mr in UK.

oedema   Swelling.

oestrogen   Female sex hormone.

ophthalmoscope   Magnifying torch with which the doctor looks into your eyes.

oral   Taken by mouth.

paediatrician   Doctor who specialises in the management of children's conditions. Usually called Dr.

palpitations   Awareness of irregular or abnormally fast heart beat.

pancreas   Abdominal gland producing digestive enzymes, insulin and other hormones.

paraesthesiae   Pins and needles or tingling.

-pathy   Disease or abnormality, e.g. neuropathy, retinopathy.

peripheral nervous system   Nerves supplying the skeletal muscles and detecting body sensation such as touch, pain, temperature.

peripheral neuropathy   Abnormality of peripheral nerves, e.g. those supplying arms or legs.

peripheral vascular disease   Abnormality of blood vessels supplying arms or legs.
photocoagulation   Light treatment of retinopathy.
physician   Doctor who specialises in the management of medical conditions. Always called Dr.
podiatrist (also chiropodist)   Someone who prevents and treats foot disorders.
podiatry (also chiropody)   Treatment and prevention of foot disorders.
polydipsia   Drinking large volumes of fluid.
polyunsaturated fats   Fats containing vegetable oils such as sunflower seed oil.
polyuria   Passing large volumes of urine frequently.
postural hypotension   Fall in blood pressure on standing.
potassium   Essential blood chemical.
progesterone   Female sex hormone.
proteins   Nitrogen-containing compounds performing many functions throughout the body. Dietary constituents required for body growth and repair (found in meat, eggs, cheese for example).
proteinuria   Protein in the urine.
pyelonephritis   Kidney infection.
receptor   Place on the cell wall with which a chemical or hormone links.
renal   To do with the kidney.
renal glycosuria   The presence of glucose in the urine because of an abnormally low renal threshold for glucose.
renal threshold   Blood-glucose concentration above which glucose overflows into the urine.
retina   Light-sensitive tissue at the back of the eye.
retinopathy   Abnormality of the retina.
saturated fats   Animal fats such as those in dairy products, meat fat.
sodium   Essential blood chemical.
steroid hormone   A hormone produced by the adrenal gland.
subcutaneous   The fatty tissues under the skin.
systolic blood pressure   Pumping pressure of heartbeat.
testosterone   Male sex hormone.
thrombosis   Clotting of blood.
thrombus   A blood clot.
thrush   Candidiasis or moniliasis. Fungal infection which produces white creamy patches and intense itching and soreness.
transplantation   The replacement of a non-functioning body organ with one from someone else (e.g. kidney transplant, pancreas transplant).
triglyceride   A form of fat which circulates in the bloodstream.
Type I diabetes   Diabetes due to complete insulin deficiency, for which treatment with insulin is essential. Lack of insulin leads to rapid illness and ketone production. Juvenile onset diabetes, insulin-dependent diabetes.

Type II diabetes Diabetes due to inefficiency of insulin action or relative insulin deficiency, which can usually be managed without insulin injections, at least initially. Ketone formation is less likely. Maturity onset diabetes, non-insulin-dependent diabetes.

uraemia High blood-urea concentration.

urea Blood chemical, waste substance excreted in urine.

ureter Tube from the kidney to the urinary bladder.

urethra Tube from the urinary bladder to the outside world.

urinary tract infection UTI. Infection in the urine drainage system.

vein Vessel which carries blood back to the heart.

visual acuity Sharpness of vision.

vitreous Clear jelly in the eye between the retina and the lens.

vitreous haemorrhage Bleed into the vitreous.

USEFUL ADDRESSES

UK

British Diabetic Association
10 Queen Anne Street
London W1M 0BD

British Mountaineering Council
Crawford House
Precinct Centre
Booth Street East
Manchester M13 9RZ

Business and Technician Education Council
Central House
Upper Woburn Place
London WC1H 0HH

Careers Information Unit
in your telephone directory
see under your county council

Careers and Occupational Information Centre
Manpower Services Commission
Moorfoot
Sheffield S1 4PQ

Careers Research Advisory Centre
(books on careers)
Hobsons Publishing
Bateman Street
Cambridge CB2 1LZ

Citizens' Advice Bureau
in your telephone directory

City and Guilds of London Institute
76 Portland Place
London W1N 4AA

Department of Education and Science
Elizabeth House
York Road
London SE1

DVLC (Drivers and Vehicles Licensing Centre)
Swansea SA99 1AB

Institute of Advanced Motorists
IAM House
359 Chiswick High Road
London W4 4HS

Keep Fit Association
16 Upper Woburn Place
London WC1A 1AH

Medic-Alert Foundation
11/13 Clifton Terrace
London N4 3JP

National Bureau for Handicapped Students
336 Brixton Road
London SW9 7AA

Outward Bound Eskdale
Eskdale Green
Holmrook
Cumbria CA19 1TE

Outward Bound Trust
Chestnut Field
Regent's Place
Rugby CV21 1TE

Ramblers' Association
1–5 Wandsworth Road
London SW8 2LJ

Royal Society of Arts
8 John Adam Street
London WC2N 6EZ

SOS Talisman
Talman Ltd
21 Grays Corner
Ley Street
Ilford
Essex IG2 7RQ

The Sports Council
16 Upper Woburn Place
London WC1A 1AH
Tel: 01 388 1277

Standing Conference on University Entrance
29 Tavistock Square
London WC1H 9EZ

Youth Hostels Association
Trevelyan House
8 St Stephen's Hill
St Albans
Hertfordshire AL1 2DY

UNITED STATES

The American Diabetes Association
National Service Center
1660 Duke Street
Alexandria, VA 22314

Juvenile Diabetes Foundation
60 Madison Avenue
New York, NY 10010

National Diabetes Information Clearing House
Box NDIC
Bethesda, MD 20205

CANADA

The Canadian Diabetes Association
(National Office)
78 Bond Street
Toronto
Ontario M5B 2J8

AUSTRALIA

Diabetic Association
86 Hampden Road
Bay Point
Hobart, Tas. 7000

Diabetic Association
19 Irwin Street
Perth, WA CO91

Diabetic Association of NSW
250 Pitt Street
Sydney, NSW 2000

Diabetic Association of Queensland
Ann Street
Brisbane, Q1d 4000

Diabetic Association of SA
Eleanor Harrald Building
Frome Road
Adelaide, SA 5000

Diabetes Education and Assessment Centre
74 Herbert Street
St Leonards, NSW 2065

Diabetes Foundation (Vic)
100 Collins Street
Melbourne, Vic 3000

Diabetic Information Centre
Woden Valley Hospital
Yamba Drive
Garran, ACT 2605

Diabetes Research Foundation of WA
Queen Elizabeth II Medical Centre
Hollywood
Perth, WA 6000

Diabetes Youth Foundation of Australia
370 Victoria Avenue
Chatswood, NSW 2067

SOURCES OF INFORMATION

M. Ardron *et al.*, 'Educational achievements, employment and social class of insulin dependent diabetics: a survey of a young adult clinic in Liverpool', *Diabetic Medicine*, 4, p. 546, 1987.

British Broadcasting Association, Schools Broadcasting Service.

British Diabetic Association.

Her Majesty's Stationery Office for the driving licence application form on page 91.

K.E. Jones and G.V. Gill, 'Diabetes and insurance – expensive business', *Diabetic Medicine*, 4, p. 577A, 1987.

H.A.W. Neil *et al.*, 'The Oxford Community diabetes study', *Diabetic Medicine*, 4, p. 539, 1987.

Oxfordshire County Council Careers Service.

INDEX

Page numbers in *italic* refer to the illustrations

132